AF776081

Confronting Corruption

Confronting Corruption

Past Concerns, Present Challenges, and Future Strategies

FRITZ HEIMANN

MARK PIETH

Foreword by

JIMMY CARTER

OXFORD
UNIVERSITY PRESS

OXFORD
UNIVERSITY PRESS

Oxford University Press is a department of the University of Oxford. It furthers the University's objective of excellence in research, scholarship, and education by publishing worldwide. Oxford is a registered trademark of Oxford University Press in the UK and certain other countries.

Published in the United States of America by Oxford University Press
198 Madison Avenue, New York, NY 10016, United States of America.

Library of Congress Cataloging-in-Publication Data

Names: Heimann, Fritz F., author. | Pieth, Mark, author.
Title: Confronting corruption : past concerns, present challenges, and future strategies / Fritz Heimann, Mark Pieth ; foreword by Jimmy Carter.
Description: First edition. | New York, NY : Oxford University Press, 2018. | Includes bibliographical references and index.
Identifiers: LCCN 2016039548 | ISBN 9780190458331 (hardback : alk. paper) | ISBN 9780190458348 (paperback : alk. paper)
Subjects: LCSH: Corruption—Prevention—International cooperation. | Bribery—Prevention—International cooperation. | Political corruption—Prevention—International cooperation. | Corruption—Law and legislation.
Classification: LCC JF1525.C66 H45 2017 | DDC 364.1/323—dc23
LC record available at https://lccn.loc.gov/2016039548

Note to Readers

This publication is designed to provide accurate and authoritative information in regard to the subject matter covered. It is based upon sources believed to be accurate and reliable and is intended to be current as of the time it was written. It is sold with the understanding that the publisher is not engaged in rendering legal, accounting, or other professional services. If legal advice or other expert assistance is required, the services of a competent professional person should be sought. Also, to confirm that the information has not been affected or changed by recent developments, traditional legal research techniques should be used, including checking primary sources where appropriate.

(Based on the Declaration of Principles jointly adopted by a Committee of the American Bar Association and a Committee of Publishers and Associations.)

CONTENTS

FOREWORD BY PRESIDENT JIMMY CARTER

Over the centuries, the pervasive perils of corruption have had devastating and complex effects on democracy and human rights. But even in contemporary times, no country—irrespective of how rich or poor it may be—is free of corruption. With the pillaging of government resources drastically limiting any government's capacity to provide fundamental services to the citizenry, the corrosive repercussions of corruption hit the world's poor the hardest. At the Carter Center—which my wife and I founded after my presidency—we have embarked upon a program to reduce corruption in the Americas since 1998. Not least through this work, we have once more learned that few things are as debilitating for the principle of rule of law and economic improvement as is corruption.

I have been deeply concerned about corruption since the beginning of my political career: my first election as Georgia state senator in 1962 was almost made impossible by fraudulent ballots, which we, however, succeeded in throwing out. After becoming president of the United States in 1976, my administration put the plight of citizens victimized by corrupt incumbents at center stage: we strongly pushed for legislation criminalizing the bribery of foreign public officials. As a result of these efforts, in December 1977, I signed the Foreign Corrupt Practices Act (FCPA) into law, marking the first time in history that bribery of foreign officials was declared a crime. The landmark piece of legislation has brought about a profound difference in the ways US corporations have operated ever since.

It was clear, however, that the United States could not overcome corruption on its own. In this regard, Mark Pieth deserves praise for his work and his leadership as the chairman of the OECD's Working Group on Bribery and for bolstering the realization of internationally binding rules on foreign bribery in the major exporting and investing nations. The adoption of the OECD Convention on Bribery, which came at a time when the vast majority of exporting nations still allowed tax deductibility of bribes, dramatically intensified the effort that had started with the FCPA.

In this illuminating book, Fritz Heimann and Mark Pieth do not only capture the magnitude of corruption and the evolution of the resistance against it: they also reveal the personal lessons they learned while being at the heartbeat of the anticorruption agenda. They take us with them on a journey behind the façade of massive international institutions and grant us a glance at the inner workings of key policymakers and leading nongovernmental organizations.

Apart from the assessment of the current state of affairs, the authors also chronicle the steps that have been taken since the issue of corruption has been pushed to the top of the international political agenda. Again, we enjoy their profound firsthand experience. Fritz Heimann's commitment to furthering transparency and honesty is exemplified by his inspirational work to establish and organize Transparency International, and I was honored to be the recipient of the TI-USA Integrity Award in 2015. The work that TI-USA does reminds us of the importance of enabling citizen oversight and the strengthening of institutions, which is why the recognition that the Award bestowed was so significant.

Since the enactment of the FCPA and its internationalization through the OECD Convention, many countries have passed legislation aimed at fighting corruption and deepening the public's confidence in their governments. Therefore, the center of gravity of anticorruption is nowadays moved from law to application. In this spirit, Fritz Heimann and Mark Pieth deserve great credit for the many years they have spent at the forefront of the fight against global corruption. I hope that the many personal experiences, accomplishments, and pieces of advice, the defeats, and success stories that have been collected in this book do their part to create a stronger, cleaner, and fairer world economy, and I am delighted to have contributed the foreword to this work.

Plains, Georgia
July 20, 2017

ACKNOWLEDGMENTS

The authors would like to thank Mr. Stefan Mbiyavanga and Ms. Nora Schneider for their intensive work on this book. Without their contribution this project would not have been possible. We would also like to thank Ms. Kirstin Bentley, Mr. Stuart E. Eizenstat and Mr. Al Larson for their valuable contributions. Furthermore, we would like to express our thanks to Mr. Alden Domizio and Mr. Blake Ratcliff of Oxford University Press for their great support.

We further want to express our appreciation for the work of the following organizations and individuals:

OECD: Ángel Gurría, Nicola Bonucci, Patrick Moulette, and Drago Kos
UNODC: Dimitri Vlassis
Transparency International: Peter Eigen, Huguette Labelle, Jose Ugaz, Alan Larson, Gillian Dell, and Nancy Boswell
General Electric: Jack Welch, Ben Heineman, Brackett Denniston, and Alex Dimitrief
ICC: François Vincke

Fritz Heimann
and
Mark Pieth

ABBREVIATIONS

1MDB	1 Malaysia Development Berhad
ACC	Anti-Corruption Commission
ADB	Asian Development Bank
AFC	Asian Football Confederation
AfDB	African Development Bank
AFP	Agence France-Presse
AG	Attorney General/Aktiengesellschaft (joint stock company)
AML	Anti Money Laundering
ANC	African Nationalist Congress
ANTICORRP	Anticorruption policies revisited
B20	Business 20
BAE	British Aerospace
BAT	Basel Art Trade Guidelines
BBC	British Broadcasting Corporation
BGE	Bundesgerichtsentscheid (Swiss Federal Supreme Court Decision)
BIAC	Business and Industry Advisory Committee to the OECD
BIG	Basel Institute on Governance
BPI	Transparency International Bribe Payers Index
BRICS	Brazil, Russia, India, China, and South Africa
BSI	Banca della Svizzera Italiana
BVGE	Bundesverwaltungsgerichtsentscheid (Decision of the Swiss Federal Administrative Court)
CAF	Confederation of African Football
CBC	Canadian Broadcasting Corporation
CEO	Chief Executive Officer
Cf.	confer
CFATF	Caribbean Financial Action Task Force

CFE	Comisión Federal de Electricidad
CHF	Swiss Frank
CH-StGB	Schweizerisches Strafgesetzbuch (Swiss Criminal Code)
CIDA	Canadian International Development Agency
CIME	OECD Committee on International Investment and Multilateral Enterprises
CME	Continuing medical education
CoE	Counsil of Europe
CONCACAF	The Confederation of North, Central America and Caribbean Association Football
CONMEBOL	South American Football Confederation
COSP	Conference of the State Parties to the United Nations Convention against Corruption
COSP	Conference of State Parties
CoST	Construction Sector Transparency Initiative
CPI	Transparency International Corruption Perception Index
CPS	Crown Prosecution Service
Crit.	critical
CSO	Civil Society Organization
Ct	Court
DAFFE	Directorate for Financial, Fiscal and Enterprise Affairs
DII	Defense Industry Initiative
DOJ	Department of Justice
DPAs	Deferred Prosecution Agreements
Dr.	Doctor
D-StGB	Strafgesetzbuch (German Criminal Code)
e.g.	Exempli gratia (for example)
EADS	European Aeronautic Defence and Space
EBK	Eidgenössische Bankenkommission (Swiss Federal Banking Commission)
EBRD	European Bank of Reconstruction and Development
ECOSOC	United Nations Economic and Social Council
EDGAR	Electronic Data-Gathering, Analysis and Retrieval System
EFPIA	European Federation of Pharmaceutical Industries and Associations
EITI	Extractive Industries Transparency Initiative
Et al.	Et alia (and others)
Et seq.	Et sequens
EU	European Union
ExCo	FIFA Executive Committee
FAC	Federal Administrative Court

FATF	Financial Action Task Force (on Money Laundering)
FAZ	Frankfurter Allgemeine Zeitung
FCPA	US Foreign Corrupt Practices Act
FDF	Swiss Federal Department of Finance
FIDIC	International Federation of Consulting Engineers
FIFA	Fédération Internationale de Football Association
FINMA	Eidgenössische Finanzmarktaufsicht
G7	Group of 7
GAC	Governance and Anti-Corruption Policy
GAFILAT	Financial Action Task Force of Latin America
GAFISUD	Financial Action Task Force of South America
GDP	Gross Domestic Product
GE	General Electric
GSK	GlaxoSmithKline
GTZ	Gesellschaft für Technische Zusammenarbeit
GWG	Geldwäschereigesetz
HLRM	High Level Reporting Mechanism
IAB	Independent Advisory Board
IADB	Inter-American Development Bank
ICAR	International Centre for Asset Recovery
ICC	International Chamber of Commerce/International Cricket Council/International Criminal Court
ICIJ	International Consortium of Investigative Journalists
ICSID	International Centre for Settlement of Investment Disputes
IFBEC	International Forum on Business Ethical Conduct
IFIs	International Financial Institutions
IFPMA	International Federation of Pharmaceutical Manufacturers & Associations
IFRI	Institut Français des Relations Internationales
IMF	International Monetary Fund
INT	Integrity Vice Presidency
IOC	International Olympic Committee
IP	Intellectual Property
IRG	Implementation Review Group
ISL	International Sports and Leisure
ISMM	International Sports Media & Marketing
KPMG	Klynveld Peat Marwick Main Goerdeler (Swiss auditing company)
KYC	Know your customer
MAI	Multilateral Agreement on Investment
MAN	Maschinenfabrik Augsburg-Nürnberg AG

MEDEF	Mouvement des entreprises de France
MENAFATF	Middle East and North Africa Financial Action Task Force
MIT	Massachusetts Institute of Technology
MNE	Multinational Enterprise
Mr.	Mister
NBFI	Non-Bank Financial Institutions
NCB	Non-Conviction Based
NCCT	Non-Cooperative Countries and Territories
NGO	Non-Governmental Organization
No.	Number
NPAs	Non-Prosecution Agreements
NY	New York
NZZ	Neue Zürcher Zeitung
OAS	Organization of American States
ODCP	Order on the Dismissal of the Criminal Proceedings
OECD	Organisation for Economic Co-operation and Development
Op-ed	opposite the editorial page
PACI	Partnering Against Corruption Initiative
Para.	paragraph
PBS	Public Broadcasting Service
PEPs	Politically exposed persons
PT	Partido dos Trabalhadores
PwC	PricewaterhouseCoopers
Q&A	Question and Answer
QOG	Quality of Government Institute
R&D	Research and Development
RAD	Rheinmetall Air Defence AG
RBA	Risk based approach
Rec.	Recommendation
RIAA	Swiss Restitution of Illicit Assets Act
RICO	Racketeer Influenced and Corrupt Organizations Act
RMP	Royal Mounted Police
S.A.	Sociedade Anônima/Société Anonyme
SEC	Securities and Exchange Commission
SFO	Serious Fraud Office
SGS	Société Générale de Surveillance S.A.
SIPRI	Stockholm International Peace Research Institute
SMEs	Small and medium sized enterprises
SOE	State owned enterprise
StAR	Stolen Asset Recovery Initiative
SVT	Sverige Television

TEFAF	European Fine Art Foundation
TI	Transparency International
TTLs	Task Team Leaders
TUAC	Trade Union Advisory Committee to the OECD
UBS	Union Bank of Switzerland
UEFA	Union of European Football Associations
UK	United Kingdom
UN	United Nations
UNCAC	United Nations Convention against Corruption
UNGC	United Nations Global Compact
UNIDROIT	Institut international pour l'unification du droit privé (International Institute for the Unification of Private Law)
UNODC	United Nations Office of Drugs and Crime
US	United States of America
US AID	United States Agency for International Development
USD	United States Dollar
VBF	Verordnung über die berufsmässige Ausübung der Finanzintermediation
WB	World Bank
WEF	World Economic Forum
WGB	Working Group on Bribery
WTO	World Trade Organization
WWF	World Wildlife Fund

PART ONE

Setting the Scene

This part leads into the book by telling some dark recent case examples that bring the reader up to speed by recalling the main events out of the world of anticorruption over the past two years. Subsequently, the authors introduce themselves and provide some personal background. Thereafter, this part features in-depth profiles of the politics of the anticorruption movement, as well as the phenomenology of corruption. It asks why it was possible to push anticorruption on the political agenda at this moment in time.

1

Introduction

MARK PIETH ■

The last two years have brought unprecedented movement into the world of anticorruption. The growing concern about corruption has come to a head in particular with a series of huge scandals:

1. FIFA, A CRIMINAL ORGANIZATION?

At dawn on May 27, 2015, Swiss police officers raided the prominent luxury hotel Baur au Lac where a regular room costs over $1,000 a night. They arrested seven top soccer officials, especially from the United States, the Caribbean, and Latin America, who had come to Zurich to attend a crucial meeting of the Executive Committee of the world soccer regulator FIFA (International Federation of Association Football). The same day US attorney general Loretta Lynch and Swiss attorney general Michael Lauber hosted press conferences in the United States and in Switzerland explaining that the officials had been arrested based on extradition requests from the United States. The US authorities presented indictments against them and called the hemispheric soccer Confederations (CONMEBOL for South America and CONCACAF for Central and Northern America) criminal organizations under the RICO Act (Racketeer Influenced and Corrupt Organizations Act). The arrested were accused of participating in a conspiracy involving fraud, bribery, and money laundering of over $200 million to gain preferential access to marketing contracts.[1]

1. Department of Justice, News Release, May 27 2015: "Nine FIFA Officials and Five Corporate Executives Indicted for Racketeering Conspiracy and Corruption"; *United States of America*

Shortly afterward the Swiss authorities stepped up enforcement. They raided FIFA offices in Zurich and opened criminal investigations against the president of FIFA, Sepp Blatter, as well as the president of the European Confederation (UEFA), Michel Platini, for misuse of corporate funds, based on allegations that Platini had received CHF2 million, supposedly for his services for FIFA nine years back. The payment was executed exactly when Blatter needed the European votes most for his re-election in 2011. There was no written contract, the work product still remains unclear, and, as far as we know, there were no traces of the debts on the books of FIFA between the supposed services in 2001 and the payment in 2011. Based on the announcement by the Swiss Attorney General's office the internal FIFA Ethics Committee suspended both FIFA president Blatter and then Candidate Platini from all official activities in soccer on a provisory basis. The drama has since further unfolded. The suspensions have been upheld by appeal courts with only minor reductions of sanctions. Furthermore, to date, close to forty FIFA officials have been suspended and debarred from soccer-related activities based on their unethical behavior. It is a story of one of the richest organizations in the world run like an old boys' club. Officials full of themselves, seemingly above the law, freely distributed the proceeds of sponsoring for FIFA programs privately amongst themselves. What has evolved into one of the most blatant abuses of power, led to major law enforcement activities; suddenly the officials were called to account for their behavior (see details below in Chapter 15).

2. THE MALAYSIAN WEALTH FUND "1MDB"

In 2015 another major corruption and money laundering scandal came to public notice. The new prime minister of Malaysia, Najib Razah, had turned the fund created by the oil-rich state Terengganu into a sovereign wealth fund under the name of 1MDB (for 1 Malaysia Development Berhad). Its goal was to promote the economic development of the country.[2] In September 2009, it set up a $2.5 billion joint venture with Petrosaudi International, a startup managed from Geneva and formally incorporated in London. According to *The Guardian*, Petrosaudi's business was "access capitalism: opening doors with the help of

v. Jeffrey Webb et al. 15 CR 0252 (District Ct of New York) filed May 20, 2015; Department of Justice News Release, December 3 2015: "Sixteen Additional FIFA Officials Indicted for Racketeering Conspiracy and Corruption."

2. Bloomberg, 2 February 2016: "Timeline: Malaysia's spiraling 1MDB state fund controversy."

friends in high places."[3] A former companion of the founders of Petrosaudi felt cheated by his colleagues and—after leaving the company—attempted to raise farewell payments by blackmail.[4] He actually handed over to journalists ninety gigabytes of data, including 227,000 emails from his former employer. Upon publication, law enforcement agencies, primarily in the United States, Singapore, and Switzerland, began to work on the case. It appears that around $1 billion of 1MDB's investment in the joint venture ended up in a web of bank accounts held by shell corporations based in offshore resorts.[5] According to an indictment of the US Department of Justice, published in July 2015, overall $3.5 billion were stolen from 1MDB. US attorney general Loretta Lynch called the 1MDB-scandal "the largest kleptocracy case in US history".[6]

The whistleblower was convinced by his former buddies to plead guilty against a promise to help him out of prison in Thailand, where he had been incarcerated for blackmail. After 'eighteen months in prison he has now been pardoned by the new Thai king.[7]

Four national investigations into the losses of 1MDB have all been stopped or have led to no visible result in Malaysia. In the meantime, financial supervisors in Singapore and in Switzerland have closed banks[8] and sanctioned bankers[9] for the blatant lack of compliance. Whereas this case demonstrates how political power, graft, money laundering, and whistleblowers play hand in hand, the following example, a Brazilian mega-case, starts off as a traditional corruption case in the area of public procurement, but rapidly takes on systemic dimensions when the corruption becomes crucial for the survival of political parties and governments.

3. The Guardian, 28 July 2016: "The inside story of the world's Biggest Financial Scandal," 4.

4. Ibid., 8.

5. Ibid., 5 et seq.

6. Ibid., 2.

7. Neue Zürcher Zeitung, 21 December 2016, 28: "Kronzeuge auf dem Weg in die Schweiz, 1MDB—Ermittlungen gehen weiter."

8. In particular the Swiss bank Banca della Svizzera Italiana, see FINMA Press Release, 24 May 2016: "BSI in serious breach of money laundering regulations"; Reuters, 5 October 2016: "Swiss prosecutors probe suspected $800 million misappropriation from Malaysia's 1MDB."

9. South China Morning Post, 21 December 2016: "Ex-BSI banker found guilty in Singapore of charges linked to 1MDB probe."

3. ODEBRECHT, PETROBRAS, LULA DA SILVA, AND MICHEL TEMER

On December 21, 2016, the US Department of Justice announced in a news release that two companies, Odebrecht S.A. (the biggest construction company in Latin America based in Brazil) and the Brazilian petrochemical company Braskem S.A. had pleaded guilty to corruption charges and agreed to pay penalties of at least $3.5 billion (maybe up to $4.5 billion, depending upon an "inabil ity to pay analysis") to resolve charges with authorities in the United States, Brazil, and Switzerland.[10]

According to the plea agreement Odebrecht maintained an internal "Division of Structured Operations," termed a "Department of Bribery" by Deputy Assistant Attorney General Suh.[11] It used a separate computer system and a shadow budget as well as a complex web of offshore companies to process the bribe payments of the company.[12] The statement of facts in the plea agreement lists recipients in Brazil, in particular executives of the state-owned oil company Petrobas, and politicians, as well as foreign officials (in Angola, Argentina, Colombia, Dominican Republic, Ecuador, Guatemala, Mexico, Mozambique, Panama, Peru, and Venezuela).[13] Braskem used the bribery structure created by Odebrecht and participated in the scheme. Odebrecht was sanctioned to fines and forfeiture of ill-gotten gains. It agreed to be supervised by a compliance monitor. The US DOJ in turn was ready to credit the sanctions agreed on with Brazilian and Swiss enforcement agencies.

The Odebrecht and Braskem case needs to be understood as a component of an even larger scandal: The entire state of Brazil seems to have been captured by a corruption network, whereby politicians of all parties participated.[14] The impeachment of Dilma Rousseff[15] and the court case against Lula da Silva for

10. Department of Justice, News Release, December 21 2016: "Odebrecht and Braskem Plead Guilty and Agree to Pay at Least $3.5 Billion in Global Penalties to Resolve Largest Foreign Bribery Case in History"; *United States of America against Odebrecht S.A.*, 16-643 (RJD) (Eastern District Ct of New York) [Plea Agreement]; *United States of America against Braskem S.A.*, 16-664 (RJD) (Eastern District Ct of New York) [Plea Agreement].

11. Department of Justice, News Release, 21 December 2016: "Odebrecht and Braskem Plead Guilty and Agree to Pay at Least $3.5 Billion in Global Penalties to Resolve Largest Foreign Bribery Case in History."

12. Annex B to Odebrecht's Plea Agreement, B-7 et seq.

13. Ibid., B-12 et seq.

14. Financial Times, 28 December 2016: "A Brazilian bribery machine."

15. Sputnik Brazil, 31 December 2016: "Retrospectiva 2016: Impeachment da presidenta Dilma Rousseff."

contempt of court (allegedly for influencing witnesses)[16] are only one side of the coin: the main allegations are that the "Partido dos Trabalhadores" (PT), the worker's party of Lula and Rousseff, had systematically taken bribes in exchange for favors. However, the reputation of the current president, Michel Temer, is no better, even if he and his cronies have not (yet) had to defend themselves in court.[17] Overall the Brazilian situation contains all the components of a global corruption scandal.

4. PANAMA PAPERS

The last five years could be called the "Era of the Whistleblower": to some extent the US legislation providing for remuneration for whistleblowers has encouraged employees to come forward with information about corporate misbehavior.[18] Independently from these incentives, disgruntled employees have increasingly used whistleblower platforms such as "WikiLeaks" to expose their (former) employer (cf. "offshore leaks," "LuxLeaks," "Swiss leaks").[19] In early 2015, an unknown person started offering data from the fourth biggest offshore law firm *Mossack Fonseca* to the paper *Süddeutsche Zeitung*.[20] The volume rapidly grew to dimensions that required the involvement of other investigative journalists. A worldwide network of around 400 journalists in over 80 countries emerged, largely organized around the "international consortium of investigative journalists" (ICIJ). Over twelve months they analyzed—under extreme secrecy—11.5 million files (2.6 terabytes of information) containing data on close to 215,000 offshore entities.[21]

The data makes it possible to identify the money laundering trails of serious organized criminals, like a Mexican drug cartel,[22] or potentially even a child

16. Neue Zürcher Zeitung, 31 July 2016: "Ex-Präsident Lula unter Anklage."

17. NZZ, 13 December 2016: "Ein Schatten auf Präsident Temer"; Foreign Affairs, 2 October 2016: "Timid Temer."

18. Dodd–Frank Act of 2010, § 922(a) Sec. 21F(b)(1).

19. With the decision of August 19, 2016, Rudolf Elmer, a former employee of Bank Baer Cayman Islands was freed from the accusation of breach of banking secrecy, but sanctioned by the Zurich appeals court for illegal cohesion.

20. Obermayer/Obermaier 2016; cf. also www.panamapapers.sueddeutsche.de. (13 March 2017).

21. The Guardian, 5 April 2016: "What are the Panama Papers? A guide to history's biggest data leak."

22. Center for Public Integrity, 25 April 2016: "Cartel-linked suspects arrested after Panama Papers revelations."

prostitution ring.[23] They offer examples of how oligarchs took control over state owned enterprises (SOEs) of former Eastern Europe, and they show how kleptocrats hid their funds with the help of the offshore industry.[24] Apart from straightforward tax evasion and fraud, the Panama Papers contain multiple proofs of harmful tax practices: companies using offshore constructions to shift their earnings to places with minimal or zero tax rates (applying techniques of transfer pricing or by transferring intellectual property rights to offshore companies).[25]

Overall the Panama Papers are a treasure trove of information on all sorts of illegal activities, including fraud, organized crime, corruption, kleptocracy, tax evasion, and sanctions busting. There is nothing fundamentally new in the methods detected: opaque structures are built using offshore instruments (shell companies, trusts, etc.) together with bank accounts in places with strong banking secrecy legislation and little likelihood of providing international cooperation in administrative or criminal matters, all held together by the professional privilege of lawyer and fiduciaries. Stooges act as nominee directors and bearer shares are widely used. However, it makes a big difference to actually see what one always assumed in its concrete detail. Furthermore, the Panama Papers have sparked off or invigorated many investigations and trials (including arbitration procedures).

The "shadow economy"[26] using offshore instruments is a key component of the world of so-called "grand corruption"[27] (see below Chapter 9).

23. Obermayer/Obermaier 2016, 217 et seq.

24. For current and former heads of state named in the papers: Wikipedia, Panama Papers, 15 et seq.

25. Joseph E. Stiglitz/Mark Pieth, Overcoming the Shadow Economy, November 2016, 6.

26. Cf. Stiglitz/Pieth 2016.

27. Georg Moody-Stuart, Grand Corruption, Oxford 1997.

2

Why the Growing Concern About Corruption?

FRITZ HEIMANN AND MARK PIETH

1. PRESENT AT THE CREATION

These four cases discussed in Chapter 1 are merely some examples that have come to light recently. Nowadays, everybody seems to be talking about corruption. The media are full of scandals, politicians run on anticorruption tickets, international organizations have drafted anticorruption conventions and soft law instruments, and national legislators are adopting new laws to prevent and to suppress bribery and other forms of corruption. The question needs to be answered: why all this activism has evolved after centuries of fatalism or even acceptance of corruption as an alternative to brute force. What has happened to push the issue up the political agenda over the last twenty-five years? And for all the efforts, we do need to ask ourselves whether we are really making a difference. Or isn't corruption as widespread as ever, in particular in challenging markets in the developing world and in emerging economies? Could it be that some politicians are using the anticorruption discourse as lip service, without wanting to change the status quo? Why is corruption so difficult to overcome? What should be done to make a real difference: Isn't there far too much talk and too little action?

We are going to address these and other pressing questions head-on. We are particularly well placed to do so as we have played a key role in the development of anticorruption standards over the last twenty-five years. We have had multiple roles in the course of our professional lives, Fritz Heimann as one of the most senior lawyers of General Electrics (GE) and later on as a co-founder of the NGO Transparency International (TI) and chairman of TI-USA, Mark Pieth as chairman of the OECD Working Group on Bribery and as an academic and adviser to governments and corporations worldwide.

The book will give a narrative of the development, interspersed with deliberately personal anecdotes, told from the vantage point of the individual coauthor (cf. the "boxes").

Fritz Heimann

For me, the story began in 1992 when Jack Welch, the CEO of General Electric, turned a review of GE's compliance programs upside down. He told Ben Heineman (GE's general counsel) and me that we were not focusing on the key issue. Of course, GE must comply with the US Foreign Corrupt Practices Act (FCPA), but that was routine legal work. The biggest problem was that GE was losing hundreds of millions of dollars in orders every year to foreign competitors who were free to continue to bribe customers and treat bribe payments as tax-deductible business expenses.

Welch insisted that the FCPA's prohibition of foreign bribery had to be internationalized. When we indicated that we did not know how that could be done, he made clear that we had to come up with a better answer. The first step forward came when I met with Michael Hershman, the head of the Fairfax Group, who introduced me to Peter Eigen, a German official at the World Bank.

Peter Eigen explained that he was planning to resign from the Bank to establish a nongovernmental organization to combat corruption. Eigen had become increasingly frustrated by the Bank's refusal to deal with corruption. The turning point came when the Bank refused to suspend loans to Kenya after President Moi had arranged the murder of Kenya's finance minister with whom Eigen had established a close working relationship as director of the Bank's programs in East Africa.

Eigen's proposed NGO was to be a coalition of individuals from international organizations, governments, and the private sector. His goal was to combat grand corruption by advocacy and public awareness campaigns. His model was Amnesty International, with its network of national chapters. He introduced me to the members of his planning team. When I reported back to GE, I was told to help Eigen get started.

Eigen asked me to go to London with Kamal Hossain, a former attorney general of Bangladesh, to visit Amnesty International in order to develop the legal structure for the new NGO. We drew up the papers for Transparency International, which was incorporated at the Dutch Foreign Ministry in The

Hague in early 1993. In May 1993 I participated in the Launch Conference of Transparency International held at a villa on the outskirts of Berlin. At that meeting the vice president of Ecuador, Alberto Dahik, invited the TI Board to come to Quito.

In Quito, we met with a local citizens group who made clear that campaigning against grand corruption was not enough to mobilize interest in a national chapter. TI would have to broaden its scope to deal with petty bribery, the myriad of small payments that citizens of Ecuador had to make to obtain public services, including admission to schools and clinics, government jobs, police protection, and permits of all kinds. These payments aroused much greater public outrage than large payoffs to ministers to win government contracts. That understanding became a central element of TI strategy.

TI's network of national chapters began to grow rapidly. GE helped to establish chapters in the United States, Canada, Italy, and several other countries. I also became TI's contact with the Organization for Economic Cooperation and Development, which had established a study group to consider possible ways to deal with corruption. The chairman of that group, Mark Pieth of the Swiss Justice Ministry, invited me to Basel in 1994. With that visit began a close collaboration of two decades recorded in this book.

Mark Pieth

Looking back on twenty-five years of work on corruption one needs to be frank: few of us actually chose the topic out of conviction, most stumbled into a specific role. I was a young lawyer with the Swiss Federal Office of Justice who had just been named "Head of Section on Economic and Organized Crime." My department sent me to participate in the nascent international activities on illicit drugs, on money laundering, on corruption etc. in 1988/1989. So I was sent off to help defend Swiss interests in the early days of the Financial Action Task Force on Money Laundering, to chair a UN Intergovernmental Expert Committee to determine the extent of the illicit trafficking in drugs, and to see what the OECD (Organization for Economic Cooperation and Development) was cooking up on corruption in business transactions—in those days code-named "illicit payments." Becoming Chair had more to do with strategic thinking of the larger powers: frequently they tried to prevent each other from taking the helm (and maybe they thought the Swiss would be neutral), and I was being rather straight forward (as I had just left academia for a time with government).

At the time it seemed that all these activities were a coincidence. As I will elaborate later, I no longer believe so—these activities are, in hindsight, all parts of an evolution. Again, it was part of this same development that Transparency International (TI) was founded to address. The appearance of TI concurrently with the United States' pressure on the United Nations and the OECD helped largely to advance the international work on corruption.

This, of course, was the moment when I got to know my coauthor, Fritz Heimann. We first met in Switzerland in 1994, just after the OECD had enacted its first anticorruption instrument, the Recommendation 1994, and when TI held its first Congress in Italy. It may seem funny in the aftermath that I did not really understand Fritz's corporate background. It turned out that he had run the legal department concerned with atomic power operations for GE, including the project of an atomic power station close to Basel, my home, which the population had effectively prevented. I had spent a good part of my university term helping to occupy the building site rather than to study. So, we found out, that we had been on opposite sides in the 1970s and were now united in the work against corruption. It was an interesting experience for me that a corporate lawyer could lead an NGO. Only later I understood that this made a lot of sense, especially as foreign bribery also went against fair competition. Furthermore, we were moving into the times where multinational enterprises (MNEs), such as oil companies, teamed up with NGOs, such as Greenpeace and others, to prevent environmental damage and to foster sound labor relations.

---

2. PUTTING CORRUPTION ON THE INTERNATIONAL AGENDA

Our involvement in the fight against corruption in the early 1990s came at an opportune time. With the end of the Cold War changes in long-prevalent positions became possible. For most of the twentieth century global corruption was a non-issue, regarded with apathy, cynicism, and denial. The United States, the Soviet Union, and their allies widely utilized bribery to promote their objectives in the Cold War. Many governments permitted their companies to treat bribe payments to win foreign orders as tax-deductible business expenses. Economists even justified corruption as a useful lubricant that enabled over-regulated economies to function.

International organizations ignored corruption. The World Bank relied on a legalistic rationalization, maintaining that its Bretton Woods Charter authorized work only on economic issues, not political ones, and that corruption was off limits because it was a political issue.

At the United Nations efforts to deal with corruption in the 1980s were stalemated by finger-pointing. Governments from the global South claimed that corruption was caused by bribe-paying businessmen from the North. Governments from the North claimed that corrupt officials in developing countries made bribe payments a condition for getting orders. These self-serving stereotypes prevented rational consideration of reforms.

Beginning in the 1990s, following the end of the Cold War, attitudes about corruption began to change. The first breaks in the ice were the organization of Transparency International and the OECD Working Group on Bribery in which the authors were actively involved.

Transparency International was launched in 1993 as a global NGO to combat corruption. From its headquarters in Berlin TI began to develop a network of national chapters around the world. In 1995 TI published an index ranking countries on their level of corruption, which received front page coverage in the *New York Times* and numerous other newspapers. The TI Index, which is published annually, raised the visibility of the corruption issue and played a key part in TI's campaign to raise public awareness of the widespread nature and damage done by corruption (see below Chapter 5).

The OECD Working Group on Bribery started as a low-key study group to identify possible actions against bribery for consideration by the governments belonging to the OECD in 1989. By 1994 it made a recommendation, urging all OECD members to end tax-deductibility of bribes. In 1997 the OECD took the much more advanced step of adopting a convention to combat bribery of foreign public officials. Because its parties include most of the leading exporters, the OECD Convention became the leading tool for addressing the supply side of bribery (see below Chapter 7).

By the first decade of the twenty-first century the public dialogue about corruption had been transformed. Awareness-raising by TI and research by the World Bank Institute provided widespread evidence of the damage done by corruption. Prominent international media, including the *New York Times*, the *Financial Times*, the *Guardian* and the *Wall Street Journal* have provided extensive coverage of corruption scandals and conducted in-depth investigative reporting.

The damage done by corruption is now widely recognized. Leaders of governments, international organizations, and corporations all claim to oppose corruption. The critical question has now become: Who is taking action against corruption, and who is only paying lip service to opposing corruption? Governments have ratified the OECD Convention, but half have taken little or no enforcement action a decade after the Convention went into effect. Numerous companies have adopted policy statements opposing bribery; far fewer have adopted rigorous compliance programs.

It is clear that there is strongly entrenched resistance to reforms. Government officials and companies benefitting from corruption are able to prevent or delay change. This was dramatically demonstrated by the ten-year battle in the United Kingdom to enact a modern anti-bribery law meeting OECD requirements. Opponents argue that prohibiting foreign bribery hurts their ability to win orders against competition from China and India, which—they allege—do not prohibit foreign bribery by their companies. Opponents also contend that anticorruption programs have done little to reduce levels of corruption, that corruption is too deeply entrenched in too many countries to be affected by international treaties, and that international organizations, operating by consensus, are incapable of forcing lagging governments to reform.

3. NEED FOR ACTION

In our view, the need for further action is compelling. Corruption undermines democratic institutions and the rule of law. It impairs government regulations, such as environmental protection and human rights. It obstructs international development programs and distorts competition for business and investment.

Public demand for action against corruption is escalating, including in China, Korea, India, South Africa, Nigeria, Brazil, France, Italy, Mexico, and the United States.

Corruption hurts all parts of society, but its most devastating effect is on the poor who are widely extorted by government officials to pay for public services that should be freely available such as admissions to clinics and schools, and access to water and electricity. Corrupt interests have taken over failed states in different parts of the world and utilize them as bases for illicit activities including drug trafficking, prostitution, and smuggling of counterfeit goods.

Anticorruption programs started in the past quarter century have laid a solid basis for making progress. Perseverance and redoubled efforts are required. Failure to confront corruption would be totally irresponsible.

4. REASONS FOR CONTINUING RESISTANCE

Corruption is a continuing problem because politicians need money to stay in power and the wealthy want political influence. Corrupt funds serve both interests. Efforts to curb corruption meet powerful political resistance because reforms impact political power.

Practitioners of corruption are resilient. Forms of corrupt behavior keep changing, becoming ever more sophisticated. Suitcases filled with large bills have been replaced by money transfers laundered by intermediaries through multiple jurisdictions.

Corrupt organizations operate readily across national borders. Law enforcement bodies are often constrained by traditional limits of national jurisdiction.

5. GROWTH OF ANTICORRUPTION CAPABILITY

The growth of extensive anticorruption capability around the world has been an important development of the last two decades. There are now thousands of experts working for governments, corporations, international bodies, law firms, financial organizations, and NGOs actively coping with corruption. This provides momentum and professional expertise to the anticorruption movement (even if some of the experts are engaged in covering up bribery). Where TI initially played a solitary role, there are now scores of NGOs actively fighting corruption.

6. EXPANSION OF GLOBAL ECONOMY

The need for action is accentuated by the expanding global economy. The volume of business conducted across borders continues to expand rapidly. Large companies have become truly multinational, with their activities spread over numerous markets. Companies that in the past did most of their business at home now have the predominant share of their business abroad. This has created an increasing need for a global level-playing field, requiring international conventions and collective action.

7. DIGITAL COMMUNICATIONS

The digital revolution is profoundly affecting how corruption is conducted and the ways to overcome it. On the negative side, digital communications have facilitated money laundering through transactions involving multiple countries. On the positive side, digital communications are eroding the cover of secrecy that is necessary for carrying on corrupt activities. It is becoming ever more difficult to preserve secrets, and as soon as they are uncovered, secrets will instantly be communicated around the world.

Prosecutors have learned that copies of emails don't disappear, and therefore provide an indelible trail of corrupt transactions. They are learning to cooperate with foreign prosecutors, through mutual legal assistance procedures, to unravel complex cover-ups.

Most dramatically, the so-called "Arab Spring" has demonstrated that mass resentment against corruption, communicated digitally, can result in the overthrow of dictators who had been in power for decades. The aftermath of the Arab Spring has been disappointing, with the exception of Tunisia. Lengthy periods of disruption have been followed by successor governments with uncertain anticorruption credentials. A challenge for the future is to learn to build on prospective Arab Spring revolutions to develop lasting reforms. This will be difficult because digital revolutions occur quickly with little advance warning, whereas lasting reforms take time to plan and even longer to implement.

In sum, the future of confronting corruption is challenging, but the prospects for success are promising.

3

The Politics of Anticorruption

FRITZ HEIMANN ■

During the two decades since corruption has emerged as an issue on the global agenda, the politics of anticorruption has gone through five phases. In the first phase, Transparency International began a solitary effort to combat global corruption. In the second phase, international organizations including OECD and UNODC became active developing anticorruption conventions. In the third phase, governments adopted national laws and regulations implementing these conventions. In the fourth phase, companies developed compliance programs. In the fifth phase, popular mass movements are playing an increasing role opposing corrupt governments.

1. TRANSPARENCY INTERNATIONAL AND ITS POLITICS

Peter Eigen founded Transparency International (TI) based on a critical political insight: the need for a unique organization focusing solely on combating corruption. He recognized that all established organizations would inevitably give priority to their primary mission. Even in organizations whose functions are seriously impaired by bribery, anticorruption will at best be a secondary objective.

TI sought support from development agencies, governments opposed to corruption, and professional groups. TI had to be politically nonpartisan, maintaining an independent identity, without becoming identified with any government or organization. Because a majority of the founders came from the World Bank and were US residents, separation from the World Bank and

Confronting Corruption. Fritz Heimann and Mark Pieth.

from the US government was important. Establishing its headquarters in Berlin helped to establish TI's independent status.

The internal politics of TI have turned around the relationship between the International Secretariat in Berlin, which has grown to more than 150 employees, and the national chapters, of which there are over one hundred.[1] At TI's Annual Meeting, each national chapter has one vote. In addition, thirty Individual Members (IMs) have one vote each. The Individual Members are selected based on long-standing service to TI. This structure is designed to provide balance between the national interests of the national chapters and a systems-wide perspective provided by the Individual Members.

TI's Management Accreditation Committee (MAC) plays a critical screening role. Both national chapters and individual members are accredited by the MAC for three years. The three-year terms avoid the need for dis-accreditation in case chapters or IMs become inactive.

The choice of Huguette Labelle as Peter Eigen's successor in 2005 reflected the desire to overcome strains between Berlin and the national chapters. The choice of Jose Ugaz from Peru in 2014 reflected the desire for a leader from a developing state, Peru, following a German and a Canadian chair.

Transparency International is discussed in greater detail in Chapter 5.

2. INTERNATIONAL ORGANIZATIONS

a. OECD

OECD's emergence as an important player in the anticorruption field was the result of two political factors: First, the desire of the United States to internationalize the US Foreign Corrupt Practices Act (FCPA) and thereby create a level playing field for global trade. OECD was a natural choice because its membership consisted of most of the leading exporters. Second, European governments preferred to assign anticorruption responsibility to OECD and not to expand the more powerful European Union.

Taking on responsibility for anticorruption transformed OECD's role. From a think tank making non-binding recommendations, OECD turned into the sponsor of a binding treaty, the OECD Convention, prohibiting foreign bribery. OECD's transformation was the result of strong leadership by Mark Pieth from the Swiss Ministry of Justice. He was chosen to lead a study group to develop non-binding recommendations on bribery. He turned the study group into the Working Group on Bribery, which drafted the Convention and then

1. See: https://www.transparency.org/about/ (February 13, 2017).

conducted a rigorous follow-up monitoring process to ensure that the member states implemented the Convention.

Mark Pieth chaired the Working Group for two decades. He was supported by OECD's Secretary-General, initially Don Johnston of Canada and then Ángel Gurría of Mexico. When the time came to find a successor to Pieth, Drago Kos of Slovenia was selected. Kos had extensive experience with anti-bribery programs first in Slovenia and then at the European Union. The Working Group on Bribery has functioned smoothly under Kos's leadership.

OECD is discussed in greater detail in Chapter 7.

b. UNODC

The UN Office on Drugs and Crime (UNODC) started in 1997 as the UN agency responsible for dealing with illicit drugs. Its scope was subsequently expanded to cover organized crime and then corruption. (It is sometimes referred to colloquially as the Office for Drugs and Thugs.) UNODC led the effort to draft the UN Convention against Corruption (UNCAC) and then became the secretariat administering UNCAC. The quality of UNODC's work has come as an encouraging surprise for many UN skeptics.

UNCAC has a very comprehensive scope, far broader than the OECD Convention's prohibition of bribery of foreign public officials.[2] UNCAC has been ratified by over 180 governments, more than 90 percent of UN members and more than four times OECD's membership. UNCAC's membership has great diversity in political and economic systems, and ranges from the most powerful and effectively organized governments down to very weak states.

The combination of a convention with a very broad scope and a large and very diverse membership presents UNODC with difficult management challenges. It has met these challenges with flexibility and patience. Many UNCAC provisions are discretionary, not mandatory. Controversial provisions, such as follow-up monitoring of compliance, have been introduced slowly. UNCAC was adopted in 2003 without provision for monitoring. A monitoring mechanism was enacted in 2009 and began functioning in 2010 with a ten-year schedule for country reviews.

The politics of UNODC are complicated by requirements for consensus and a practice of not taking votes. The resistance to follow-up monitoring was long led by a group of governments including China, Russia, Venezuela, and Ecuador. UNCAC has made progress because it has support from a substantial majority of governments. Importantly, the leadership of UNODC, particularly

2. See below Chapters 7 and 8.

Dimitri Vlassis of Greece, are adept at functioning within the constraints of the UN system.

Involvement of TI and other civil society organizations met resistance but has made progress on a step-by-step basis. The formation by Gillian Dell of TI of an UNCAC Civil Society Coalition, with more than three hundred member organizations has greatly strengthened civil society influence. The Civil Society Coalition played an active role in promoting UNCAC ratification and in follow-up monitoring.

UNCAC and UNODC are discussed in greater detail in Chapter 8.

c. G20

Started in 1999 with meetings of finance ministers and central bankers, G20 was elevated in 2008 to meetings of heads of state. G20 has become an important forum for action against corruption.

The main attraction of G20 is that it brings together the leaders of the twenty most powerful governments in the world. It includes the governments of the old G7: United States, Canada, Germany, United Kingdom, France, Italy, Japan, and the European Union; the five BRICS states: Brazil, Russia, India, China, and South Africa; plus eight other significant states: Nigeria, Indonesia, Saudi Arabia, Mexico, Argentina, Australia, South Korea, and Turkey. The participation of world leaders assures substantial media coverage for G20's work.

G20 utilizes an annual rotating leadership system. This can be a problem when the leader of the year has different priorities from his predecessor or his successor. For example, working on anticorruption is of less interest to Putin or Erdogan than to Obama or Cameron. G20 does not have an independent staff. The leader of the year will be supported by a staff from his or her government.

An important benefit of G20 is that it is complemented by B20 consisting of business leaders and C20 consisting of civil society leaders, coming from the same twenty countries as the G20. B20 and C20 have separate meetings, followed by a meeting with the G20. The B20 and the C20 provide greater continuity than the G20. For example, on anticorruption continuity comes from the participation of TI at the C20 and of General Electric at the B20.

d. World Bank

The politics of the World Bank on corruption provides a checkered story. For several decades, the policy of the Bank was set by the Bank's general counsel,

Ibrahim Shihata of Egypt, a respected expert on international law. Shihata insisted that the Bretton Woods agreements, under which the Bank was established, allowed the Bank to deal only with economic issues, not political ones. Shihata contended that corruption was a political issue and therefore off limits for the Bank.

The founding of TI by Peter Eigen was, in effect, a rebellion against the Shihata policy, and TI was regarded as a renegade. That changed when James Wolfensohn became the Bank's president. Wolfensohn, born in Australia, was a successful international banker in London and in the United States. He had become a US citizen and developed close ties to President Clinton, who proposed his nomination as World Bank president

In his second Annual Meetings address as World Bank president Wolfensohn called on the Bank to combat "the Cancer of Corruption."[3] He invited Peter Eigen and several others from TI—including myself—to a full day meeting with the Bank's top staff. When TI mentioned Shihata's opinion that the Bank could not oppose corruption because it was a political issue, not an economic one, Wolfensohn commented: "That is bullshit—corruption is as much a political issue as it is an economic issue."

The change in high-level policy met resistances at the working level. The Bank's staff regarded its prime mission to make loans. Not making loans because of concerns about corruption did not fit their interests. New employees had to be recruited to ensure compliance with the anticorruption policy. This resulted in protracted internal political tensions between loan officers and the compliance staff. Wolfensohn's first two successors, Paul Wolfowitz and Robert B. Zoellick, maintained firm anticorruption policies. Dr. Jim Yong Kim, who had a medical background and had been president of Dartmouth, de-emphasized anticorruption, which resulted in departures from the compliance staff.

The politics of the Bank are complicated by its complex organization. Seats on the board of directors are given to member countries, including both donor countries that provide the Bank's capital and countries that borrow from the Bank. Each director has a separate staff not controlled by the Bank's president. (John Maynard Keynes, one of the Bank's founders, was prophetic in identifying the problems raised by the Bank's structure, but his concerns were overridden by the United States.)

3. James D. Wolfensohn, Address to the Board of Governors at the Annual Meetings of the World Bank and the International Monetary Fund, Washington DC, October 1, 1996.

e. International Chamber of Commerce (ICC)

The ICC, with headquarters in Paris and scores of national committees around the world, has actively assisted the business community in overcoming corruption for several decades. It developed the pioneering ICC Rules of Conduct to Combat Extortion and Bribery, and published the ICC handbook *Fighting Corruption: A Corporate Practices Manual*; it also conducts advocacy at OECD and UNDOC, and organizes training courses for companies.

f. FIFA

The organization managing worldwide soccer has been of interest because it utilized corruption as the central tool to build its power and to manage its affairs. Because World Cup and regional soccer tournaments are extremely lucrative, FIFA is able to collect huge sums for allocating the right to hold such tournaments.

On paper FIFA appears to be a democratic organization of over two hundred member states, each having one vote. The reality is that FIFA was run by Sepp Blatter, a Swiss national, through his control over FIFA's vast funds. Switzerland is the headquarters location for FIFA and numerous other sports organizations, but until recently has done little or nothing to prevent questionable activities. This appears to be changing as part of a broader Swiss effort to improve its international image.

FIFA is discussed in greater detail in Chapter 15.

3. GOVERNMENTS

Government policies regarding corruption have varied greatly. Some countries make combating corruption a high priority in their international relations and in their domestic policies. Others seek to prevent domestic corruption, but do not control foreign bribery by their exporters, or by their foreign aid and intelligence agencies. Finally, there are governments where corruption is not on the agenda. A few examples should be mentioned.

a. United States

The US government has long been regarded as the 800-pound gorilla in the anticorruption arena. This reflects its political and economic power, as well as moralistic concerns. President Carter's decision made foreign bribery a crime in 1977, two decades before any other country did so. Opposition to corruption has had consistent bipartisan support. Despite business lobbying against the extension of the FCPA, it was passed by an overwhelming 436-0 margin.[4] Members of Congress knew that their opponents would accuse them of supporting corruption at the next election if they failed to support the FCPA extension.

There has been strong enforcement by the Justice Department and the SEC for violations of the FCPA. Actions have been brought against both US and foreign firms. Fines of hundreds of millions of dollars have been collected. The United States collected $400 million from British Aerospace (BAE), compared with $40 million levied by the UK. Enforcement has been based on an expansive jurisdictional approach. Actions in US courts could be brought against foreign companies based on trading of their shares on US exchanges or use of US communication facilities, such as email servers.

The US government has actively supported action against corruption at the UN, the OECD, G20, and in other international forums. The power of the United States has produced a backlash of increasing strength. China, Russia, Venezuela, and Ecuador among others have frequently opposed US positions on corruption. China is now sponsoring rival organizations to compete with the World Bank.

b. UK

The UK government's policies on corruption have reflected divergent influences. There has been long-standing pride in the UK's rule of law tradition, going back nine centuries to the Magna Carta. The UK's international development department has been one of the leading bilateral donors and an influential supporter of anticorruption programs. The Commonwealth Secretariat promotes the rule of law and related policies in the former British dominions.

Less constructive has been the UK's effort to preserve London as a major source for questionable financing in Eastern Europe, the Middle East, and South Africa. Prime Minister Tony Blair carried on a prolonged rearguard action to preserve Victorian and Edwardian bribery laws that included broad loopholes. He ordered prosecutors to drop a suit against British Aerospace (BAE) for payments to a Saudi prince to win a huge order for fighter planes. The BAE case defied Article 5 of the OECD Convention, which provides that enforcement shall not be influenced by considerations of national economic interests. After

4. Noonan 1984, 677.

a decade-long dispute with the OECD, Prime Minister Gordon Brown revered UK policy and supported passage of the very advanced Bribery Act of 2010.[5] In 2016 Prime Minister David Cameron organized an international conference to promote anticorruption enforcement.

Relations between OECD and the UK are discussed in greater detail in Chapter 7.

c. Nordic Countries

Denmark, Finland, Norway, and Sweden enjoy an outstanding reputation, as reported in TI's Corruption Perception Index, where they have consistently ranked among the top ten countries. However, companies from the Nordic countries carry on extensive trade with Russia and other corrupt Eastern European countries. There are indications that Nordic governments turn a blind eye to bribery in such trade.

d. China

Chinese politics has been seriously impacted by corruption for many decades. The government of President Mao Tse-tung is widely credited with ending the endemic corruption that prevailed before the Communist revolution. When Deng Xiao Ping reintroduced private enterprise in the late 1970, corruption re-emerged. Deng's successors conducted several anticorruption drives. But these were used primarily to purge corrupt officials from the preceding regimes, with corruption continuing under the new government.

The government of President Xi Jinping is conducting a massive drive against corruption within China. Thousands of government officials and officials in the private sectors—in Xi Jinping's words "tigers" as well as "flies"—are being dismissed and punished.[6] Xi Jinping's commitment to combating corruption is strong. However, there can be questions about the long-term effectiveness of a top-down approach that does not utilize checks and balances such as an independent judiciary, NGOs, and whistle-blowers.

Whether OECD can succeed in establishing a global, corruption-free level playing field will be strongly influenced by Chinese actions. Government policy prohibits foreign bribery by Chinese companies, but has not been effectively

5. See below 93 et seq.

6. The Guardian, 22 January 2013: "Xi Jinping vows to fight 'tigers' and 'flies' in anti-corruption drive."

enforced. China has observer status at the OECD but has not signed OECD's anti-bribery Convention. It has adopted UNCAC and has participated in UNODC's implementation reviews.

e. Bangladesh

Bangladesh presents some interesting paradoxes. It has provided outstanding leaders for TI, including Kamal Hossain and Iftekhar Zaman. It has a very large number of NGOs that have received extensive support from international development agencies. TI-Bangladesh has the largest staff of any TI national chapter. Nevertheless, Bangladesh has remained in the bottom quartile of TI's Corruption Perception Index.

4. ROLE OF MEDIA

The media play a powerful role in the politics of corruption. There clearly is a symbiotic relation between the media and the anticorruption movement. Corruption scandals sell newspapers. Investigative reporters cooperate with corruption fighters. When governments fail to control corruption, more scandals are sure to erupt, resulting in new media coverage and increased popular pressure for government action.

The digital revolution is reducing the number of newspapers, but is enhancing the effectiveness of other ways to provide news. It has become much harder to maintain secrecy, which is crucial for bribe payers and bribe takers. Secrets once uncovered circulate instantaneously around the world.

5. GROWTH OF ANTICORRUPTION MOVEMENT

The anticorruption movement began in 1993 with a single NGO in a two-person office in Berlin. There are now tens of thousands of people with full-time careers in the fight against corruption. They provide political momentum as well as specialized expertise for the anticorruption movement.

6. GOVERNMENT DEPARTMENTS

There are anticorruption programs in most developed governments, as well as in many developing countries. In the United States this includes the Departments of Justice, State, and Commerce, as well as the SEC, FBI, and CIA. Most of the forty-two OECD members have programs in their ministries dealing with foreign affairs, law, and trade. In China, employee totals in the four to five figure range from the Ministry of Supervision and the Disciplinary Committee of the Central Committee are involved in Xi Jinping's anti-bribery campaign.

7. PRIVATE INDUSTRY

Practically all major multinational enterprises (MNEs) now have substantial compliance programs. For example, Siemens has a compliance staff of over six hundred people.[7]

8. NGOS

TI has about 150 employees in Berlin, plus over a hundred chapters with several thousand employees, members, and active supporters. There are dozens of other NGOs with active anticorruption programs, including TRACE, Human Rights Watch, and Oxfam.

9. PROFESSIONAL ORGANIZATIONS

Major law firms serving MNEs have staffs with anticorruption expertise. Washington firms have recruited so many former Justice Department and SEC employees that the fight against corruption has become a local cottage industry. Law firms in such cities as New York, Chicago, Boston, Atlanta, Houston, Dallas, San Francisco, and Los Angeles have anticorruption lawyers. Law firms in Europe and Asia are following the same trend.

The major accounting and financial services firms, including PWC, Ernst &Young, KPMG, and Deloitte have large staffs working on anticorruption compliance.

10. UNIVERSITIES

Many universities in Europe and the United States have anticorruption and corporate governance experts on their faculties. The University of Basel has an

7. Manager-Magazin, January 26, 2016: "Wo waren Sie, Herr Cromme?."

associated Governance Institute with a staff of over thirty professionals with Mark Pieth as Chairman of the Board.

11. ILLICIT ACTIVITIES

Large numbers of experts, probably numbering in the hundreds, are actively engaged in extortion, counterfeiting, smuggling, and money laundering. This creates the need for a much larger number of anticorruption experts.

12. MAJOR POLITICAL INFLUENCES

Anticorruption politics has been influenced by several major factors:

a. Tone at the Top

In governments, corporations, and international organizations the level of corruption will be strongly influenced by the tone at the top. Leaders with a strong commitment to anticorruption can create an organizational culture in which corruption will not flourish. Corrupt leaders set bad examples; as a result, corruption can readily expand to endemic levels.

b. Power of the Legal Establishment

In countries where the rule of law is well established, independent prosecutors and judges can serve as effective checks and balances, deterring corruption by government leaders and elsewhere in society. Successful prosecution has often served as a steppingstone to high-level political office.

c. Role of Civil Society

NGOs and individual whistle-blowers can play an influential role in combating corruption.

d. People Power

Popular mass movements have demonstrated their ability to overthrow corrupt leaders, even dictators who have been entrenched in power for decades. This is a major new factor in anticorruption politics, dating back to the Arab Spring. However, building better institutions following a revolution is a difficult challenge, because the time frame and the actions required are different from what it takes to organize a successful revolution.

e. Counteractions

Opposition to reforms has taken many forms. Bribe payers and bribe takers have become much more sophisticated, using money laundering and intermediaries in multiple countries to cover their tracks. Repressive governments bar NGOs and whistle-blowers and use sedition laws and libel laws against those who attack bribery.

The fight over corruption has no foreseeable end date. However, the developments of the last two decades provide reasons for optimism that the balance is shifting in favorable directions. The growth of a large anticorruption movement provides momentum and expertise. The digital revolution is eroding the secrecy without which corruption cannot function. Developing closer linkage between people power and the anticorruption movement will ensure that revolutions can result in better successor governments.

4

What Is Corruption?

MARK PIETH ■

1. A "CANCER" TO BE ROOTED OUT?

Many modern books about corruption start out with the broadest of possible definitions, associating corruption with filth, moral decay, and all things bad.[1] These authors find support in the famous 1996 speech of Jim Wolfensohn, then president of the World Bank, calling corruption a "cancer" to be rooted out.[2] They typically go on to call for all-out "war on corruption".[3] The authors of this book find matters more complex. It is unlikely that the phenomenon will simply go away as a consequence of concrete activism. It is a very old phenomenon, deeply engrained in many societies, even if in very different forms. It is true that over the ages at least some forms of corruption have been legally or at least morally sanctioned in most societies. Judge John Noonan[4] gives a detailed account of the ways societies have dealt with the issue over 5,000 years. In this and other narratives, however, it emerges that historically the phenomenon was not always criticized wholeheartedly. In certain phases it was considered a preferential option to brutal force: a quite explicit example are the agreements concluded amongst British noblemen in the seventeenth century to avoid unnecessary bloodshed and to replace their power

1. The Oxford English Dictionary defines corruption as the "perversion or destruction of integrity in the discharge of public duties by bribery or favour. . . ."

2. World Bank 2005, 45 et seq.

3. Vogl 2012.

4. Noonan 1984.

Confronting Corruption. Fritz Heimann and Mark Pieth.

management by an elaborate system of corruption, bribery, and patronage. The acquisition and the sale of public office and parliamentary seats became acceptable.[5]

A series of questions need to be discussed in this chapter:

- Is there a common understanding of what corruption means?
- Why has corruption been historically so ubiquitous, and why is it still nowadays such a widespread phenomenon?
- Is corruption really harmful?
- What made Western states and societies suddenly turn against corruption towards the end of the twentieth century?
- Are we successful in combating bribery?

Answers to these introductory questions will allow us to focus better on the different forms of corruption and their prevalence. It will also allow us to distinguish between problematic and less harmful forms of reciprocities.[6]

2. GIVING AND TAKING

Corruption is frequently set in the context of giving and taking (*"do ut des"*). Now, giving in order to receive something in return is a normal thing in life: even in the most intimate relations we rarely act purely out of altruism. We want to be loved. In business, we are used to concluding contracts for the exchange of goods and services. Again, giving and taking is what keeps everyday business going. Nothing is a priori problematic. Obviously, the relationship gets more delicate if I give what does not belong to me (e.g., access to the commodities of my state) to a third party in exchange for a non-deserved personal favor. Frequently, however, situations are not so clear-cut: let's say, I am a private engineer as is my classmate, who is now planning an infrastructure project on behalf of the government. I am perfectly qualified to get the job and my bid is within the official parameters. Is there a problem if I get the contract? The example—even though it may be debatable if one can call this corruption—leaves a stale taste: as a minimum, transparency would prevent a possible conflict of interest, the next-door neighbor to corruption.

5. Noonan 1984, 366 et seq.; Richter 1989, 64 (referring to the Treaties of 1660 and 1688).

6. Noonan 1984, 687 et seq.

3. LEGAL DEFINITIONS

Looking at the topic from a legal perspective, "corruption" is actually not a term of art. It is rather a broad umbrella term for an entire field of concrete offences:

Bribery is the traditional core notion. Typically, laws address so-called active bribery (bribing) and passive bribery (receiving) by *officials* separately,[7] even if it has become customary to consider one behavior as bad as the other. Formerly, taking bribes by officials was considered worse because officials violated their official duties. Nowadays though, it is next to universally recognized that the "supply side" of bribery is equally problematic, as sometimes the briber is the stronger part.[8] The criminal act is usually described as an exchange (of a promise) of an undue advantage to a (foreign or domestic) official for an act or omission in the execution of his or her duties. Some countries differentiate further between genuine bribery, whereby the briber fosters a breach of duty by the official, and subsidiary forms of offenses, where they are merely encouraged by the undue payment to do their duty.[9] Typically, though, discretionary acts would fall under the breach-of-duty rule. Internationally, there is a common understanding that the actual bribery of domestic or foreign officials in exchange for a breach of duty should be criminalized.[10] Whether countries want to go beyond that and criminalize domestic or foreign "facilitation payments" (advantages in furtherance of the official's duty) or even so called gratuities (payments in the aftermath of an act or omission) is left to them.

Beyond the bribing of officials, most countries also criminalize *private* commercial bribery. However, this is a totally different type of offense: instead of putting the general trust of the population in the public order in question, it entices an employee to breach his duty toward his principal and typically, it affects the employer's assets. This is why, in many countries, it is left to the employer whether she wants to bring a case.

Still, under the umbrella term "corruption" an entire series of *related crimes* need to be mentioned. "Graft" or "embezzlement" of public funds is used where an official is not actually bribed, but illegally helps himself to public funds (the famous "hand in the till"). Typical are those cases where kleptocrats divert public funds into their private accounts.[11] Fraud is another crime that

7. Cf. UNCAC 2003, Article 15(a) and (b).

8. Pieth 2013a, 687 et seq.

9. Cf. for facilitation payments see Germany: §§ 331, 333 D-StGB; Switzerland: Article $322^{\text{quinquies}}$ and ^{sexies} CH-StGB.

10. Cf. UNCAC 2003, Article 15; OECD Convention 1997, Article 1.

11. See below 132 et seq.

may—according to some national laws (cf. the United States)—be used in the context of corruption. However, generally it is seen as an offense by an outsider rather than by an official or an employee working from within the institution.

Sometimes officials offer preferential treatment to relatives or friends (the term "nepotism" is used where a public position is given to a relative). A further related area is the so-called *"traffic in influence,"* whereby a "friend" promises to curry favors with officials in exchange for remuneration by the favored person. All these activities have in common that they are variations of conflicts in interest. At least "traffic in influence" is considered a crime by international law[12] and according to many national legislations.

It is far more difficult, however, to come to terms with the help of traditional criminal law, where a *"quid pro quo"* relation is not obvious at all: in Italy, the large scale *mani pulite* investigations detected that entire networks of "friends" kept track of *"favors"* to be repaid over long stretches of time and in kind rather than in money. These mechanisms are especially widespread in so-called "patronage cultures." A study of Swiss engineers amongst their professional colleagues came up with the finding that there was hardly any straightforward corruption in construction; however, friends and schoolmates were inclined to offer and expect favors of each other.[13] We will revisit this type of exchange of favors when we come to the mismanagement of Sports Governing Bodies (below Chapter 15).

4. CORRUPTION COMES IN DIFFERENT FORMS

Overall, the term "corruption" is extremely wide and encompasses a whole range of questionable situations. If we look at them from a political science rather than a legal perspective, a few traditional examples may help define the scope:

Maybe the simplest of forms, to be found in all parts of the world, is the public official demanding a personal favor in exchange for preferential treatment to an applicant for a license, permit, or contract. This type of extortive behavior is not uncommon also in the developed world; it is frequently a form of embezzlement by a person believing himself to be underpaid. The culprit is not far off from any other criminal caught with his hands in the till. His motivation could be greed, but frequently corruption goes far beyond this individualistic interpretation.

12. CoE 1999, Article 12; UNCAC 2003, Article 18.

13. Bircher and Scherler 2001; Pieth 2013a, 683.

The person targeted to become a briber will typically go along either because it makes sense economically or because he or she is desperate. The latter form is more frequent where this type of solicitation is systemic and where simple everyday government acts are not to be had or not to be obtained within reasonable time without the extra payment (take a birth certificate, a driver's license, a passport, a visa etc.). Frequently this method is also used to siphon off funds in everyday business (a container is "lost" in the harbor upon arrival and needs to be "found" against a small fee; customs refuses to give the necessary stamps to clear the goods if the client refuses to make the extra payment). The goal here is not to qualify this behavior morally, as in many parts of the world government actually expects its officials (be it traffic police, customs agents, or hospital personnel) to generate part of their own income "proactively": the official's salary frequently does not allow a decent life, let alone schooling of the official's children, or salaries are only paid irregularly, if at all.[14]

Bribery can get far more systemic yet. For example, in India it is not uncommon to buy public office. The necessary funds will need to be raised with a loan and then repaid in the aftermath. In fact, there is evidence that in many aspects of public life an entire pyramid of payoffs has been established. While procuring funds from the population at large, from farmers dependent on water for irrigation purposes, or from patients seeking access to the healthcare system, only a part of the funds is kept by the immediate recipient; other parts are handed up the ladder to more senior officials, in order to finally reach the minister or the chief minister of a state.[15]

What may seem like a complex system of capital accumulation, through a multitude of petty-payments affecting the entire society, could also be represented by direct big-time embezzlement of public funds: the typical model is the cooperation of Western multinational enterprises and representatives of new elites in resource-rich states of the global South. The new elites of yet unstable but resource-rich states find it easy to sell off natural resources for private benefit. Frequently, multinational enterprises have been willing partners in what was called "business as usual".[16] The lack of procedures and controls in the new states makes their endeavors easy.

Where heads of state and the interests of entire nations get involved, it is far more difficult yet to unravel a corruption network. We have observed several large-scale bribery schemes involving the defense sector, virtually inaccessible

14. Ben Jelloun 1994.

15. Cf. Davis 2004; Stålgren 2006, 7; Centre for Media Studies 2011, 18 et seq.; Centre for Media Studies 2012, 17 et seq.

16. Pieth 2000, 51.

for ordinary justice, because the exporting and the importing state place these deals outside judicial scrutiny:

The French frigate scandal has become a famous example: French businesses (including Elf, Thompson-CSF and the Chantiers Navals) bribed representatives of the potential buyer, the Taiwan Defense Department, to give their product preference over that of others; they also bribed mainland Chinese officials to mitigate their protests against the arms deal with Taiwan. However, the main scandal were the retro-commissions to finance a French electoral campaign. Documentation was rapidly centralized in a building in France and declared off limits for judicial supervision when the scandal broke.[17] It proved to become a model for the French "secret de la defense" to avert law enforcement action against highest level corruption.[18]

A second cause célèbre was the BAE (British Aerospace) bribery to promote the sale of fighter planes to Saudi Arabia, the so-called "Al Yamamah" contract. After evidence emerged that over £60 million had been paid to several members of the Saudi royal family through a London travel agent ("petty-cash")[19] and more evidence pointed toward much bigger payments to Prince Bandar through Riggs Bank in Washington, the case run by the Serious Fraud Office (SFO) in London was closed upon intervention by the prime minister, Tony Blair, in December 2005.[20] The reasons given by the prime minister were on the one hand, the safeguarding of the international relations with Saudi Arabia, and on the other hand, the protection of employment in Britain, both considerations outlawed by Article 5 of the OECD Convention.[21] This case will be analyzed in greater detail in Chapter 7. Here it may serve as a simple illustration of how law enforcement becomes an uphill battle as soon as vital public and economic interests are involved.

A last case to illustrate the difficulties relating to arms and similar exports is the *Steyr/Daimler/Puch*-case: Steyr/Daimler/Puch, an Austrian defense

17. Swiss Federal Supreme Court Decision, BGE 130 II 217, 3 May 2004; Jean-Pierre 2003, 223 et seq.; AFP, October 3, 2008: "French judge dismisses Lafayette case."

18. Critical OECD in its phase 2 and phase 3 monitoring of France: OECD WGB 2012, France Phase 3, 47 et seq.

19. The Guardian, October 5, 2004: "BAE chief linked to slush fund: Documents suggest system of false accounting covered £60 million payments to leading Saudis."

20. The Guardian, December 15, 2006: "National interest halts arms corruption inquiry"; cf. in more detail below 87 et seq.

21. OECD WGB 2008, UK Phase 2[bis], 37 et seq.

company, found its production line empty, awaiting a new tank design to mature. In the meantime, it considered acting as a trading house: it procured the sale of 315 fire trucks and 30 firefighting boats and other equipment to the Bangkok Municipal Authority (BMA). The trucks themselves were assembled by a Belgian company. In order to secure the contract, Steyr/Daimler/Puch expended over 20 percent "commission payments," even though—based on the actual work product of the intermediaries—a maximum of 2 to 3 percent would have been justified.[22] So far, the newly created Austrian law enforcement agency on corruption has refused to become involved, even though documentation was available and testimony possible.[23] Whereas Austrian courts have closed the case, the Supreme Court of Thailand has sent the former minister of interior and the fire chief of Bangkok to prison for over ten years each for accepting bribes.[24]

5. A SYSTEMIC PERSPECTIVE

So far, the examples have been focusing on the individual infringement of rules. As in the criminology of economic crime in general, there is a tension between explanations centered around personality and incentives (greed, peer pressure, clan pressure) on the one hand, and objective (so called "environmental") factors, standing for opportunity or need (monopoly, discretion, low level of supervision, low pay, culture, loyalty to clan rather than to state) on the other.

All these considerations, however, remain within the *individualist* realm of explanations. Serious corruption comes in a *systemic* way. Political scientists have stressed this for quite a while. Johnston has talked of "syndromes of corruption."[25] More recently they have concentrated on distinguishing different types of corruption-prone systems. They address various forms of "autocracies," "patronage networks" based on family, clans, "oligarchies," or other kinds of "elites."[26] A multitude of case studies has been published, focusing in particular

22. Cf. OECD WGB 2009 Typologies, 20.

23. Regional Court (Landesgericht) for Criminal Matters Vienna, Decision No. 130 BI 51/13h, 27 August 2013.

24. Supreme Court of Thailand, Criminal Division for Holders of Political Positions, Decisions No. 5/2554 and 7/2556, 10 September 2013 (subject: malfeasance in office, violations of the 1999 Act Concerning Offences Relating to the Submission of Bids to Government Agencies).

25. Johnston 2005; Johnston 2014, 5, 16 et seq., 86 et seq., 235.

26. Johnston 2014, 86, 119, 151 et seq.

on fragile states or oligarchic regimes. Although it is true that life in such a state may be determined by the need to ensure nearly all public or even private services with the help of extra payments, these studies tend to deflect from the risks faced by established democracies and states of law.

Democracy does not protect from corrupt behavior. Even in such traditional and well-established democracies as France, the United Kingdom, or the United States[27] mechanisms to secure power for wealthy elites exist. It starts with schooling, and goes on to party financing and selective access to senior public or private positions. All these countries know local corruption scandals, but in particular in France nearly every president is said to have been involved in party financing scandals.[28] Economists and social scientists have criticized that even in established democracies certain industries or elites may obtain preferential access to goods: Johnston quotes Stiglitz[29] when he talks of "private-sector rents created and protected by the law" in the United States and other Western democracies. As examples he mentions "the non-competitive drug purchase program" or "reduced tax rates for the wealthy".[30] The obvious snag with this theory is that inequality may seem illegitimate under the circumstances mentioned; the elites, however, manage to obtain their rents legally. This raises the question whether we can seriously talk of "legal corruption" as some authors do,[31] or whether this is not an oxymoron. Maybe it is better to speak of "legalized corruption." Nevertheless, what is legal is not merely the object of criminological theory; policy and politics need to work toward changing the law. Even as a lawyer, one should not give up too easily: Would the constitutional concept of equality not offer legal arguments against publicly protected private rent-seeking? Parliaments and constitutional courts need to give especially party financing and lobbying a much closer look.[32]

6. WHAT IS THE COMMON DENOMINATOR?

Books on corruption traditionally distinguish between "grand" and "petty" corruption.[33] They also differentiate between bribery and other forms of corruption.

27. Teachout 2014; Johnston 2014, 197 et seq.

28. Johnston 2014, 194 et seq.

29. Stiglitz 2012, chapters 1–4; cf. also Johnston 2014, 208 et seq.

30. Johnston 2014, 209.

31. Kaufmann and Vicente 2005.

32. Teachout 2014, 246 et seq.; Johnston 2014, 199 et seq.

33. Moody-Stuart 1997, 4 et seq.

Nevertheless, there are common traits binding the above-mentioned examples together: corruption is always a form of abuse of power for private benefit.[34] As shown above, there are common legal definitions emerging in particular in international treaties and in national implementing laws. They differentiate between actual bribery (promising or giving an undeserved favor to promote a breach of duty) and simpler forms of favors. They distinguish public from private (commercial) bribery, and they all deal with the briber (active bribery) and the bribee (passive bribery) separately. Typical for public and commercial bribery are: the offering or giving, demanding, or taking of an undue advantage in furtherance of (illicit) behavior.[35]

There is, however, a wider common thread between the examples, which also explains why corruption is so prevalent and seems to have been so for such a long time: corrupt behavior (in the broadest of senses) has been a traditional means of *power management*. Already historic authors such as Niccolò Machiavelli[36] (1469–1527) or Thomas Hobbes[37] (1588–1679) have made it clear that to obtain power and to stay in power are dependent upon the ability to buy the loyalty of essential followers. Historical examples illustrate what is meant. No one is able to wield power alone. All the powerful, including autocrats, need followers or cronies. Even Louis XIV (1638–1715) had to secure his reign by creating a new caste of followers (court officials) and by controlling the old guard of noble men by forcing them to be permanently present at his court.[38] What may seem logic when regarding past or present autocrats is less obvious with politicians in democracies. True, you would assume they cannot simply turn around and distribute public goods to a small group of followers. They must be perceived to foster the general good. And yet, those candidates for office promising the greater advantage to the bigger part of the electorate are more likely to win. This may seem simplistic, but also democrats and their electorate are not necessarily pure idealists. The population of a democracy wants to live, and it will cast its vote for those making the most attractive promises.[39] Of course, there is a high tension—in particular in democratic countries—between the need to be seen promoting the public good and the necessity to remunerate the narrow group of essential followers (what Bueno de Mesquita and Smith call the

34. Moody-Stuart 1997, 1, Appendix.

35. OECD Convention 1997, Article 1 (1); UNCAC 2003, Article 15 (a).

36. Machiavelli 1513.

37. Hobbes 1651.

38. Bueno de Mesquita and Smith 2011, 1 et seq., 128.

39. Bueno de Mesquita and Smith 2011, 19, 41, 65 et seq.; Johnston 2014, 186 et seq.

"winning coalition"[40]). One paradigm allowing to explain this ambiguity is the differentiation between formal democracy and rule of law and the remaining informal mechanism of power management (in Italy you still may need friends at high places to get the administration to do its job—and you will repay the help, maybe in the same coin, using your own network of friends).

The case for corruption as a means to obtain and retain power has been made in different ways, either as a description of a simple fact[41] or its being portrayed as a necessary evil. In some cases, authors have even used the argument in a form of paradox intervention: Horst-Eberhard Richter writes his "arguments for corruption" as a wake-up call.[42] And yet, especially economists have used similar arguments in all earnest, in an attempt to move away from a moralizing discourse.[43]

7. ARE WE SURE THAT CORRUPTION IS HARMFUL?

The imagery of the "cancer" that needs to be rooted out leaves no doubt: corruption is harmful, and there are good reasons for this position.

Especially in developing states corruption leads to dangerous misallocations of resources: the healthcare system frequently malfunctions, education is not delivered, housing cannot be funded, and, in extreme cases, hunger relief does not reach those in need. Also, in more affluent societies corruption typically leads to a waste of taxpayers' money (the cost of infrastructure projects, such as tunnels and motorways, is inflated, the best briber, rather than the best bidder gets the job), or shareholders suffer from commercial bribery. Overall, there are also more abstract damages to consider: bribery in business relations or political corruption are forms of unfair competition, and ultimately, corruption undermines the trust of the population in the public institutions of a country.[44]

All this may be true and yet one needs to explain why not more energy has gone into reducing the risks of bribery. The current drive against bribery is very recent, barely twenty to thirty years old.

One reason could be seen in a certain ambiguity: it is true that from a short-term and very egoistic perspective—the kind of approach we know from some "law and economics"-students—there may be benefits for the position of

40. Bueno de Mesquita and Smith 2011, 4 et seq., 119.

41. Bueno de Mesquita and Smith 2011, xi.

42. Richter 1989, 16.

43. Neugebauer 1978, 132 et seq.

44. Pieth 2013a, 687 et seq.; Pieth 2013b, Vor Art. 322[ter] N 11.

the individual briber. This is the background of the frequently cited "prisoner's dilemma."[45] The context is clearly a simplistic theory of capitalist egoism derived from the thinking of John Stuart Mill and his epigones.[46]

Only slightly different are those theories that go beyond describing bribery as a classic means of power management: there have been authors throughout history actually defending the need for bribery as an essential item in the politician's toolkit.[47] Until recently it was even considered an essential means of foreign policy to secure political alliances worldwide. So, authors[48] are right, there is a tension between fighting corruption as "good policy" and corruption as "good politics."

However, for all the ambiguity, we need to consider why we are suddenly so concerned about corruption and bribery.

8. HOW BIG IS THE PROBLEM?

For all we know, the problem is huge. Some scholars have tried to estimate the total amounts spent on bribes worldwide. They come out with the amazing figure of $1 trillion per year. Now, the methodology of such "guesstimates" is problematic. They remind us of the efforts in the early 1990s to affix a number to the global drug trade and drug money laundering.

Estimating Global Drug Money Laundering

Those who have witnessed the initial moments of the worldwide anti-money-laundering movement, with the UN Vienna Convention of 1988[49] and the early days of the Financial Action Task Force on Money Laundering (FATF) from 1989 on[50] will remember that the contemporary estimate of laundered funds was $300 billion per year.[51] Nobody was really able to explain where the figure came from. This led the UN to create an "Intergovernmental Expert

45. Pieth 2012, 3.

46. Mill 1859.

47. Machiavelli 1513; Bueno de Mesquita and Smith 2011.

48. Bueno de Mesquita and Smith 2011.

49. UN 1988: United Nations Convention against Illicit Traffic in Narcotic Drugs and Psychotropic Substances.

50. FATF Report 1989.

51. Intergovernmental Expert Group 1991, para. 28.

Group to Study the Economic and Social Consequences of Illicit Traffic in Drugs."[52] From 1990 onward, a group of experts met in Vienna, amongst them the Italian anti-mafia-hero, Giovanni Falcone.[53]

Having been sent to the meeting by the Swiss Federal Office of Justice as draftsperson of government texts on money laundering and organized crime at the time, I rapidly found myself engulfed in international politics: the United States was opposing the prestigious head of the Indian Anti-Drug Agency, Mr. Bhatnagar, being named chair. They preferred a Mexican colleague. The Indian delegate, realizing that he could not have his will, insisted that the "neutral" Swiss become chair. The entire masquerade was organized behind the scenes by a Spanish Head of Section of the United Nations Office on Drugs and Crime (UNODC) and one of the long sequences of Italian undersecretaries running the Vienna office of the UN. My Mexican colleague[54] (who ended up being named vice-chair) and I tried to use academic criteria in a highly politicized environment. We spent a long and hot summer in Vienna discussing whether $300 billion or rather $500 billion annually were laundered in the early 1990s.[55]

Diplomats will excuse me if my lesson was to be yet more skeptical about what politicians can do with a straightforward criminological or economic topic. The contribution of a bunch of French diplomats in particular, after hard days of work of condemning drug trafficking in all its forms, was in the evening—over a drink—to discuss the merits of legalizing drug consumption and trafficking.

The World Bank Institute[56] has suggested that the right figure for bribes paid worldwide would be annually over $1 trillion. One thing is sure: it is big. Everything else is less certain. One problem is that this figure mixes together very diverse types of bribery: the multitude of petty bribes paid especially in the Third World and the major bribes paid in infrastructure or the defense industries all over the world. It furthermore does not distinguish between actual bribery and broader forms of embezzlement, graft, and other abuses of power.

52. UN 1989: International Action to Combat Drug Abuse and Illicit Trafficking, para. 9.

53. Cf. Falcone and Padovani 1992.

54. Mr. Miguel Ruíz Cabañas, in the meantime the deputy Minister of Justice of Mexico.

55. Intergovernmental Expert Group 1991, para. 11 et seq.

56. Cf. World Bank online, News & Broadcast: "Six Questions on the Cost of Corruption with World Bank Institute Global Governance Director Daniel Kaufmann."

Another difficulty is that the figure of total bribes paid is next to meaningless: its aim is to impress us and remind us to take the issue seriously. What would be far more relevant, though, would be figures on the damage caused through bribery and corruption. Again, the methodology available cannot realistically come up with concrete figures.

Furthermore, quantitative studies of corruption try to measure very different facts: some authors use the Rule of Law Index developed by the World Justice Project.[57] Other texts use as reference indices: the World Bank's Rule of Law Index, the Government Effectiveness Index, and the Corruption Risk Index from the International Country Risk Guide of the Political Risk Services Group.[58]

Another indirect way of measuring corruption is to use perception indices.[59] Transparency International (TI) achieved a political coup by publishing its Corruption Perception Index (CPI), and is doing so annually.[60] It remains uncertain, though, whether the ratings can really be compared from year to year, as their bases change. TI followed soon after with a "Bribe Payers Index" (BPI) assessing the perception of the home country of large bribers of foreign public officials.[61] Malicious observers have maintained that perception indices are primarily there to replicate prejudice and may amount to little more than organized slander. At least, this is how some active corruption fighters in difficult markets felt (such as the auditor general of Brazil after his huge efforts reaped merely a worsening of Brazil's rating[62]). Obviously, in hindsight one may hold that the perceptions were not totally inaccurate.

What is possible, though, are micro-studies of for example, what a judge on an island in Indonesia typically demands[63] or what access to hospitals in Bulgaria would cost.[64] Such tariffs are available, but again they do not in themselves indicate the actual harm done to the institutions and society; expressing it in figures is difficult, but not impossible.

57. Cf. WJP Rule of Law Index 2014.

58. Klitgaard 2014, 18; Mungiu-Pippidi 2014, 3.

59. EU: Special Eurobarometer 397; World Bank: Worldwide Governance Indicators (WGI); The Quality of Government Institute (QOG): ANTICORRP European survey 2013.

60. Cf. TI CPI 2014, 1 et seq.; crit. Recanatini 2013, 59; Rose-Ackerman and Søreide 2011, xiv.

61. TI: Bribe Payers Index (BPI); Johnston 2014, 200 et seq.

62. Statement by the Controller General of Brazil in the OECD WGB (Working Group on Bribery).

63. UN 2006, 35 et seq.

64. Datzova 2003, 21 et seq.

9. WHY HAVE WE CHOSEN TO FIGHT CORRUPTION NOW?

On a national level, probably all states have laws against domestic public bribery. Traditionally, bribe-taking was considered as a breach of trust by officials. Bribe-giving was subjected to varying interpretations: it was either defined as a form of aiding and abetting of bribe-taking or as an independent (but typically lesser[65]) offense. It needs to be added, though, that these traditional laws were rarely applied.

A new concept emerged when the United States enacted the Foreign Corrupt Practices Act (FCPA) in 1977.[66] The context and the reason for the timing will be discussed in greater detail below in Chapter 6. For our purposes here it will be noted that the focus shifted from the defense of domestic administration to international competitiveness. Initially, the FCPA remained unilateral, though, and served the defense of US export interests.

This approach developed into a multilateral concept with the fall of the Berlin Wall and the opening of the East. During the Cold War the superpowers had themselves systematically resorted to corruption in order to secure their influence worldwide; now, opening up markets and doing away with irrational trade barriers has become a priority interest. In our view, this is one of the key reasons for the breakthrough of the OECD Convention[67] as well as regional treaties[68] and ultimately the United Nations Convention against Corruption (UNCAC).[69]

In short, the new policy needs to be seen as a consequence of intensified globalization towards the end of the twentieth century.[70] Obviously, the rationale has been broadened since then by nongovernmental organizations (NGOs) and especially multinational development banks (MDBs) considering corruption as one of the major impediments to development (see below Chapter 16).

Some authors explain the recently found interest in corruption less with economic demands than with a change of moral attitude: the psychoanalyst

65. Balmelli 1996, 60 et seq.; Pieth 2013a, § 22 N 18; Pieth 2013b, Vor Art. 322[ter] N 12 et seq.

66. FCPA 1977.

67. Pieth 2014a, 8 et seq.

68. EU 1997: European Union Convention against Corruption Involving Officials; CoE 1999: Council of Europe Criminal Law Convention on Corruption; OAS 1996: Inter-American Convention against Corruption; African Union 2003: Convention on Preventing and Combating Corruption.

69. UNCAC 2003: United Nations Convention against Corruption.

70. Pieth 2014a, 17.

Horst-Eberhard Richter[71] reminds us of our need of enemies to help us deflect from our own shortcomings. The rise of *"moral entrepreneurs"* is explained as a kind of cleansing process due to the common enemy, communism, no longer being available for us to project our collective needs. And Noonan with his highly moralistic approach plays into Richter's hands. Noonan even goes as far as comparing corruption with sex crime and witchcraft,[72] exactly where Richter wants to push us.[73]

10. ARE WE MAKING A DIFFERENCE?

As we will describe, we have spent twenty years in the international arena developing policies against corruption. They have led to a multitude of conventions, recommendations, action plans, and other soft law tools. National legislators have implemented the international legal texts and translated them into domestic practice. Monitoring mechanisms[74] in international organizations, in particular in the OECD, but also the Council of Europe, the UN, the Organization of American States (OAS), and the African Union, are seeing to it that the texts do not stay dead letters.

However, corruption remains a major issue: in particular, chief executive officers (CEOs) of large companies pushed to expand into even more difficult markets are feeling the heat. They increasingly find themselves between a rock and a hard place. Either their sales force uses illicit means and the company risks law enforcement abroad and at home, or they abstain from bribery and risk losing essential contracts.[75] This problem has (in a yet more accentuated way) been highlighted by a recent survey with 5,000 business leaders: the PwC's 2014 Global Economic Crime Survey (Figure 4.1).[76]

In particular, the pharmaceutical industry is finding itself in difficulties in Eastern Asia, above all in China.[77] Its sales force is usually remunerated on the

71. Richter 1989, 1 et seq.

72. Noonan 1984, xvii et seq.

73. Richter 1989, 59.

74. Bonucci 2014, 534 et seq.

75. Pieth 2011, 105.

76. PwC 2014, 16 et seq.

77. Cf. NZZ, May 23, 2014, 27: "Chinas Aufsichtsbehörde stattet Roche einen Besuch ab"; The Financial Times, April 3, 2014: "Big pharma fights back from China scandal"; Reuters, September 5, 2013: "China probes against foreign pharma unfair: EU business lobby"; Shanghai Daily, August 14, 2013: "Novartis saleswomen told to bribe doctors."

Bribery and corruption: The C-Suite gets the message

While it is not the most common form of crime reported, of all the types of fraud covered in our survey, bribery and corruption may pose the greatest threat to global businesses because of the number of business processes it threatens. Sales, marketing, distribution, payments, international expansion, expense reimbursement, tax compliance, and facilities operations are all vulnerable processes.

Every region reported a significant number of incidences of bribery and corruption. Twenty-seven per cent of all respondents who reported economic crime experienced corruption during the survey period, making it the third-highest crime specified and a relative increase of 13% from the 24% reported in 2011.

Figure 10: Rising CEO concern regarding bribery and corruption

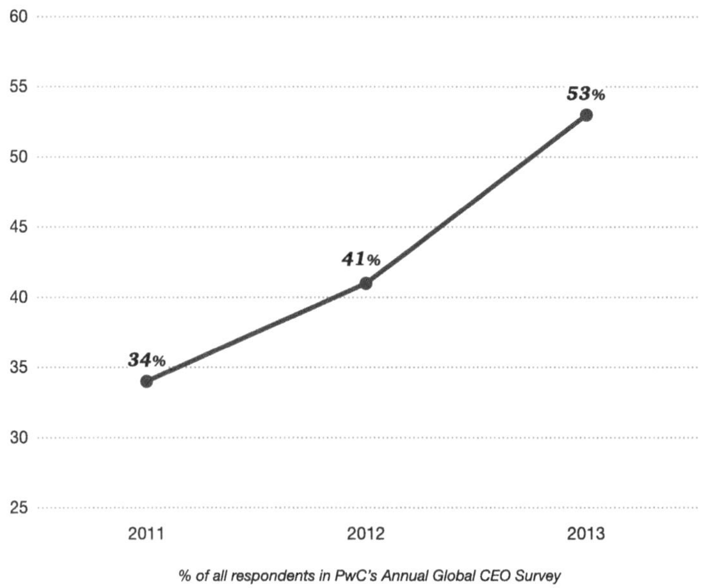

When an economic crime threatens a company in so many ways, it deserves CEO attention—which could explain the sharp increase in CEO focus on the risks of corruption and bribery in this year's CEO Survey.

Figure 4.1 Bribery and corruption: The C-Suite gets the message.
SOURCE: PwC's 2014 Global Economic Crime Survey. Page 18.

basis of performance, that is sales figures. Doctors, be it general practitioners or hospital staff, usually expect to be paid off for prescriptions or the acquisition of medication. The market seems to be rather decentralized. To date there is no obvious way out of the dilemma, as the annual growth rate in China is up to 20 percent and the government has not shown an inclination to step up preventive action. The issue was recently brought to mind, when Chinese authorities turned on GlaxoSmithKline (GSK)[78] in an unprecedented domestic investigation. An investigation by the SFO and the regulators in London followed.[79] Many observers have considered it a political move to force businesses to lower prices. One of the main challenges of doing business in China is that it may be very hard to tell in advance which direction the party policy may go (see below Chapter 23).

If pressure is high in difficult markets, law enforcement, in particular in exporting nations, is not overzealous. Both the OECD Phase 3 evaluations[80] and the TI assessment of investigations and prosecutions by OECD countries[81] show a very ambiguous picture: although a part of the countries are active or moderately active investigators, virtually half have never ever had a case of foreign bribery. As the secretary-general of the OECD, Ángel Gurría, has repeatedly said, it just might be possible that companies of these countries and their managers are markedly more virtuous than their competitors, but it is rather unlikely.[82]

We will revisit the topic of what has been achieved and which challenges remain after giving detail on agents of change and on continuing trouble spots (see below Chapter 21).

78. Cf. Fox 2013: "GSK in China: A game changer in compliance"; The Guardian, May 14, 2014: "GlaxoSmithKline executive could face prison in China over bribery claims"; Financial Times, April 3, 2014, 17: "Big pharma fights back from China scandal"; Financial Times, December 4, 2013: "Q&A: China's investigation into GlaxoSmithKline."

79. The Guardian, May 28, 2014: "GlaxoSmithKline faces criminal investigation by Serious Fraud Office."

80. OECD WGB 2013, 13.

81. TI Progress Report 2015.

82. OECD online, December 11, 2013: "Roundtable on the impact of the OECD Anti-Bribery Convention 15 years on: Webcast."

PART TWO

Drivers of Change

This part provides the reader with the necessary historical background to complete the understanding of the current anticorruption landscape. It tells of how the main anticorruption bodies—the Foreign Corrupt Practices Act (FCPA), OECD Convention and the United Nations Convention against Corruption (UNCAC)—came into existence, and how the prime anti-corruption NGO—Transparency International—was founded.

Evolution of Transparency International

FRITZ HEIMANN

1. PETER EIGEN AND THE WORLD BANK

The evolution of Transparency International (TI) is the remarkable story of the transformation of a personal idea into one of the world's most influential non-governmental organizations (NGOs). TI was founded by Peter Eigen in May 1993 after two decades at the World Bank, in response to his frustration over the refusal of the World Bank to take action against corruption.[1]

Eigen is a remarkable individual: intellectually gifted, articulate, multilingual (fluent in German, English, French and Spanish). He has a warm, outgoing personality and attracts and maintains personal relationships around the world. He is also a talented musician performing at near-professional level on the saxophone and the clarinet. Above all, he is tireless, capable of continuing meetings when everyone else is getting hungry and exhausted. (From personal experience, the latter capability is not an unmitigated pleasure.)

Eigen's World Bank career began serendipitously in 1973. Peter was studying antitrust law at Georgetown University in Washington, planning to return to Germany where antitrust was a growing field. He was offered a job by the Bank because the Bank's jazz band needed a saxophonist.

During the next twenty years Eigen worked at Bank headquarters in Washington as well as at field offices in Latin America and Africa, switching from the legal staff to management positions. By the mid-1980s he was the

1. See above Introduction.

Confronting Corruption. Fritz Heimann and Mark Pieth.

director of Bank programs in East Africa, stationed in Nairobi, Kenya. He had grown increasingly concerned about corruption in the Bank's international development programs. The Bank provides billions of dollars in loans and grants to governments in poor countries, many with corrupt leaders. Before making commitments the Bank's staff carefully analyzed projects. However, in Peter's view, efforts to track how the money was actually spent were inadequate, and the Bank did not know how much money was siphoned off by government officials and intermediaries.

The turning point for him was the refusal of the Bank to take action after Kenya's finance minister was murdered at President Daniel arap Moi's ranch. Eigen had developed a close relationship with the finance minister and they were working on several projects that would avoid the usual payoffs to Kenyan officials by foreign bidders. Eigen's demand that loans to Kenya should be suspended following the murder of the finance minister put Eigen on a collision course with Ibrahim Shihata, the Bank's long-serving Egyptian general counsel.

Shihata, a renowned authority on international law, had issued a legal opinion after the Bank was founded, holding that the Bank's Bretton Woods Charter authorized the Bank to work on economic issues, but not on political ones. Shihata concluded that corruption was off limits because it was a political issue.

Shihata's opinion on corruption fitted squarely with the Bank's prevailing politics and culture. It was consistent with the views of the wealthy countries that provided the Bank's funding and it accommodated the desires of the leaders of poor countries, the recipients of Bank funding. The Bank's management culture focused on getting loans out. Employees were measured and rewarded based on the volume of loans; no one received credit for blocking loans because of concerns about corruption. It was widely recognized that prominent leaders of developing countries, such as Suharto of Indonesia, Mobutu of Zaire, and Moi of Kenya, were corrupt. They remained in power for decades because they were adept at securing continuing funding by playing off the United States and the Soviets against each other.

2. THE GENESIS OF TI

Peter Eigen concluded that an independent organization focusing specifically on corruption was needed. In organizations with a broader scope, concerns about corruption would inevitably be subordinated to other interests. He decided to leave the World Bank and establish an autonomous NGO.

During 1991 and 1992, he refined his ideas through discussions with an informal brainstorming group of friends and colleagues from the international development community. The group was diverse in nationality and professional background but shared Peter's conviction that corruption should no longer be overlooked and that a new organization had to be formed. The participants had extensive practical experience with the politics and economics of international development. They were doers, not theorizers.

The brainstorming group included Hansjörg Elshorst, the head of the German international aid agency GTZ (agency for technical cooperation); Frank Vogl, a former *London Times* foreign correspondent who had been head of public relations for the World Bank; Dieter Frisch, the head of the European Union's aid program; Kamal Hossain, former foreign minister and attorney general of Bangladesh; Michael Hershman, former deputy inspector general of US AID and president of a Washington-based international investigations firm; Joe Githongo of Coopers & Lybrands in Nairobi, who brought in Paul Batchellor and Gerald Parfitt from Coopers & Lybrands headquarters in London; and Laurence Cockcroft, an English development economist with extensive African experience. The group met twice in Africa and once at Coopers & Lybrands' training center outside London. I joined the group before the UK meeting.

By the end of 1993 the central ideas on which TI was founded had crystallized and obtained the support of the whole group:

- TI's primary role was to be an activist organization capable of advocacy at both national and international levels.
- It was essential to raise public awareness of the damage done by corruption. This would require research and dissemination of ideas. But TI should not just be a think tank cranking out intellectual papers. Advocacy was crucial to TI's mission.
- TI should be a broad-based coalition with participation and support from corporations and national governments, as well as from international development organizations.
- The organization structure should consist of an international headquarters and national chapters around the world.
- The name *Transparency International* would be most appropriate, conveying openness and accountability. It would highlight the need to overcome the secrecy on which corruption depends.
- Berlin would be a good headquarters location, recognizing that a location in the United States would be inappropriate.

The name *Transparency* met some initial resistance. Michael Hershman and I felt that the word had no resonance in American legal or commercial usage. The only association was with Scotch Tape and see-through blouses. Peter pointed out that *transparence* had much broader understanding in France and Germany, but invited consideration of other names. But possible alternatives all sounded sanctimonious (e.g., *Integrity International*) and it was decided to proceed with *Transparency International*. A surprising by-product of the growth of TI has been how quickly the term *transparency* achieved widespread usage in the United States. It is an unusual example of European usage moving West.

The choice of headquarters location reflected a clear recognition that TI's ideas would achieve more objective consideration if they did not carry a "Made in America" label. Initially, locations in the Netherlands and in London were discussed. This was cut short when Peter's wife inherited a large house in Berlin. Peter was attracted by the idea of going back to Germany after two decades and witnessing German reunification firsthand.

No one involved in the choice of headquarters saw any objection to Berlin. In hindsight, the Berlin location brought with it some unanticipated problems. A serious shortcoming was that Berlin in the 1990s lacked a pool of manpower with international expertise. Another problem was the rigidity of German employment laws, which complicated hiring and made discharge of employees extremely difficult. In addition, the existing rules for NGOs were designed for local soccer clubs and were not entirely suitable for an NGO with an international mission. Over time, the quality of Berlin as a place to live has improved greatly, which has made it much easier to attract new employees.

3. ORGANIZING TI

a. Meeting with Amnesty International

Peter sent Kamal Hossain and me to London in early 1994 to meet with Amnesty International management to explore how suitable their organization and legal structure would be for TI. Amnesty had been organized in 1961 to campaign for amnesty for two Portuguese human rights activists who had been imprisoned for seven years by the Portuguese government.[2] Following the successful outcome of that campaign, it was decided to continue the organization and take on a broad human rights mission. (The *Amnesty* name was retained even though amnesty campaigns were not an active part of the agenda.)

We had a detailed discussion with Ian Martin, the managing director, and his colleagues in which they explained how they operated and what they considered relevant for TI. They gave us copies of the documents setting up the legal structure for their international headquarters and their national chapters, which were very helpful for TI. They pointed out that their financial model

2. The Guardian, 27 February 2005: "The man who fought for the forgotten."

based on small grants from large numbers of individuals would not work for TI. (At the time, they were raising $10 million through annual $10 grants from 1 million individuals; this has grown to $60 million coming in from 6 million individuals.) Martin did not think that fighting corruption would have a similar appeal to individuals, and that TI would have to rely on raising money from international organizations, foundations, and companies, a forecast that proved accurate.

b. Organization Meeting at Dutch Foreign Ministry

The next step was a February 1994 meeting at the Dutch Foreign Ministry in The Hague, hosted by Jan Pronk, the minister for Development Cooperation. TI's corporate documents were signed by the founding members, Peter Eigen, Frank Vogl, Hansjörg Elshorst, Kamal Hossain, Michael Hershman, Peter Conze, and myself. Crucial to the start was a commitment by Elshorst that GTZ would underwrite any deficits incurred during TI's first year.

c. Berlin Launch Conference

To secure public recognition for TI a launch conference was held at the Villa Borsig in Berlin on May 4–6, 1993, attended by seventy participants from twenty countries. Prominent participants included Richard von Weizsäcker, the president of Germany; Robert McNamara from the United States who had been president of the World Bank for ten years; Oscar Arias, president of Costa Rica; and Alberto Dahik, vice president of Ecuador.

At the opening session McNamara stated that with the founding of TI "our chances of curbing corruption effectively are now better than in the last 50 years." Coming from a person with McNamara's record as president of Ford Motor Company, US defense secretary and World Bank president, that statement boosted TI's credibility with governments and international organizations both in industrialized and developing countries.

McNamara utilized the meeting to promote the development of "integrity pacts," agreements between corporations and government procurement agencies to prevent extortion and bribery. He regarded the idea of integrity pacts to be of such importance that he conditioned his coming to Berlin on General Electric's (GE) participation in a discussion of integrity pacts. Peter Eigen, Robert McNamara, and I spent several hours discussing the key elements of integrity pacts and how best to launch them. McNamara offered to contribute $10 000 to TI when the first integrity pact was signed.

George Moody-Stuart, a prominent member of the British corporate establishment (and brother of Mark Moody-Stuart, chairman of Royal Dutch Shell), spoke about the prevalence of grand corruption, large payments by multinational enterprises (MNEs) to government leaders to win big orders. He circulated his book on fighting "Grand Corruption".[3]

Alberto Dahik's speech emphasized the need for direct involvement of TI in developing countries and invited the TI Board to come to Ecuador as guests of his government: an invitation that TI accepted, and that turned out to be highly influential for the development of TI strategy.

Due to Frank Vogl's outstanding media contacts the launch conference received widespread coverage all over the world. Most memorable was a cartoon in *The Economist* portraying Peter Eigen as Don Quixote charging a windmill labeled *Corruption*. In coming years *Economist* coverage of TI became much more favorable.

d. Ecuador Meeting

The visit to Ecuador took place in the fall of 1993. Vice President Dahik was one of a new generation of Latin American leaders with graduate degrees from Ivy League universities.[4] Dahik took on an active role as the host of the meeting, setting up meetings with ministers, judges, and business executives. One of his most important contributions was to organize a meeting with a local citizens group in Quito.

As already mentioned in our introduction, that meeting was an influential eye-opener. Prior to Quito the prime focus for TI strategy was on corruption in international development programs and business deals between MNEs and governments in the global South. To our surprise, the citizens of Quito showed no interest in high-level corruption. For them it was something that occurred on another planet. They made clear that they would only join a national chapter if it addressed their real concern, the myriad petty bribes they had to pay to obtain public services and permits of all kinds.

The Quito meeting showed that corruption looked very different at the ground level than from the top level. This foreshadowed an important issue for TI. Programs conducted by TI's national chapters would have to be based on local concerns. Global programs such as promoting international conventions would be of little interest to chapters in developing countries. Differences about

3. Moody-Stuart 1997.

4. He was the de facto head of Ecuador, in place of a largely inactive octogenarian president.

priorities would inevitably result in political tensions between the center and the chapters.

A highly-visible member of the TI team in Ecuador was Olusegun Obasanjo of Nigeria. An imposing figure, well over six feet tall and dressed in flowing tribal gowns that were changed several times each day. Obasanjo had risen to the top of the Nigerian army, and become president in a military coup. At the end of his term he took the unprecedented step of turning the presidency over to a popularly elected successor. He then became an active world figure. An unforgettable recollection of the Ecuador trip was Obasanjo in his long robes lying across the dividing line between the North and South sides of the equator on the highway outside Quito.

In 1995 Alberto Dahik was forced to flee Ecuador and take refuge in Costa Rica.[5] He was accused of using special presidential funds to influence votes on reform legislation. The details remain murky and it is unclear whether his downfall was caused by legal or by political troubles, or more likely a combination of the two. The difficulty of staying clean in the fight against corruption is a recurring problem. It also arose again in Obasanjo's career, after he was re-elected president of Nigeria.

e. Jeremy Pope Becomes Managing Director

In the fall of 1993 Jeremy Pope, a brilliant lawyer from New Zealand, became TI's Managing Director. He came from London where he had been director of legal programs for the Commonwealth Secretariat. This gave him detailed experience with most of the issues TI needed to deal with, as well as a circle of contacts with leading lawyers around the world. Jeremy was amazingly productive, the fastest writer I have ever worked with.

The first project on which Jeremy and I worked together was to get a grant from the Ford Foundation. This was strategically important because Ford had the biggest staff and was known to conduct the most meticulous reviews. Getting a grant from Ford would signal to the rest of the foundation world that TI was an acceptable recipient. Jeremy provided the key ideas for our application. My involvement added a GE connection and an office only an hour from the Ford Foundation, while Jeremy was 3,500 miles away.

5. Cf. University of Minnesota, Human Rights Library (available at: http://www1.umn.edu/humanrts/cases/93-01.html (last visited February 10, 2017).

We knew that getting a Ford grant would be hard, but were surprised just how difficult it turned out to be. Our grant proposal was transmitted by Obasanjo, a Ford trustee. That got us in the door, but resulted in strong resentment by the staff reviewing our proposal. We had to go through innumerable meetings and rewrites. We never worked so many hours for $75,000, but it was worth it. The grant paid for the TI Integrity Sourcebook, which covered Jeremy Pope's ideas for TI's intellectual work. The grant also laid the basis for a continuing relationship with Ford, including a $2 million contribution to TI's endowment. The Ford grant also opened other doors. A grant from the MacArthur Foundation came a year later.

Jane Polin of the GE Foundation provided important advice for the TI foundation strategy, including the need to win the first Ford grant. She also taught us that in approaching foundations: "If you ask for money, they will give you advice. If you ask for advice, they will give you money." A pithy way of emphasizing the importance of getting foundation staff interested in the substance of TI's work.

---

f. Growth of National Chapter Network

During TI's first year, national chapters were established in Kenya, the United States, Bangladesh, Great Britain, Germany, and Ecuador. Ground rules for the organization of chapters were developed that have been followed in the growth of the present network of over one hundred chapters. Each chapter is a separate legal entity, incorporated in its own country, and has its own board of directors. It raises its own funds and decides on its own program.

Because international development agencies support chapters in developing countries, but not in developed countries, many of the developing country chapters are better funded and have a much larger staff than those in developed countries. For example, TI-Bangladesh has several hundred employees,[6] TI-Colombia has about fifty,[7] TI-USA[8] and TI-France each have five.[9]

6. By October 2015, TI-Bangladesh had a total staff of 251; (cf. http://www.ti-bangladesh.org/beta3/index.php/en/about-us/administrative/staff) (last visited February 10, 2017).

7. Cf. http://transparenciacolombia.org.co/quienes/ (last visited February 10, 2017).

8. Cf. http://www.transparency-usa.org/who-we-are/staff/ (last visited February 10, 2017).

9. Cf. http://www.transparency-france.org/ewb_pages/o/organisation_transparence_international_france.php (last visited February 10, 2017).

g. Publication of TI Index

In 1995 the first TI Corruption Perception Index (CPI) was issued, ranking countries around the world by their level of corruption. It was published on the front page of the *New York Times* and numerous other papers and caused a sensation. The Index instantaneously transformed the public visibility of TI and of the corruption issue.

On the day of publication GE's head of public relations called me, praising the TI index as a master stroke. "Any time you can make a complex political issue look like baseball batting averages, the media will eat it up." An hour later Professor Susan Rose-Ackerman, a distinguished Yale economist (and member of the TI-USA board), called to express a somewhat more reserved view: "Great publicity, but somewhat dubious social science."

The TI Index was the work of a German economist Johann Graf Lambsdorff, a professor at Passau University. He had developed a statistical technique for combining the results of more than a dozen different assessments of corruption, by business organizations, government agencies, and academics. One criticism of the Index is that it is based on perception of corruption, not hard data. This fails to recognize that hard data is not available because bribery is always conducted in secrecy. Bribe payers and bribe recipients go to great lengths to cover up their tracks, and don't provide data to students of corruption. The Index is given credibility because it is based on information from a substantial number of sources using different techniques for obtaining their information. This diversity of sources provides corroborating credibility to the TI Index.

Ranking countries individually can be criticized as overly refined. A country ranked 54th may not be more corrupt than the country ranked 53rd. However, there is no argument that countries ranked in the fourth quartile belong there, as do those in the higher quartiles. Ironically, many of the questions about the CPI have focused on relative rankings of neighboring countries, rather than on where they are ranked overall. (For example, Sweden versus Finland, both near the top, or Brazil versus Colombia, both much further down.)

The Index has been published annually since 1995 and its methodology has been revised to incorporate data from an ever-increasing number of studies; currently there are twelve sources.[10] It is now compiled in-house by TI's research staff headed by Dr. Robin Hodess. The 2016 CPI ranks 176 countries.[11] Although no country comes close to achieving perfect scores, Scandinavian

10. For the 2014 CPI cf. Transparency International 2014, 1 et seq.

11. Corruption Perceptions Index 2016 (http://www.transparency.org/news/feature/corruption_perceptions_index_2016) (last visited February 10).

countries, New Zealand, and Switzerland are ranked at the top (least corrupt); Yemen, Syria, North Korea, South Sudan, and Somalia are ranked at the bottom.

Bribe Payers Index

TI also publishes a Bribe Payers Index (BPI), which ranks leading exporting countries based on their proclivity to bribe in major importing markets. Unlike the CPI, which is based on existing studies, TI had to commission new studies for the BPI. In each of the approximately thirty countries responses to questionnaires were obtained from 100 business persons active in a wide range of business sectors. Netherlands, Switzerland, Belgium, and Germany were ranked as least likely to bribe in 2011. Russia, China, Mexico, and Indonesia were ranked as most likely to bribe. The BPI is published approximately every three years.[12]

Rapprochement with the World Bank

Getting the World Bank to fight corruption was a high priority for TI from the outset because the Bank is the largest and most influential international development organization. However, during the first three years of TI's existence Peter Eigen was considered persona non grata by the leadership of the Bank, who regarded TI's pleas to deal with corruption as a personal affront. In their view TI was a protest organization.

The ice began to crack following the appointment of James Wolfensohn as president of the Bank in July 1995. Wolfensohn had a reputation as an independent thinker and as a multifaceted character, including Olympic fencer and outstanding cellist. His appointment to the Bank followed a highly successful career as an investment banker in Australia, London, and on Wall Street. He was a top fundraiser for Bill Clinton, which almost certainly helped with his appointment to the Bank.

Wolfensohn quickly concluded that major changes were needed at the Bank. When Peter Eigen first met with Wolfensohn in early 1996 he was pushing an open door. Wolfensohn invited Peter to come back with a TI team for an in-depth discussion of what the Bank should do about corruption. The meeting took place in April. Peter brought with him Jeremy Pope, Frank Vogl, Luis Moreno Ocampo of TI-Argentina, and me. Wolfensohn brought fifteen top Bank executives. When Peter introduced me, Wolfensohn asked: "What is one of Jack Welch's lawyers doing in bed with Peter Eigen?." I explained that for Welch creating a level playing field for international competition was a high priority.

12. The results of the latest BPI from 2011 are shown in Appendix C.

The meeting began with the issue of why the Bank had failed to address corruption. We pointed to the Shihata opinion that corruption was off limits as a political issue, that under the Bank's Charter it could only deal with economic issues. Wolfensohn replied "that is bullshit; corruption is as much an economic issue as it is a political issue."

The meeting lasted from 9:30 am until after 2 pm. The TI team explained the magnitude of corruption around the world and its adverse impact on the Bank's development agenda. Peter and Frank Vogl talked about their firsthand experience while working at the Bank. Luis Moreno Ocampo described the havoc wrought by corruption in Argentina. We laid out a number of proposals for Bank action, including requiring strict procurement rules, preventing bribery and kickbacks for all Bank financed procurement. Wolfensohn was interested in our ideas and was taking extensive notes. It was apparent that his associates remained largely unconvinced.

Six months later, in his presidential address at the World Bank's annual meeting in October 1996, Wolfensohn called on the Bank to "[. . .] deal with the cancer of corruption [. . .]."[13] This received worldwide publicity. Bringing the Bank bureaucracy around would be a long-term project, even for a leader of Wolfensohn's strong convictions; the way the Bank functions, employees look primarily to the directors from their own countries, who appoint them. Over time Wolfensohn's influence has been substantial. The World Bank Institute has become a foremost source of research on corruption, and an internal organization to control corruption in Bank operations has been set up.[14]

4. CONVENTIONS ADVOCACY

a. OECD Convention

TI recognized from the beginning that international conventions would be essential to creating a level playing field for international competition. The OECD was a key arena because its members were the major exporting states. In the early 1990s the OECD had established a Working Group on Bribery (WGB) to develop steps that governments could consider to address corruption. After

13. World Bank 2005, 45 et seq.

14. Chapter 16 on Development Assistance will discuss in greater detail with the World Bank's role on dealing with corruption.

the WGB published a list of possible steps, I called Mark Pieth, the chair of the Working Group, and was invited to spend a day with Mark in Basel.

Mark explained the low-key nature of their work: identifying a range of proposals for government consideration. He noted that criminalizing foreign bribery was highly controversial, and that the single-minded US pressure for criminalization was an obstacle to progress on less controversial issues. Ending tax-deductibility of bribes would be a better objective because OECD finance ministers were increasingly concerned about the resulting large losses of tax revenues. He urged me to meet with the State Department and ask them to support ending tax-deductibility. Action on tax-deductibility would build the credibility of the Working Group and make it possible to take on tougher issues thereafter.

On his return, I met with Daniel Tarullo, the assistant secretary of state for Economic Affairs (now a director of the Federal Reserve Bank). Tarullo readily agreed to support Mark's approach, recognizing that US pressure for criminalization was not working.

Mark's game plan succeeded. In 1995 the Working Group approved a resolution calling on OECD governments to end tax-deductibility of bribes. In 1996 consideration of a resolution on criminalizing foreign bribery began. In the spring of 1997 the criminalization issue took an unexpected turn. Several leading OECD members, including France, Germany, and Japan, objected to a resolution, but indicated that they would support a treaty on criminalization. That was a surprise because OECD had never before sponsored a treaty, preferring the soft-law approach of resolutions.

Both TI and the US government were suspicious, fearing that the treaty approach would bog down in endless negotiations of treaty provisions followed by long delays in securing ratification by national legislatures. Mark proposed that time limits be established, that treaty negotiations be concluded within six months, and that the treaty be submitted for ratification within two years. Remarkably, the Working Group produced an excellent treaty draft in five months, which was signed by OECD foreign ministers in Paris in December 1997. Enough legislatures had ratified the Convention to enable it to enter into force in December 1999.

TI's participation in the development of the OECD Convention established TI as an influential player. TI national chapters were active in securing ratification by their legislatures.

The US Senate Hearing

I testified as chair of TI-USA before the Senate Foreign Relations Committee in July 1998. My appearance resulted in an interesting exchange with Senator

Jesse Helms, the chairman of the Committee. Helms began by stressing his long-standing position that treaties are worthless pieces of paper that do not produce results. I responded that the OECD Convention was different. It recognized his concerns and provided for a follow-up monitoring program. After some questions about the monitoring program, Helms stated that he would support the Convention, and add a requirement that the State Department had to report annually to his Committee on the progress of the monitoring program. Helms concluded the hearing, stating that he would ensure that the Senate would ratify the Convention before it recessed for the summer in two weeks.

When I went up to the dais to thank Senator Helms for his support, he put his arm around me and remarked: "you and I are working together in the best Judeo-Christian tradition." True to his word Helms secured passage before the Senate recessed. He also followed up on the requirement for State Department reports on the monitoring process.

The Canadian ratification of the Convention was approved by the House of Commons at a hearing where Michael Davies of TI-Canada was invited to participate in the debate on the floor of the House. Canada's ratification brought the Convention over the threshold where it entered into effect.

In subsequent years, TI national chapters participated actively in the monitoring reviews. The order of reviews had been arranged to begin with Finland, Canada, the United States, and other countries that provided for NGO participation. When Berlusconi's government objected to TI-Italia participation, Mark overruled their objection as a violation of established precedents.

b. TI Progress Reports on Enforcement

In October 2004 Peter Clark of the US Justice Department organized a meeting of OECD prosecutors in Paris. The prosecutors recommended that annual reports be prepared covering the overall status of Convention enforcement. They felt that such reports could provide a comprehensive assessment of the Convention's progress that could not be obtained from the Working Group's reports on individual countries, which covered only one-fifth of the countries each year.

The following day the Working Group agreed with the proposal for annual progress reports, but suggested that TI should do these reports. TI has done so every year since 2005, and the reports have become one of TI's major work projects. The reports assess the overall status of enforcement, provide updates on individual countries, and make recommendations for improving enforcement.

TI is in a unique position to do the progress reports because it has national chapters with experienced lawyers in all OECD countries. The reports classify countries into four categories: active enforcement, moderate enforcement, limited enforcement, and little or no enforcement. The reports are reviewed in draft with the WGB before publication. This allows government representatives with an opportunity to provide additional information and avoids criticism of the report after publication.

The progress reports reveal very uneven levels of enforcement. The 2014 report[15] shows four countries with active enforcement, five with moderate enforcement, nine with limited enforcement, and twenty-two with little or no enforcement. On the positive side, it is noteworthy that the four countries in the active enforcement category, the United States, Germany, the United Kingdom, and Switzerland, are all large exporters. In addition, the number of investigations and prosecutions brought in these countries is continuing to increase.

On the negative side, it is disturbing that a decade and a half after the Convention entered into force over half the parties have little or no enforcement. As a result, the goal of the Convention, to create a level playing field for international business, is still far from achieved. Companies based in countries that enforce the prohibition against bribery are still losing orders to companies from countries that do not prohibit bribery.

TI's progress reports have concluded that the principal cause of inadequate enforcement is lack of government commitment, resulting in poor funding and staffing. TI has repeatedly recommended that advocacy programs demanding better enforcement be launched in countries with lagging enforcement.[16]

c. United Nations Convention against Corruption

The UN Convention against Corruption (UNCAC) has potential for curbing corruption far greater than OECD, because it has global membership. As of 2014 more than 170 countries have ratified UNCAC.[17] UNCAC also has a comprehensive scope, extending far beyond OECD's focus on criminalizing foreign bribery. UNCAC includes extensive preventive measures, broad criminal provisions

15. TI, Progress Report 2014: Assessing Enforcement of the OECD Convention on Combating Foreign Bribery.

16. Chapter 7 covers the OECD Convention in greater detail.

17. Cf. https://www.unodc.org/unodc/en/treaties/CAC/signatories.html.

covering domestic as well as foreign bribery, and covering bribery in the private sector as well as bribery of government officials. UNCAC also has innovative provisions for asset recovery and other forms of international cooperation.

TI had a team led by Jeremy Pope at the Geneva negotiations in 2002 that drafted the text of UNCAC. Jeremy was able to play an influential role because of his extensive connections with delegates from his years as legal director of the Commonwealth Secretariat. Jeremy deserves substantial credit for UNCAC's broad scope. I did not go to Geneva because I was skeptical about the likelihood that a UN initiative would produce a strong Convention, but changed my mind after reading it.

UNCAC's global membership and ambitious scope are a great plus but make achieving its potential difficult. The issue of monitoring implementation was highly controversial from the start. A group of countries led by Russia, China, Cuba, Venezuela, Egypt, and Algeria blocked inclusion of follow-up monitoring in the text of the Convention adopted in the Geneva negotiations, and the issue was deferred for future consideration.

The signing conference for UNCAC was held in Merida, Mexico, in December 2003. Peter Eigen and I were invited by the UN Office of Drugs and Crime (UNODC). We published an op-ed piece in a leading Mexican paper on the opening day, pointing out that the Convention would not be successful without a follow-up monitoring process. We were called in by the chairman of the conference, UNODC director Antonio Maria Costa, an Italian who had long headed UN's anti-drug program. Costa assailed us as "skunks at the lawn party" who abused a celebratory occasion. Peter responded that he had told UN Secretary-General Kofi Annan that UNCAC would never get anywhere as long as Costa was head of UNODC. Costa and Eigen left in a huff. As the meeting broke up, I suggested to Dimitri Vlassis (the head of treaty affairs under Costa) that something needed to be done to improve relationships. He invited me to come to see him in Vienna.

The Vienna meeting was constructive. We agreed that the best way to proceed would be to move away from debating the pro and cons of monitoring in principle and move to consider the specifics of how a UNODC monitoring program should function. TI would form a study group in which Dimitri Vlassis would participate as UNODC's liaison representative. Vlassis arranged to have the proposals developed by the study group considered at conferences of States Parties in 2005 and 2007. The discussions were inconclusive, but led to an agreement at the 2009 Conference of States Parties in Doha to proceed with an "Implementation Review Mechanism," UN-speak for monitoring.[18]

18. UNODC, March 2011, Mechanism for the Review of Implementation of the United Nations Convention against Corruption—Basic Documents, 21.

To promote progress with UNODC, Gillian Dell of TI formed a civil society coalition that enlisted more than three hundred organizations from around the world. The coalition sent sizeable delegations to conferences of States Parties where they actively lobbied the government representatives. The agreement finally reached at Doha was a compromise that in effect gave objecting governments opt-out rights on three issues: country visits by reviewers, NGO participation in country reviews, and publication of the full text of country reports (not just executive summaries).

Many representatives of the civil society coalition and of TI felt that the compromise reached at Doha was a sellout and should be publicly criticized. Others felt that agreement to proceed with the Implementation Review Mechanism was a crucial step forward, and that the opt-out rights would not seriously weaken the operation of the review process. The debate was as bitter as the previous debate among governments. Some civil society groups in fact issued critical press releases. History has shown that the optimists were right. More than 90 percent of country reviews have included country visits by the reviewers as well as participation by NGOs.

A monitoring process for a convention with more than 170 parties and fifty-nine substantive articles is by its nature a very complex and time-consuming undertaking. UNODC seeks to schedule sixty country reviews each year, covering the implementation of all fifty-nine UNCAC articles in two five-year phases. Each country is reviewed by two governments, one from the same region, one from another region, UNODC has built an excellent staff that manages the review process.

TI published a progress report on UNCAC enforcement in 2013. It focused on the procedural aspects of the review process—whether there were country visits by review teams and whether NGOs participated. Beginning in 2015, TI's progress report will go beyond the procedural aspects and also cover how well key articles have been implemented in key countries.

Most important, UNCAC implementation is underway and gathering momentum. With sustained progress, UNCAC will achieve its goal of becoming the key instrument for addressing global corruption.[19]

d. Evolution of TI Management

In its initial years TI was a small, cohesive organization: Peter Eigen and an enthusiastic group of followers. The warm glow was sustained by the

19. Chapter 8 covers UNCAC in greater detail.

positive reaction to TI's ideas, the rapid growth of national chapters, the successful reception of the TI Index, and the rapprochement with the World Bank. Peter Eigen's stature was enhanced by the ready reception he received from government leaders and others in both developing and industrialized countries.

Tensions began to develop over time. The growth of national chapters around the world raised concerns about the relative power of the group in Berlin and the power of the chapters. Some argued that the chapters should be regarded as the core of the movement. Others argued that the Berlin secretariat remained the center of TI. In response, changes had to be made in TI's management structure. The result has been a more complex and politicized system.

The original TI board had been elected by members of the founding group. A new system was developed under which each national chapter has one vote at the annual management meeting where board members are elected and other issues are decided. Voting rights were also given to "independent members," individuals with long service to the movement who can provide a broad international perspective. The number of independent members is limited to maintain a 70:30 balance with the votes of national chapters. In effect, constructive tension has been institutionalized.

Another important management innovation has been the application of a three-year accreditation process, for both national chapters and independent members. This was set up after several instances where the quality of chapter management had deteriorated seriously. Because the politics of dis-accrediting chapters is very awkward, it was concluded that establishing three-year terms and requiring re-accreditation was preferable. The same approach also serves well when individual members no longer remain active.

After five years as managing director Jeremy Pope decided to move back to London, where he set up a research office for TI. He was succeeded as managing director by Hansjörg Elshorst, who had retired from GTZ, the German aid agency. His long-standing relation with Peter eased the strain of Jeremy Pope's departure.

An outstanding addition to TI's management was the arrival of Jermyn Brooks who had been the head of Pricewaterhouse Coopers (PwC) in London. Brooks added to the Berlin team financial discipline and wide private sector connections. After working for PwC in the Middle East, he had spent more than two decades in Germany, becoming head of PwC German practice, before he was promoted to London. There he led the merger of Coopers & Lybrands with Price Waterhouse to form PwC. Recruiting Brooks was facilitated by personal factors. He had a German wife and they had retained their home in Wiesbaden when they moved to London. Brooks served first as TI's financial manager and then became managing director.

In May 2002 David Nussbaum was recruited as managing director from the World Wildlife Fund (WWF), an environmental organization active around the world. He strengthened TI's management and relations with national chapters. Personal considerations made it impossible for Nussbaum to move to Berlin, as originally planned. He brought in Cobus de Swardt, a South African human rights activist as his deputy. When Nussbaum returned to WWF in May 2007, de Swardt became TI's managing director. Nussbaum stayed involved with TI as an independent member and as a member of the international advisory council. He became CEO of WWF in 2007.

Cobus de Swardt brought an infectious personality and a remarkable background to TI. He came from a prominent Boer family. Both his parents had been cabinet members in apartheid governments. While a college student, Cobus had become the leader of the underground chapter of the African Nationalist Congress (ANC) at Witwatersrand University. He was arrested and tortured by the Boer police. His parents managed to extricate him from prison. He had to move to Australia where he completed his education. He taught at universities in Australia and England and worked in human rights organizations.

Cobus has prodigious work habits, commonly working 100-hour weeks. His enthusiasm enlivens even the largest meetings. He hired Christiaan (Chrik) Poortman from the World Bank as his deputy. Chrik, a Netherlander, had risen to become vice president for Africa and the Middle East. He resigned from the Bank and came to TI after Paul Wolfowitz became president of the Bank, succeeding James Wolfensohn.

e. The 2005 Election

Peter Eigen could not run for re-election as chairman in 2005 because of term limits, but offered to become head of the Advisory Committee. Two highly regarded board members, Huguette Labelle of Canada and Rosa Inés Ospina Robledo of Colombia, became candidates for the chairmanship. Both had strong support, and Huguette Labelle won in a 44-43 cliffhanger.

The succession of a charismatic founding father is inevitably a traumatic event that many organizations do not survive. Huguette Labelle's personality and experience made possible a smooth transition. She had served as vice minister, the senior civil-service position, in a number of Canadian cabinet departments and was used to deferring publicly to the minister, while effectively running the department. She and Peter Eigen liked and respected each other, and she welcomed his desire to become chair of the Advisory Council, a position that includes attendance at board meetings. After her election, Labelle offered to let Eigen share the chairman's office, as she would only spend limited time in Berlin.

Huguette brought a more low-key style to the TI chair. Participants at meetings she ran never felt disregarded or offended. However, her meetings almost always reached the result she favored. (They may take even longer than Peter's meetings.) She has an amazing work ethic and is indefatigable, constantly traveling around the world. Two days after getting back to her home in Ottawa from a trip to Berlin, Paris, and London, she will be off again on a trip to Seoul, Jakarta, Zimbabwe, and Brasilia. She has visited almost all of TI's hundred national chapters. A typical country visit includes meetings with the chapter's board, with the country's president or prime minister, with the leading media, with corporations, with donor organizations, and with other NGOs—morning to night for three or four days.

She has developed close relations with the Secretary-General of the OECD, the Secretary-General of the United Nations, the president of the World Bank, and the director general of UNODC, and has served as vice chair of the World Economic Forum in Davos.

Huguette and Cobus developed a close and comfortable working relationship, based on a clear understanding of where she wanted to play an active role and where he could exercise managerial discretion. They talked for an hour every Monday morning Berlin time, regardless where in the world Huguette may have been.

After three years in Berlin, Chrik Poortman decided to move back to Washington where he became a TI-USA director. Miklos Marschall became deputy managing director of TI. A former deputy mayor of Budapest, he had worked with NGOs in the United States and had long been active in TI. He has an unusual ability to get contesting TI components to work together, a crucial skill now that the Berlin Secretariat has grown to more than 150 persons with competing skills.

6

The United States

Foreign Corrupt Practices Act and Campaign Financing

FRITZ HEIMANN ■

Corruption has been a persistent issue in American history. This chapter will discuss the colonial period, the enactment of the US Constitution, the Yazoo land rights controversy, the construction of the Panama Canal, the Watergate scandal, and the Foreign Corrupt Practices Act (FCPA) and involvement with OECD. It concludes with a discussion of the Citizens United case.

1. COLONIAL HERITAGE

Gifts from the British Crown to influential persons played a prominent role in English politics and also in the American colonies. Gifts of diamond-studded snuffboxes to Benjamin Franklin, Thomas Jefferson, and Silas Deane, who represented the American colonies in London and in Paris, became controversial matters at home. Should such gifts be refused, should they be turned over to the home government, or is disclosure sufficient? Such gifts were commonly presented after the foreign service had been completed, and the recipient had gone home. However, that did not make them less controversial.[1]

1. Teachout 2014, 17 et seq.

Confronting Corruption. Fritz Heimann and Mark Pieth.

2. CONSTITUTIONAL DEBATES

Preventing corruption was a very prominent issue in the Philadelphia debates at which the Constitution was hammered out. James Madison's handwritten notes include fifty-four references to corruption, more than for any other subject.[2] A study by American historians in the 1960s showed that "[c]orruption fears—fears of a conspiracy against liberty . . . nourished by corruption lay at the heart of the Revolutionary movement."[3] George Mason, a prominent delegate from Virginia, stated: "if we do not provide against corruption, our government will soon be at an end."[4]

The core metaphor of corruption was a rotting of positive ideals of civic and public integrity. Corruption was compared to cancer "eating at the vitals of the body politic and working a progressive dissolution."[5]

Article I, Section 9 of the Constitution, commonly referred to as the gifts clause, provides that "No person holding any office of profit or trust . . . shall, without the consent of the Congress, accept any present, emolument, office, or title of any kind whatever from any king, prince or foreign state." The gifts clause was designed to prevent corruption. It was a ban on a culture of gift giving and made no exception for token gifts.

3. YAZOO CONTROVERSY

From the time of the first settlements in the early seventeenth century, gaining rights to previously unoccupied land was a crucial political and legal issue. (George Washington, it should be noted, was a surveyor.) It remained a key issue as the United States expanded from the East Coast to the Pacific Ocean, and on to Alaska.

The Yazoo dispute followed the decision of the Georgia State legislature in 1789 to sell thirty-five million acres of land along the Yazoo River for $500,000. A contemporary commentator called it the "greatest real estate deal in history."[6] Purchases and resales of the land were made under questionable circumstances. Much of the land was gobbled up by Georgia legislators.

2. Chicago Press and Tribune, 29 March 1860; Teachout 2014, 57 et seq.

3. Teachout 2014, 38, with reference to Pocock 1975, 507.

4. Teachout 2014, 38.

5. Banning, 1980, 47; Teachout 2014, 40.

6. Teachout 2014, 83, with reference to Beveridge 1919, 551.

The western boundary of Georgia was poorly defined, and portions of the Yazoo land became part of the newly established state of Mississippi. Whether purchasers held proper titles was a common issue. Many prominent political and legal figures, including Patrick Henry, John Randolph, Thomas Jefferson, John Marshall, and Joseph Story were on different sides of Yazoo disputes. In *Fletcher v. Peck* the US Supreme Court decided in 1810 that a subsequent purchaser of Yazoo land had valid title, notwithstanding questions regarding the initial sale of Yazoo land.

4. CONSTRUCTION OF THE PANAMA CANAL

The Panama Canal was started by the French government, under the leadership of Ferdinand de Lesseps, who had previously built the Suez Canal. De Lesseps used bribery to secure support from French officials and French newspapers. Large bribes were also paid to Colombian officials. (Panama was a province of Colombia at the time.) De Lesseps planned to build a sea-level canal, which proved to be prohibitively expensive, resulting in the bankruptcy of his company after expenditures of approximately $260 million.[7]

The second phase was undertaken by the US government under the leadership of President Theodore Roosevelt and his secretary of war, William Howard Taft. Roosevelt promoted the secession of Panama from Colombia, sending naval vessels and troops to Panama, and recognized Panama as an independent state. In return, Panama made available to the United States a corridor from the Atlantic to the Pacific for the construction and operation of the Canal.

The construction of the Canal was by far the most expensive engineering project undertaken by the US government before World War II, costing $375 million.[8] It was completed ahead of schedule, below budget, and without bribe payments; results attributed to able management by Secretary Taft who spent a great deal of time in Panama.

5. WATERGATE

The initial focus of the Watergate investigation established in 1973 was the break-in by President Nixon's operatives into the headquarters of the

7. Panama Canal Museum, Factsheet (http://cms.uflib.ufl.edu/pcm/facts.aspx) (last visited March 6, 2017).

8. Panama Canal Museum, Factsheet (http://cms.uflib.ufl.edu/pcm/facts.aspx) (last visited March 6, 2017).

Democratic party at the Watergate office complex in Washington, DC. The scope of the investigation expanded to cover the sources of the funds raised by the aptly named CREEP, the Committee to Re-elect the President. Investigators from the SEC made the surprising discovery that much of the money came from foreign bank accounts of US corporations, accounts used to pay bribes in the United States. The SEC proceeded to establish a voluntary compliance program under which cooperating corporations were offered amnesty providing they disclosed past bribe payments and enacted anti-bribery compliance programs. Over 400 companies admitted to making payments in excess of $300 million; of these companies 117 were among the Fortune 500.

6. FOREIGN CORRUPT PRACTICES ACT

When he became president in 1977, Jimmy Carter was deeply troubled by huge foreign bribery scandals involving Lockheed and Gulf Oil. He pushed the enactment of the Foreign Corrupt Practices Act (FCPA) through a reluctant Congress.[9] The FCPA took the unprecedented step of making bribe payments to foreign officials a crime under US law. Carter's hope that other exporting states would also prohibit foreign bribery was disappointed.[10] Major foreign exporters, such as Siemens, British Aerospace, Alstom, Toshiba, and Hitachi, regarded the FCPA a quixotic step depriving US exporters of a powerful competitive tool. Their governments continued to allow their companies to treat foreign bribe payments as tax-deductible business expenses, in effect subsidizing foreign bribery. In an unequal playing field, American exporters lost numerous large orders to foreign competitors.

This created a politically intolerable situation. Efforts to repeal FCPA were unavailing. Members of Congress made clear that voting against FCPA would be politically suicidal because their opponents at the next election would attack them for voting in favor of corruption. FCPA was originally enacted with a ten-year time limit, expiring in 1987. Notwithstanding extensive industry lobbying, FCPA was extended in 1988 by an overwhelming margin, without time limit and with only small changes relating to facilitating small payments to low-level officials.[11]

9. Noonan 1984, 604 et seq.

10. Cf. the work of, first, the ECOSOC's Commission on Transnational Corporations, and later of its Committee on an International Agreement on Illicit Payments; Pieth 1999, A-1039.

11. FCPA 1988.

With the FCPA politically invulnerable in the United States, the only way to build a level playing field was to internationalize the FCPA. This required an international forum, the OECD in Paris, and support from a broad constituency, including Transparency International and the International Chamber of Commerce. Taking the issue to the OECD in Paris was a logical move because OECD's member governments included the world's leading exporters.[12] In 1997 OECD adopted the "Convention on Combating Bribery of Foreign Public Officials in International Business Transactions," which mirrored the FCPA; it became effective in 1999.[13] The Convention included provisions for follow-up monitoring of compliance by member governments. The OECD Convention is discussed in detail in Chapter 7. The US government also played an active role in the adoption of the UN Convention against Corruption (UNCAC), which is discussed in Chapter 8.

Enforcing of the FCPA is facilitated by flexible jurisdictional provisions that require only minimal US contacts. Sending an email, a phone call, or transferring money to or from the United States is sufficient to provide the jurisdictional basis to bring a lawsuit in the United States.

7. CITIZENS UNITED CASE

After two centuries during which prohibitions on bribery were applied to campaign contributions and gifts to politicians and government officials, the Supreme Court in the Citizens United case held that the First Amendment's protection of free speech was applicable to campaign contributions and gifts to politicians. By broadening the interpretation of protected free speech to include campaign contributions and gifts, the Court correspondingly narrowed the scope for prosecution of corruption. It held that bribery could only be prosecuted when there was a clear quid pro quo.[14] This flies in the face of the experience that bribe payers and bribe recipients are careful to structure their transactions to avoid any appearance of quid pro quos. In practice only very careless bribe payers or bribe recipients are likely to flunk the US quid pro quo test.

12. See OECD 1989.

13. Cf. Pieth 2014, 19.

14. Teachout 2014, 238 et seq.

Citizens United v. Federal Election Commission (FEC)

The Citizens United case involved a documentary film organization. As a film it produced had been partially funded by a nonprofit company, the FEC placed restrictions on its availability and ordered Citizens United to disclose the main contributors to FEC.

On appeal the US Supreme Court held these restrictions to be "prior restraints" that violated the First Amendment. It is now legal for corporations to make independent expenditures in any amount they want. Corporations can also form political action committees (PACs). Thereby, direct contributions to a candidate are permitted.

7

Bribing Foreign Officials

The OECD Anticorruption Instruments

MARK PIETH

1. IS BRIBERY A NECESSARY EVIL?

Before the year 2000 bribery was considered a "necessary evil" by most exporting countries. Of course, it was perceived as a nuisance to those having to pay, and the exporters realized that local judiciaries were rarely able to deal with it. In fact, in many instances local law enforcement agencies and judges were part of the problem. Therefore, an attitude *"when in Rome do as the Romans do"* prevailed. Even companies based in countries culturally averse to bribery (such as the Nordic States) rarely saw a problem when bribing in the Third World. Lawyers in developed states helped bolster this attitude with the corresponding theory: host states of companies are not responsible for the protection of the public interest of foreign states, they said. Overall, this attitude was very much embedded in (post-)colonial thinking.

This cynical approach was even reinforced in many exporting states by tax-deductibility of bribes (as so-called "necessary expenses"). Tax authorities claimed their role was to be ethically "neutral."

It is true that bribery was rampant and that in many instances exporters were solicited for bribes. The attitude of these companies and of their host states, however, contributed substantially to keeping the corruption cycle going.

In some cases, the companies bribing pursued an ulterior interest beyond obtaining a contract or a license abroad: sometimes they developed complex bribery schemes to obtain so-called "retro-commissions." Part of the corruption money would flow home to friends, frequently to clandestinely finance political campaigns.

A particularly problematic case of this type seems to be the French Karachi/ Nautilus scandal. The facts are gradually emerging from legal decisions, French secret service sources, and investigative journalism;[1] there is to date, however, no finally researched version of the facts. The following can be said on a provisory basis:

"Le dossier Karachi"

The Nautilus saga starts with the sale of three submarines on September 21, 1994, by the French shipyard DCN to Pakistan. A second arms contract followed in November of the same year. Reports claim that the two contracts were worth 90 billion French francs and that large "commission payments" were agreed upon. The reports talk of 33 million French francs alone for the second contract. The commissions were due to go through the inevitable middle men to Pakistani military commanders, in close contacts with secret service operators and Islamists. The reports, however, also claim that a part of the commissions was destined to fuel the French presidential campaign of M. Balladur in 1995. The argument was that the eventually elected new president of France, Jacques Chirac, stopped the payments in 1996. Whether there was a link to the upcoming adoption of the OECD Convention in 1997 is unclear, though. All commentators, however, see a link between the "breach" of the bribe contracts of 1994 and the bombing of a bus in Karachi, killing eleven DCN technicians. Apparently, the bomb was far less amateurish than comparable devices: it points toward military involvement.[2]

It remains unclear whether the attempt of the French legislature in 1998 to allow its companies to continue to honor bribe contracts concluded prior to the new law—the so-called "grandfather-clause" ultimately dropped by the Assemblée Nationale after intense critique by the OECD[3]—has been influenced by this experience.

1. Cf. the report by the Direction de surveillance du territoire (DST), "Nautilus," 11 September 2002; cf. also La Libération, 20 June 2009: "Karachi: derrière l'attentat, l'ombre d'une affaire d'Etat."

2. Report by the Direction de surveillance du territoire (DST), "Nautilus," 11 September 2002; cf. also Wikipedia: "attentat du 8 May 2002 à Karachi."

3. No. 2001, Assemblée Nationale, Constitution du 4 octobre 1958, Onzième législature, Enregistré à la Présidence de l'Assemblée nationale le 8 décembre 1999, Rapport fait au nom de la commission des lois constitutionnelles, de la législation et de l'administration générale de la République sur le projet de loi, adopté par le sénat, modifiant le code pénal et le code de la

So, why would legislators of all major exporting nations suddenly adopt laws outlawing foreign bribery and banning tax-deductibility of such bribes?

2. THE US FOREIGN CORRUPT PRACTICES ACT

The OECD initiative on corruption in 1989 was a consequence of the US Foreign Corrupt Practices Act (FCPA) enacted in 1977 (see also above Chapter 6).

In the aftermath of the Watergate scandal the United States embarked on a moral cleanup. An international corruption scandal involving the US defense giant Lockheed Martin and the Japanese prime minister Tanaka triggered a vast Securities and Exchange Commission (SEC) investigation.[4] For lack of a clear legal basis the SEC offered exemption from sanctions to those issuers voluntarily disclosing foreign bribery. Close to four hundred companies owned up to having bribed abroad.[5] Shocked by this fact the US legislator drafted laws subjecting foreign bribery to criminal punishment.

Authors have disputed that the origin of the Foreign Corrupt Practices Act in 1977[6] had a purely moral background. They saw economic and political advantages: companies allowed to procure contracts by bribery were in the long run going to lose their competitive edge. Furthermore, the fact that hundreds of US companies were bribing abroad and some of them—such as Lockheed—bribed prominent political allies, was going to interfere with US foreign policy. Some of the staffers participating in the legislative efforts at the time came up with even more adventurous explanations: a former high-level official of the Department of Defense explains that Jewish interest was supporting the Foreign Corrupt Practices Act, as it was feared that bribery would promote arms sales to Arab countries. There is no way of telling if these explanations are correct, except that securing a level playing field in commerce was a key factor.

procédure pénale est relatif à la lutte contre la corruption, par M. Jacky Darne, député, article 2, 47 et seq.; Intervention of M. Pieth in the Assemblée Nationale, Paris 1999 and meetings with Deputy Jacky Darne; Les Echos, 10 February 1999, 13: "Les industriels de l'armement montent au créneau contre la future loi anti-corruption."

4. Hearings on Activities of American Multinational Corporations Abroad Before the Subcommittee on International Economics Policy of the House Committee on International Relations, 94th Cong. 57, 63 et seq. (1975). For the findings of the SEC cf. the Report of the Comptroller General of the United States to Congress in 1981.

5. More than 400 companies, over 177 of them ranked amongst the Fortune 500, owned up to having paid substantial bribes in the recent past.

6. FCPA 1977.

At any rate, the unilaterally enacted legislation was bound to put US commerce into a difficult situation internationally vis-à-vis their competitors.[7] Therefore, it is not astonishing that the United States tried to internationalize the approach. The first ports of call were the United Nations. Between 1978 and 1979 the Committee on Transnational Corporations of the United Nations Economic and Social Council (ECOSOC)[8] tried to draft an international treaty mirroring the approach of the FCPA. In 1979, however, Member States had to realize that these efforts were not going anywhere. They were abandoned.

The FCPA in its first ten years of existence was used sparingly and yet, toward the end of the 1980s business interests in the United States got restless. The "Omnibus Trade Act," enacted in 1988, softened the FCPA's touch; it introduced explicit exceptions and defenses (especially for facilitation payments).[9] At the same time, it obliged the president to seriously engage in negotiations with the major trading partners to internationalize the FCPA.

This time the OECD was chosen and especially the Group of 7 (G7) Countries were targeted. In the meantime, chances had grown, as new markets were about to open with the ending of the Cold War.[10]

3. THE INITIATIVE AND FIRST STEPS IN THE OECD

Rather astonishingly, the Council, the supreme body of the OECD, accepted by unanimity a US initiative in 1989 to work toward an international instrument combating "illicit payments",[11] the code word used at the time. In 1989 a study group was created under the chairmanship of the then Legal Counsel of the OECD, Christian Schricke.[12] It basically analyzed national laws and came to the conclusion that the United States was the only country able to tackle foreign bribery. The Council, again by unanimity, created a new working party to explore options, the "Ad-hoc Working Group on Illicit Payments," a

7. Langer and Pelzman 2001, 3; Tarullo 2004, 676 (31): reference to Warren Christopher, deputy attorney general, when the FCPA was passed.

8. Cf. the work of, first, the ECOSOC's Commission on Transnational Corporations, and later of its Committee on an International Agreement on Illicit Payments; Pieth 1999, A-1039.

9. FCPA 1988; Tarullo 2004, 674; Weinstein et al. 2012, para. 1.03 (3).

10. Pieth 2014a, 13 et seq.

11. OECD 1989: United States Proposal on the Issue of Illicit Payments.

12. Pieth 2014a, 14.

subsidiary body to one of the standing OECD Committees, the Committee on International Investment and Multilateral Enterprises (CIME).[13]

How to Become Chairman

As frequently there is more than one reason for a choice: during the first year of the OECD's work on corruption I had (as a young Criminology professor) been rather pushy and critical of the usual means of comparison of law. Concurrently, the Swiss Ministry of Economy, who had sent me to the OECD, seemed interested in the issue: Marino Baldi, then deputy director of the Swiss Federal Office of Economy and Chairman of CIME even put in a voluntary contribution to get this work off the ground. As life goes in International Organizations, those who promote an issue get remunerated with a job. Up to then I was totally unaware of these power mechanics. In 1989 I was a thirty-six-year-old inexperienced, but maybe overly self-conscious young lawyer. And then I was invited to lunch by a charming representative of the Secretariat, Enery Quinones. I did not really know how to react to the suggestion that I become president of this new working group (and of course I had no idea that this job was going to cling to me for the next twenty-four years).

The first three years of work in the new Working Group were rather drab: the old hands in the OECD, in particular French (such as Henri Chavransky) and Japanese commerce officials with a long career behind them, tried to explain that everyone else was incredibly naive and why this entire effort was driven by religious fanatics from across the ocean. We spent basically three years not speaking of contents, but of form: what type of instrument would we choose if we were to do any work at all.[14]

It all changed when the Clinton administration took over in the United States. Since the new secretary of state, Warren Christopher, had been involved in writing the FCPA in 1977, there was no way back: suddenly, the level of representation in the Group was drastically raised. The US ambassador to the OECD and later undersecretary of state, Alan Larson, took the helm on behalf of the United States.

13. A Working Group that was created by the OECD Committee on International Investment and Multinational Enterprises.

14. OECD Council Decisions of March 1989 C(89)49; of June 1990 C(90)87; of February 1992 C(92)16; Ministerial Communiqué of 2 June 1998 (CES(93)22); Pieth 2000, 54 et seq.; Sacerdoti 2003, 72 et seq.

Allergic to Power Breakfasts or to Scallops?

Another anecdote illustrates the change of mind:

We were obviously stuck in these technical arguments about form over content. Alan Larson invited us to the US embassy for a "power breakfast" at 7 am. The issue was how to achieve the breakthrough. Up until now we were focused on a Convention, which seemed to get everybody worked up and the Group nowhere at all.

It was just the time when in another similar body, in the Financial Action Task Force on Money Laundering (the FATF),[15] rules against money laundering were created in a rather smooth way with the help of soft law, with Recommendations. There was no need for domestic ratification. Once the Recommendations were adopted unanimously by the Group, they could be further developed internationally and countries' compliance could be subject to evaluations.[16]

Having been a "founding member" of the FATF between 1989 and 1993 and one of the three examiners of the first monitoring exercise (of France in 1992), I advocated a soft- law approach also on anticorruption in the OECD. I know that it took the US Delegation a lot of energy to convince people at home of the change of approach—but it was worthwhile: in 1994 the OECD adopted its first Council Recommendation on Bribery.

The side effects of the breakfast were just as dramatic, even though I am sure that the cook of the US embassy is absolutely not to blame: I am probably simply allergic either to scallops or to power breakfasts altogether.

4. THE 1994 RECOMMENDATION AND THE FOLLOW-UP

To a modern reader the 1994 Recommendation may seem rather simple. It starts off with exhortative language promising collectively to do something about bribery in foreign business relations and then goes on to give a so-called "shopping list" of possible areas of further work.[17] What has been frequently overseen, though, is that this text already contains the rules of the further development: the peer process and the monitoring mechanism. Based on these

15. Cf. below Chapter 9.

16. Cf. below 124 et seq.

17. OECD Rec. 1994; OECD Travaux Préparatoires 1999, 1001 et seq.

procedural rules the Working Group, now called "Working Group on Bribery," spent the years between 1994 and 1997 developing more detailed language on the individual items of the "shopping list." The method at the time was quite simple: the Working Group had a Deputy Chair, but no Bureau. We created Subgroups for each of the issues on the "shopping list" (especially criminalization of bribery, tax-deductibility, accounting and auditing, public procurement, and international cooperation as well as accession to the Group). We held seminars on each of these topics and nominated Subgroup Chairpersons to drive the process forward. In the course of three years we managed to supplement the Recommendation drastically. Paradoxically, the failure of the so-called Multilateral Agreement on Investment (MAI)[18] helped our work in more than one way: first, we inherited the professional workforce who had been acting as Secretariat to the MAI (in particular Carolyn Ervin and the legal counsel, David Small). Furthermore, the OECD had learned its lesson from the MAI that civil society and the private sector needed to be involved in its work from an early stage. We therefore held regular open meetings and invited civil society representatives to our seminars.[19]

It must be added that during this period resistance by countries was relatively small; furthermore, other OECD bodies contributed largely to the emerging upgraded standard of 1997.[20] The toughest part, however, remained criminalization. Under the chairmanship of Deputy Chairman Professor Gorgio Sacerdoti, a subgroup developed the backbone of a text on criminal law called the "Agreed Common Elements".[21] They were added to the draft of the 1997 Recommendation as an Annex. However, several countries—amongst them Germany, France, and Japan—were opposed to enacting criminal law on the basis of soft law. The example of the FATF had gone too far for them already. They insisted that criminalization be done based on a Treaty, either by the UN or the World Trade Organization (WTO). This led to a deadlock in the run-up to the Council Recommendation of May 1997.[22] The United States now insisted

18. OECD MAI 1998.

19. From 1995 onward, the WGB held regular meetings with representatives of the private sector, trade unions, and NGOs: Business and Industry Advisory Committee to the OECD (BIAC), Trade Union Advisory Committee to the OECD (TUAC), International Chamber of Commerce (ICC), and Transparency International (TI). In the final stage of the negotiations, TI's intervention proved to be instrumental: it drafted a helpful letter signed by Chief Executive Officers (CEOs) of large international companies.

20. OECD Revised Rec. 1997: Revised Recommendation of the Council of the OECD on Combatting Bribery in International Business Transactions.

21. OECD Revised Rec. 1997, Annex.

22. OECD Revised Rec. 1997; Pieth 2014a, 18 et seq.

on a Recommendation (as they had changed their approach altogether after our 1993 breakfast), the Europeans on a Convention in the UN or the WTO.

The then-deputy director of the Directorate for Financial, Fiscal and Enterprise Affairs (DAFFE), the Department of the Secretariat servicing the Working Group, Rainer Geiger, had the decisive idea: "let's call their bluff, let's do a Convention, here in the OECD and quick." The immediate reaction was not forthcoming; the Europeans doubted it was possible and the United States had changed their mindset and strategy from Convention to Recommendation. Everybody was caught off guard. Nevertheless, the main countries agreed to give it a try and to build a strategic safeguard into the 1997 Recommendation: in case the project of a Convention should fail at the end of the year, criminal law would be enacted by Recommendation on the basis of the Agreed Common Elements.[23]

LUGANO/GANDRIA

How to draft a Convention in three days?

Imagine sunshine at the height of summer in a lovely place on the lake of Lugano with no cars. Rent the rooms of a middle-class hotel on the lake and a boathouse as your meeting room. Take a break every three hours allowing for a swim in the dark green water and to eat well. The main contenders (the so-called "friends of the Chairman"[24]) all turned up, dressed down, went for a swim, had a fight or two, then an evening together in a traditional restaurant (a grotto) across the lake in Cantine di Gandria—invited by the Swiss Federal Office of Economy—and after three days, with heavy coaching and professional draftsmanship of the OECD Secretariat and Legal Department, we had the blueprint of the Convention.

The rest were seemingly official steps typical to such a process: a full week of negotiations within the entire Working Group in October,[25] a formal Negotiation Conference on the ambassadorial level in November,[26] and then on December 17, 1997, the big ceremonial signing ceremony[27] with ministers,

23. OECD Working documents, DAFFE/IME/BR(97)12 and 16.

24. Pieth 2014a, 19.

25. OECD Agenda, DAFFE/IME/BR/A(97)4.

26. OECD Agenda, DAFFE/IME/BR/A(97).

27. Cf. OECD DAFFE/IME/BR(97)16/FINAL; DAFFE/IME/BR(97)17/FINAL.

amongst them US secretary of state Madeleine Albright, and French minister of justice Elisabeth Guigou, as well as her colleague, the then-French minister of finance, Dominique Strauss-Kahn, and many others.

What is frequently overseen, though, is that between spring and autumn of 1997 intensive lobbying took place behind the scenes. The US secretary of state sent speaking notes and instructions to all US embassies in key OECD capitals to intervene on behalf of the OECD Convention (I have received a copy of them). Nongovernmental organizations (NGOs), in particular the recently created Transparency International (TI) under the leadership of Peter Eigen and Fritz Heimann, wrote to business leaders[28] and suggested to the former German president to host meetings in Berlin with business leaders in support of the OECD Convention.[29] It was a memorable moment when Richard von Weizsäcker told the general counsel of Siemens (who had hinted at the concept of *"do as the Romans do"*) that he did not want to see him anymore in the context of these meetings.

It will be noted that at the same time resistance was rather strong. In particular in France business associations such as the *Patronat Français*, now called Mouvement des entreprises de France (MEDEF), and the Institut Français des Relations Internationales (IFRI)[30] called meetings to discuss the possible trade disadvantages for French companies, especially when exporting to Africa and Asia.

Recent media reports indicate that possibly France had good reasons to fear the new rules: *La Libération* has quoted findings that French defense corporations had acquired contracts with the help of bribery and were threatening to stop payments if the OECD Treaty went through. As indicated above, they linked the death of eleven French engineers working on a submarine contract in an explosion in Pakistan to this uncertainty.[31] Whether this is true or not, it demonstrates that the struggle for new rules against foreign bribery could have had a very serious impact indeed.

28. TI's intervention proved to be instrumental: it drafted a helpful letter signed by Chief Executive Officers (CEOs) of large international companies.

29. Two meetings were held in the Aspen Institute in Berlin on an island in the Wannsee upon invitation by the former German president, the Aspen Institute, and Transparency International.

30. Presentation by Mark Pieth at a breakfast meeting in the Paris Sofitel Hotel hosted by IFRI in late 1996.

31. Cf. above footnote 1 and 2.

5. IMPLEMENTING THE CONVENTION

With its entry into force in 1999 the Convention was ready for implementing by Member States. Overall the probably most impressive achievement was the rapid enactment of legislation by virtually all State Parties.

Monitoring helped a great deal. Several methods have been applied: in a first round ("Phase *1*")[32] the Working Group on Bribery (WGB) deliberately concentrated on laws and did not assess application yet: countries were invited to get used to the new standards step by step. This is also the procedure followed with new Members entering later. In a second phase ("Phase 2")[33] the standards were drastically raised: although adequate legislation was still an issue, now application moved center stage. Law enforcement, awareness, and other evidence that the Convention and the Recommendation were being taken seriously were addressed. Both Phases 1 and 2 were followed up regularly in oral and written follow-up reports.[34]

How Does Monitoring Work?

First, the evaluated country is invited to fill in a questionnaire and the Members of the OECD Secretariat assemble literature and press clippings on the country's track record in fighting domestic and foreign bribery. Frequently, the country is quite unhappy at being confronted with public opinion. Then a team made up of representatives of two countries together with the Secretariat visit the country and meet between eighty and a hundred representatives of government, private sector, and the civil society. They try to get a firsthand impression of the ability of the country to run anticorruption cases and to prevent further bribery. Obviously, such an on-site visit allows some quite straightforward discussions. Based on this experience the examiners and the Secretariat draft a report, which will then be discussed in the plenary of the WGB. There are three hearings within one week: the first to establish that the Group is happy with the analysis, the second to agree on Recommendations, and the third to finalize everything, including the press release. Frequently, the debates are heated, direct, and quite undiplomatic. The Group sometimes hears prosecutors and may inquire what methods

32. See Phase 1 country monitoring of the OECD Anti-Bribery Convention (available online); Bonucci 2014, 545 et seq.; Pieth 2014a, 42 et seq.

33. See Phase 2 country monitoring of the OECD Anti-Bribery Convention (available online); Bonucci 2014, 550 et seq.; Pieth 2014a, 43 et seq.

34. Bonucci 2014, 563 et seq.

have been applied in concrete cases. Especially where cases have been closed, prosecutors will expect a "grilling" in order to assess their ability to run foreign bribery cases and their political will.

The WGB developed extraordinary means of monitoring as sanctions in case the "Recommendations" by the WGB were ignored by countries. In parts, they are technical in nature: especially the rerun of the full evaluation (termed "Phase 2bis") or a technical visit to the country to support legislation in a specific area (i.e., corporate liability, including talks with officials and members of parliaments etc.)[35] fall into this category. More on the political side are letters to ministers, prime ministers, and presidents or public statements and media conferences.[36]

The procedures were redrafted in 2009 at the beginning of the so-called "Phase 3" and given a permanent format.[37] Basically, Phase 3 follows the approach developed in Phase 2 with its emphasis on implementation; it is, though, more concise in nature. Also, Phase 3 can be followed up by extraordinary measures.[38] After a period in which (too) many "Phase 3bis" evaluations have been called, the WGB had to restrict itself to less burdensome and more effective ways, in particular conditional Phase 3bis follow-ups, in case countries resisted essential Recommendations steadfastly. Currently the WGB—now a permanent Committee of its own—is getting ready to embark on a fourth Phase.

Overall, the crucial element of these evaluations is the concept of "unanimity minus one" applied in adopting the final report. The evaluated country has the right to speak but cannot prevent consensus.

Apart from these rounds of in-depth monitoring—which are very heavy, as they imply on-site visits and multiple hearings and reports—there is also an ongoing process called *"tour de table."* Its centerpiece are reports by law enforcement agencies of various countries (at each of the four meetings a year one quarter of the member countries are evaluated). On the basis of media reports a so-called "Matrix" of allegations in the public domain is established, and countries have the right to react to those news stories, if they like.[39] This matrix has served as a basis of a report recently published by the OECD Secretariat (see Figure 7.1).[40]

35. UK, Chile; Bonucci 2014, 565 et seq.; Pieth 2014a, 47 et seq.

36. E.g. to the Czech Republic, Finland, Japan, Slovak Republic and the UK.

37. OECD WGB 2009.

38. Bonucci 2014, 571 et seq.; Pieth 2014a, 47 et seq.

39. Bonucci 2014, 543 et seq.; Pieth 2014a, 42.

40. OECD Foreign Bribery Report 2014.

Figure 7.1 OECD Foreign Bribery Report: An Analysis of the Crime of Bribery of Foreign Public Officials.
SOURCE: OECD Foreign Bribery Report 2014.

Whereas other Conventions have adopted a rather soft touch and are known for their smooth functioning, the OECD Anti-Corruption Initiative was from the outset about unfair competition amongst major trading "partners." The tone in the Group and its reports was always harsh. The reports mattered, and what the Group did influenced economic positions of countries and companies. This became obvious as soon as law enforcement in countries beyond the United States picked up. In particular the German Siemens prosecution[41] served as a wake-up call.

Not everybody appreciated the tone, but the real *crisis* for the OECD's Anti-Corruption Convention came in December 2005 when the United Kingdom's prime minister suggested to the attorney general and indirectly to the director of the Serious Fraud Office (SFO) to close an investigation against British

41. Weidenfeld (ed.) 2011.

Aerospace (BAE) in the context of a large arms deal with Saudi Arabia, the so-called *"Al Yamamah"* contract.[42]

6. THE CRISIS

Saudi Arabia decided to acquire Taifun planes for £40 billion and later on additional planes for £10 billion. BAE managed to beat French and US competitors with the help of political influence (intense lobbying by the Thatcher and following administrations) as well as through bribes. It is now known that BAE paid off several members of the Saudi royal family through a London-based travel agent. The roughly £60 million expended by Peter Gardiner on behalf of BAE, however, proved to be merely the tip of the iceberg. Far bigger sums have been paid and laundered through the international banking system toward key persons in the Saudi royal family. Indicators point to several billions of dollars.[43]

Whereas some details about intermediaries and financial flows are known, the entire story will probably never be fully revealed, as shortly before the Swiss Attorney General's Office could grant the SFO mutual legal assistance, the British prime minister suggested the case be closed. His personal note to the attorney general (AG) was published in the context of the Judicial Review (see Figure 7.2).

The Legal Department of BAE had petitioned the United Kingdom's attorney general already previously for months to abandon the investigation, so far unsuccessfully.[44] (see Figure 7.3)

In autumn 2005 the Saudi ambassador to the United States, Prince Bandar, apparently threatened to stop cooperation on antiterror activities between Saudi Arabia and the United Kingdom if the investigation in the United Kingdom went ahead. Originally, the attorney general resisted these threats. One year later they became more pressing and this time met the interest of the prime minister. He as well as the attorney general leaned on the director of the SFO.

42. PBS Frontline documentary, April 7, 2009: "Interview with the Prime Minister in 'Black Money' "; Financial Times, December 16 and 17, 2006, 4; Statement of the Attorney General in the House of Lords, Hansard, HL vol. 687, cols 1711-13 (14 December 2006).

43. Some British media reports spoke of £1 Billion: The Guardian, June 8, 12, and 14, 2007; The Daily Mail, June 9, 2007; The Daily Express, June 11, 2007; US media even talked of $2 billion, such as The Washington Post, June 8, 2007.

44. The Queen on the Application of Corner House Research and Campaign Against Arms Trade v The Director of the Serious Fraud Office, Case No: CO/1567/2007, High Court of Justice, Queens Bench Division, Administrative Court, Index to Exhibit RW4, Item No. 3, Letter of 7 November 2005 by Michael Lester to Lord Goldsmith QC, attaching a Memorandum, 3 (www.thecornerhouse.org.uk/pdf/document/IACC.pdf (last visited March 6, 2017).

SECRET – PERSONAL

THE PRIME MINISTER

Personal Minute

Attorney General

AL YAMAMAH: SERIOUS FRAUD OFFICE INVESTIGATION

[…]

relationship with the Kingdom of Saudi Arabia. **It is my judgement on the basis of recent evidence and the advice of colleagues that these developments have given rise to a real and immediate risk of a collapse in UK/Saudi security, intelligence and diplomatic cooperation. This is likely to have seriously negative consequences for the UK public interest in terms of both national security and our highest priority foreign policy objectives in the Middle East.**

[…]

by the investigation, it is of course of concern to me, not least because of the critical difficulty presented to the negotiations over the Typhoon contract.

[…]

I understand and respect the constitutional position and the independent judgement you are required to make on extremely difficult and delicate issues of this nature, and I know any intervention you make in the conduct of this investigation must be your decision alone. For my part, after much careful thought I have come to the conclusion that the seriousness of these risks to the national interest is such that I would be failing in my duty if I did not bring them directly to your attention ask you to consider them. That is why I am taking the exceptional step of writing to you myself.

[…]

Tony Blair

8 December 2006

SECRET – PERSONAL

Figure 7.2 Al Yamamah: Serious Fraud Office Investigation.

BAE SYSTEMS

Michael Lester
Group Legal Director

07 November 2005

The Lord Goldsmith QC
Attorney General
Attorney General's Chambers
9 Buckingham Gate
London SW1E 6JP

LAW OFFICERS
08 NOV 2005
DEPARTMENT

Private & Confidential

Dear Lord Goldsmith

This Company has been the subject of a Serious Fraud Office (SFO) investigation instituted in November 2004. Recent developments in this investigation raise in our view serious public interest issues which we consider should be brought to your personal attention having regard to the prosecutorial discretion conferred upon you.

I enclose a brief note summarising the position and would welcome the opportunity to see you to amplify its contents and answer any questions you may have. You should be aware that I have discussed the issues referred to in the enclosed note with Sir Kevin Tebbit, the Permanent Secretary at the Ministry of Defence, who is aware that I am contacting you.

I look forward to hearing from you.

Yours sincerely

enc.

Figure 7.3 The Queen on the Application of Corner House Research and Campaign against Arms Trade v The Director of the Serious Fraud Office, Case No: CO/1567/2007, High Court of Justice, Queens Bench Division, Administrative Court, Index to Exhibit RW4, Item No. 3, Letter of 7 November 2005 by Michael Lester to Lord Goldsmith QC, attaching a Memorandum, 3, available at: http://www.thecornerhouse.org.uk/sites/thecornerhouse.org.uk/files/SecondRedactDocsRW4.pdf.

Reason enough for Mr. Wardle, then director of the SFO, to close the case. In an interview, however, he calls the Saudi move "blackmail."[45]

Two UK-based NGOs, Corner House and Campaign against Arms Trade,[46] took the case to court to force its reopening. Whereas the High Court saw the advantage of reopening,[47] the House of Lords, to which the case was ultimately transferred, opted against it.[48]

Concurrently, a worldwide media storm with over one thousand articles and quotes arose.[49] Politicians all over the world criticized the United Kingdom, amongst them Thabo Mbeki of South Africa: "Mr Mbeki spoke out in a discussion at the World Economic Forum in Davos on the fight against corruption in Africa. He voiced fears that corruption inquiries focused disproportionately on African countries rather than the Western companies on the other side of the equation."[50]

The OECD clearly saw its anticorruption work confronted with the toughest of challenges so far. Fritz Heimann and Ben Heineman wrote in *The National Interest*: "The great irony of Britain's misguided Al Yamamah decision, taken in the name of national security, is that by weakening the OECD Convention, in the end, it will only weaken the security of the United Kingdom, the rest of the developed world and the emerging nations."[51]

45. PBS Frontline documentary, April 7, 2009: "Mr. Wardle in Interview with the Prime Minister in 'Black Money'"; Financial Times, December 16 and 17, 2006, 4; Statement of the Attorney General in the House of Lords (cf. House of Lords Hansard, vol. 687, cols 1711-13, 14 December 2006).

46. Opinions of the Lords of Appeal for Judgment in the Queen on the Application of Corner House Research and Campaign Against Arms Trade v The Director of the Serious Fraud Office, House of Lords, Session 2007–08 [2008] UKHL 60, 30 July 2008.

47. The Queen on the Application of Corner House Research and Campaign Against Arms Trade v The Director of the Serious Fraud Office, Case No: CO/1567/2007, High Court of Justice, Queens Bench Division, Administrative Court, Lord Justice Moses, Mister Justice Sullivan, 10 April 2008.

48. House of Lords, session 2007–08, [2008] UKHL 60, Opinions of the Lords of Appeal for judgment in the cause R (on the application of Corner House Research and others) (Respondents) *v* Director of the Serious Fraud Office (Appellant) (Criminal Appeal from Her Majesty's High Court of Justice), 30 July 2008.

49. In a matter of three months more than a thousand media reports were registered on the Internet.

50. The Times online, January 27, 2007: "Mbeki says Blair guilty of double standards over BAE."

51. Heineman and Heimann 2007, 87; cf. also Rose-Ackerman and Billa 2008.

The OECD officials made strong statements in the media,[52] and the WGB held two hearings and came out with a press statement, distributed at a widely televised press conference. What was probably more effective in the long run, though, was an action plan:[53] the WGB called a Phase 2bis evaluation on the United Kingdom[54] and demanded the reopening of the case as well as new laws to be drafted. It demanded a progress report by the United Kingdom every three months, and it added in a statement an ominous sentence: "The Working Group stresses that failing to enact effective and comprehensive legislation undermines the credibility of the United Kingdom's legal framework and potentially triggers the need for increased due diligence over UK companies by their commercial partners or Multilateral Development Banks."[55]

Translated into ordinary language this sentence meant that all British companies could face a trade disadvantage if Britain remained underregulated the way it was. It was the first time in the history of the WGB that it threatened trade sanctions to a Member. Astonishingly, no one asked at the time whether the WGB had the necessary powers. It basically followed the model of the Financial Action Task Force in its dealings with so-called Non-Cooperative Countries and Territories (NCCTs).[56]

THE UNITED KINGDOM FIGHTS BACK

In the OECD, the United Kingdom had to defend its position at several instances, first in two meetings in January and March 2007, when the decision was taken to put the United Kingdom on probation and to re-run its evaluation. Whereas the official exchanges remained relatively civil, moves behind the scene and in the public domain rapidly deteriorated:

First, the magazine *The Economist* invited its Aeronautics Editor to write a lead article on the newly elected secretary general of the OECD! Under the title "An Angel Flies into Some Flack, Trouble at the OECD" *the Economist*, in its "top story," tried (unsuccessfully) to question the secretary general's integrity.[57]

52. The Times, January 18, 2007: "Blair faces new OECD pressure on halted BAE inquiry"; Forbes.com, January 18, 2007: "OECD concerned by U.K. move on BAE"; Financial Times, March 15, 2007: "OECD to probe Britain's anti-bribery performance."

53. Bonucci 2014, 566 et seq.

54. WGB press release, March 14, 2007: "OECD to conduct a further examination of UK efforts against bribery."

55. OECD WGB 2008, UK Phase 2bis Report, 71.

56. Cf. below 125.

57. The Economist, April 19, 2007; cf. also Le Monde, May 4, 2007: "l'OCDE agasse Londres . . . et vice-versa."

Shortly afterwards,[58] *The Guardian* reported that the United Kingdom was "covertly trying to oust the head of the world's main anti-bribery watchdog to prevent criticism of ministers and Britain's biggest arms company, BAE . . . British diplomats are seeking to remove Professor Pieth, a Swiss legal expert who chairs the anti-corruption watchdog of the Organization for Economic Cooperation and Development (OECD), claiming he is too outspoken." The article goes on to remind readers that "at the OECD meeting in Paris last month, British officials tried to stop Prof Pieth addressing a press conference at which he announced his agency was to conduct a formal inquiry into the government's decisions to terminate the BAE investigation. They then privately briefed other diplomats involved with the OECD, saying he should be removed".[59]

Whilst the political struggles went on, BAE made a move to reduce some of the tension. Although the "old guard" of BAE continued to make big noises in the House of Lords that they had never bribed, the new company president Dick Olver asked former chief lord Justice Woolf to conduct an investigation into BAE's compliance system. The analysis was moderately critical and gained some credibility; if it did not lead to the reopening of the case, it helped pave the way toward a new law.

A Very Special Seminar

As part of the Woolf inquiry, a group of about twenty persons was invited to an informal seminar: some members of civil society, including TI, but also representatives of the Ministry of Defense and of the company BAE. It so happened that I was seated next to Dick Olver. After the seminar, while the other participants went for drinks to the adjoining room, we had a private conversation: realizing that by the time (2008) I had used my power, I was keen to enroll Mr. Olver's and Lord Woolf's help to push for the new law. We struck an unofficial "deal" that I would resist from further fueling a media campaign against the company if they wrote to the Ministry of Justice supporting the new legislation. They both stuck to the deal and copied me on their letter to Jack Straw.

---

58. The Guardian, April 24, 2007: "UK tries to sabotage BAE bribes inquiry"; also NZZ, April 28 and 29, 2007, 27.

59. The Guardian, April 24, 2007: "UK tries to sabotage BAE bribes inquiry"; also NZZ, April 28 and 29, 27.

7. OVERCOMING THE CRISIS: THE UK BRIBERY ACT 2010

The crisis was ultimately overcome not by the reopening of the case, but by Britain enacting a new law, the (theoretically) toughest law on foreign bribery worldwide: the UK Bribery Act 2010.[60]

When the OECD Convention was adopted, the United Kingdom was amongst the first to ratify, since it believed that the 1906 legislation[61] was sufficient to cover the requirements. The OECD, however, from Phase 1 on had serious doubts, in particular as neither this law nor the underlying common law had ever led to a case on foreign bribery.[62] The United Kingdom tried to salvage the situation in an annex to its law on terrorism in 2001,[63] when it clarified that the 1906 law was indeed applicable also to foreign bribery. However, this left the deficiencies of the old law in place (notably the agent-principal approach and the insufficient corporate liability, based on a pure "identification theory"[64]). Continuous efforts to enact new laws in 2003 and 2005 failed in Parliament.[65] Pressure only mounted dramatically with the Al Yamamah crisis. Now the Law Commission was tasked with drafting new law. Its report[66] was a step in the right direction, but was still heavily criticized both domestically and internationally. Amongst other voices the United Kingdom heard the opinion of the WGB and of seven individual Member States of the OECD at a seminar in London.[67] The WGB suggested in particular that UK corporate liability ensure adequate capture of cases where junior company representatives had committed the crime, but the company had omitted to prevent them. The probably most creative part of the

60. The UK Bribery Act 2010 is considered "tough" even in comparison to the FCPA, cf. Warin, Falconer and Diamant 2010; Pieth 2014a, 220 et seq.

61. OECD WGB 1999, UK Phase 1 Report, 1.

62. OECD WGB 1999, UK Phase 1 Report, 24 et seq.; OECD WGB 2005, UK Phase 2 Report, para. 15 et seq.

63. UK Anti-terrorism, Crime and Security Act 2001, part 12.

64. Pieth 2014a, 219 et seq.

65. Corruption Draft Legislation, Presented to Parliament by the Secretary of State for the Home Department by Command of Her Majesty, March 2003; Bribery, Reform of the Prevention of Corruption Acts and SFO Powers in Cases of Bribery of Foreign Officials, A Consultation Paper, December 2005.

66. Law Commission, Reforming Bribery, Law Com No 313, 19 November 2008.

67. Pieth 2014a, 220 et seq.

2010 Act is its section 7, the offense "the failure of commercial organizations to prevent bribery," balanced by a defense of "adequate procedures."[68]

Overall, the British prime minister was able, in blatant breach of the separation of powers, to close an investigation. Tony Blair's legacy on anticorruption, though, was to have provided the United Kingdom with the toughest anticorruption law worldwide—if applied.

Even though the United Kingdom had enacted one of the most stringent legal texts on bribery, the crisis was not entirely over yet: in a next stage, the entry into force was delayed until a guidance was adopted, and it looked as if this could take some considerable time yet, as there was resistance from business circles. The OECD restarted its power play, involving letters to ministers and public pressure. When the guidance was published in 2011[69] the law could finally enter into force. However, at this stage of the budgetary crisis the UK government slashed 40 percent of the SFO ordinary budget, putting in question the practical effectiveness of the main investigative body responsible for implementing the law. Now the SFO has to apply to the Treasury if it needs more money on a case-by-case basis. Furthermore, it still remains unclear whether the SFO is going to survive as an independent organization.

Since 2011, the first cases[70] have been run under the UK Bribery Act, and the Act has had a marked preventative effect on companies doing business abroad. Overall the crisis of the OECD work on bribery and the lessons learned in its course have shown that the OECD and its monitoring process have the power to secure implementation of its instruments.

8. UNEVEN APPLICATION

This leads to a general problem of all anticorruption treaties and of the OECD Convention in particular: although some countries are active and a few others may be moderately active in enforcing the law, the majority, however, is hardly opening any cases at all or closes next to all of the cases again. The OECD Phase 3 monitoring has been very critical of about half of its constituency, and the TI annual survey[71] also gives a rather bleak picture of the OECD implementation. The experience is that in the area of fighting corruption there is much talk and

68. Nicholls et al. 2011, para. 4.87 et seq.; O'Shea 2011, 130 et seq.; Pieth 2014a, 220 et seq.; Pieth and Ivory 2011, 28 et seq.; Raphael 2010, 57 et seq.

69. UK Ministry of Justice Guidance 2011.

70. The Financial Times, June 24, 2014.

71. TI Progress Report 2015, 2 et seq.

little genuine action. One needs to face the realities: law enforcement agencies and judiciaries are frequently not overzealous because running corruption cases against the powerful is rarely good for one's career. Governments are typically more interested in fostering exports than in beating up on corrupt corporations and certainly when it comes to politically sensitive industries, such as defense, governments like to keep a tight control. France has extended its national security legislation to allow governments to declare head offices of corporations off limits for the judiciary.[72] Even Nordic States have closed cases in the area of defense giving problematic reasons: Swedish TV showed the senior prosecutor charged with investigating possible bribery by Saab Gripen, claiming that he was drastically understaffed and that he was politically pressured when closing the cases and when retiring from his job.[73] The Finnish Patria Case was dismissed at first instance on the basis of lack of evidence[74] after the former Slovenian president had been sentenced by a Court in his own country for taking bribes by this company. Only slightly different are a sequence of cases relating to Austria: in one case involving the payment of €13 million to the Hungarian minister of economy and his friends by a construction company. The case was closed because the Court held that preventing nationalization of motorways was not an activity "to obtain or retain business" by the construction company.[75] In another case (the deputy minister of interior of Thailand had just been sentenced to twelve years of prison for taking bribes from an Austrian provider of fire trucks[76]) Austrian authorities refused to open the case altogether.[77] Here, the problem is rather lack of competence combined with political disinterest.[78]

72. OECD WGB 2012, FR Phase 3 Report, 45 et seq.

73. SVT, Sverige Television AB, Uppdrag Granskning (Assignment: Investigate), Manuscript, The Final Battle (of the Grippenaffair), 10 June 2009.

74. At the Hämeenlinna District Court (YLE News, 30 January 2014: "Finnish court rejects Slovenian bribery charges against Patria"); the case continues at the Turku Court of Appeal; furthermore, two former Patria executives were convicted, and the company fined, for bribing officials in Croatia (YLE News, February 16, 2015: "Patria executives found guilty of bribing Croatian officials").

75. Higher Regional Court (Oberlandesgericht) Vienna, Decision No. 23 Bs 43/12k; Kurier, 9 October 2013; Der Börsianer, 9 October 2013: "The STRABAG case."

76. Supreme Court of Thailand, Criminal Division for Holders of Political Positions, Decisions No. 5/2554 and 7/2556, 10 September 2013 (subject: malfeasance in office, violations of the 1999 Act Concerning Offences Relating to the Submission of Bids to Government Agencies); cf. also Kurier (online), 11 September 2013: "Steyr: Schuldsprüche in Millionen-Korruptionsfall, Bangkok. 12 Jahre Haft für Vize-Innenminister."

77. Regional Court (Landesgericht) for Criminal Matters Vienna, Decision No. 130 BI 51/13h, 27 August 2013, 9 et seq.

78. Pieth 2014c, 367 et seq.

9. FURTHER CHALLENGES

The monitoring system developed by international organizations is a helpful tool to ensure the implementation and application of conventions and especially of soft-law instruments. Especially, where the peers turn rough with a noncompliant member state, the risk is that the members turn on the chairman.

IMPEACHMENT?

Already in 2005, a Member State had turned against the Chair of the WGB: as the concept of "unanimity minus one" did not allow a country to oppose its own report, it could only take revenge by blocking the re-election of the Chair. As Chair, I had to be re-elected annually between 1990 and 2013 by unanimity of the Members of the group. The OECD does not elect its Bureau by formal elections, but rather by negotiation. If a candidate loses the full support of the Group, he is expected to step down, but has to stay in office until another candidate is elected by full unanimity.

After I had in the evening news in Italy in 2005 criticized Italy for watering down its legislation on accounting and auditing (in particular the offense of *falso in bilancio*, in order to shorten the statute of limitation and help its prime minister Berlusconi evade law enforcement), Berlusconi tasked his personal secretary with seeing me impeached as the OECD Working Group Chair. The Group did not really know how to handle this politically sensitive issue, in particular as the Group was made up predominantly of technical experts. Ultimately, the deputy secretary general of the OECD in contact with the US undersecretary of state, Alan Larson, handled the issue and managed to dissuade Italy from further action, in particular as it became obvious that Italy was the only country opposing re-election.[79]

In a similar way the United Kingdom, through the office of Prime Minister Blair (his Secretary Powell) intended to impeach the Chair on the height of the crisis. A letter was sent to the Foreign and Commonwealth Office; it was, however, leaked to the press and published. That was the end of this move.

---

79. Facts 18/07, 3 May 2007, 26.

UK tries to sabotage BAE bribes inquiry

Attempt to oust legal expert heading European corruption investigation

David Leigh and Rob Evans

The UK is covertly trying to oust the head of the world's main anti-bribery watchdog to prevent criticism of ministers and Britain's biggest arms company, BAE, the Guardian has learned.

The effort to remove Mark Pieth comes as his organisation has stepped up its investigation into the British government's decision to kill off a major inquiry into allegations that BAE paid massive bribes to land Saudi arms deals.

British diplomats are seeking to remove Professor Pieth, a Swiss legal expert who chairs the anti-corruption watchdog of the Organisation for Economic Cooperation and Development (OECD), claiming he is too outspoken.

At the OECD meeting in Paris last month, British officials tried to stop Prof Pieth addressing a press conference at which he announced his agency was to conduct a formal inquiry into the government's decision to terminate the BAE investigation. They then privately briefed other diplomats involved with the OECD, saying he should be removed.

When that failed, the campaign against him continued unabated with further back-channel complaints.

But concern about the conduct of the British diplomats filtered back to Prof Pieth, who confirmed yesterday that he was aware of the attempts to remove him. "I am aware that the British ambassador was asking at the time for action to be taken against me," he said.

Prof Pieth refused to elaborate, but he is understood to be privately furious at the way he has been bad-mouthed.

A source at the OECD added: "The UK's representatives were sent to Paris to emasculate the [watchdog] and ensure they did not say anything publicly. They failed and were not pleased. They behaved in a manner that would not have been out of place in a boxing ring."

In recent weeks the UK has demanded that OECD officials should be prevented from making any future statements about the BAE case while the inquiry is ongoing. But the request has hit a brick wall. An OECD source said: "The British do not have support from anyone else on this."

The director general of the OECD, Angel Gurría, also believes the UK is encouraging a smear campaign against him. Last Friday he was accused in a British magazine of giving a job to his daughter, getting free football tickets, and spending €733,000 (£500,000) to refurbish his Paris flat in what was described as "the poshest bit of the swanky 16th arrondissement".

The article in the Economist quoted an unnamed north European ambassador expressing fears that "the staid old body [OECD] ... may drift into dangerous waters" under Mr Gurría, the former finance minister of Mexico.

Following the allegations, Mr Gurría issued a combative statement, saying that he was under UK media attack by "innuendo, gossip and partial truths".

"It is no surprise that this attack occurs at this time," he added.

Britain's ambassador to the OECD, David Lyscom, admitted yesterday that he had talked off the record to the Economist but added: "The UK had absolutely nothing to do with planting the story."

The UK partly controls OECD purse-strings, and also has the power to veto Prof Pieth's reappointment, due next January.

Sensitivity over the OECD inquiry has become more acute since its 36-strong panel announced last month detailed plans to mount a fresh official inspection of Britain because of the manner in which the BAE inquiry had been halted.

It also rebuked the UK for failing to keep its promises to modernise its inadequate corruption laws, under which no one has yet been prosecuted.

The UK also faces a legal challenge in London. Two campaign groups, the anti-corruption group The Cornerhouse and the Campaign Against the Arms Trade, filed detailed pleadings last week alleging that Britain had broken the treaty banning corrupt payments by companies to foreign politicians and officials.

Figure 7.4 UK Tries to Sabotage BAE Bribes Inquiry.
SOURCE: The Guardian, 24 April 2007 www.guardian.co.uk.

Even later on, other such efforts were made in the context of conflicts with individual Member States: in 2010 Canada received a particularly critical report: since Phase 2 (in 2002), it had not followed up on the Recommendations, had no new cases to speak of, and refused steadfastly to review its policy on the nationality principle (Canada remained one of the last countries to introduce national jurisdiction). The situation has since changed dramatically. However, during the hearings Canada was unable to convince evaluators (Austria and the United States) and the Group that it met the standard. The Canadian representative, however, had it out with the Chair: he was overheard assuring the newly participating Russian Delegation that they could rest assured that the Chair would be deposed before they were evaluated.

All this goes to demonstrate that the work of the OECD WGB seems to be relevant to countries, that the concept of "unanimity minus one" is crucial, but that the weak spot in the arrangement is the position of the Chair.

Unanimity and Media Policy

Although in monitoring the rule "unanimity minus one" ensures that the country monitored is heard but cannot block publication of the report, the Group needs consensus not only when adopting an international instrument, but also for such prosaic matters as publishing its *annual report*. Therefore, the United Kingdom was able to block the Working Group on Bribery's annual report 2006, hinting at the difficulties that had been encountered with the closing of the Al Yamamah case, even though thousands of new stories had been published on the issue and several OECD monitoring reports discussed it in great detail.[80]

A further issue emerged in the height of the crisis with the United Kingdom, where the United Kingdom tried to prevent a *press conference* from taking place. When the Group was uncertain whether the principal of unanimity or unanimity minus one applied here, the United Kingdom referred to a draft press policy stating that "media releases drafted by the Chair/Bureau must be approved by the Committee, unless otherwise agreed."[81] Clearly these rules were made for a "nice weather" institution, primarily focusing on economic analysis rather than on peer pressure. In the case of the United

80. Letter by the British Ambassador David Lyscom to the OECD of March 8, 2007, indicating that the UK delegation will continue to oppose the publication of a report that contains a specific reference to this case, in whatever form.

81. Position paper by the OECD Public Affairs and Communications Directorate, C/INF(2007)9.

Kingdom I actually had to threaten to step down as Chair if the Group was not prepared to hold a press conference at the height of the storm.

Of course, this all can only be understood in the context of the very heated atmosphere of the crisis. The press conference turned out to be very tense—including an attempt by the British ambassador to call an end to the event, actually holding his hand into the camera stating "enough damage has been done."

One journalist described the situation as follows:

"The Chair did an admirable job in presenting the general issues without getting into detailed responses regarding BAE. The British journalists present were clearly out to get aggressive quotes from him, but he didn't give them any. The situation with the British delegation standing behind was bizarre. The atmosphere was very tense, one of the tensest press conferences I have attended. I have rarely seen so much pressure by someone to end a press conference held at somebody's premises. (Note—that is a reference to the British Embassy press officer.) At their briefing afterwards, the British flatly contradicted what Pieth had been saying, insisting that there was no tension and that everyone was in agreement. But the (Working Group) statement is fairly damning, particularly when you consider that it concerns a G8 country."[82]

---

10. A NEW STEP FORWARD: THE 2009 RECOMMENDATION

The WGB has a peculiar way of advancing. Frequently, there are moments when nothing goes. For years the WGB has been analyzing its own work. It wrote a "mid-term-study"[83] to determine the emerging standards of Phase 3. Based on this study it discussed whether the Convention could be supplemented by an Additional Protocol, an idea given up in the following discussion very rapidly. Shortly afterward, however, the idea of reorganizing the Recommendation of 1997, a document that had somewhat lost traction next to the Convention, emerged. Much of what could have been the object of an Additional Protocol now filtered into the new Recommendation. The WGB reinvented itself and went back to "soft law." An upgraded Recommendation was presented to the

82. Mail by a British journalist of March 23, 2007 to the OECD media department.

83. OECD WGB 2006.

Council for adoption.[84] As Annex to the Recommendation two texts, one on corporate liability and one on company compliance, were added.[85]

The Annex II was actually adopted only in 2010.[86] It was the object of fierce negotiations between the leading Ministries of Commerce (in particular of Germany, France, United Kingdom, and the United States). Its contents were not really new. It covered the ground that had been already covered by many US deferred prosecution agreements,[87] by NGOs,[88] and be the "compliance industry" in general.[89] Its significance is, however, that it is an intergovernmental public standard. It serves as a blueprint for national guidance, for law enforcement agencies, etc. Thereby, the topic of Annex I, corporate liability, and Annex II, compliance, become intertwined: Annex II indicates what an adequate compliance program entails.

11. A FINAL POSITIVE EXPERIENCE

Everyday life in the WGB remained tedious up to the end of my tenure: last fights with Belgium demonstrate it; Belgium was "insulted" because the Group and especially the Chair believed that its lack of enforcement was based on a deliberate policy decision. Belgium insisted on listening to tapes of meetings and refused to participate in the following work of the Working Group to demonstrate its displeasure. Again, the critical stance of the report seemed to have struck a chord.

Once more, however, the WGB showed its strength when it came to elect a new Chair:

> Based on a call for applications a Search Committee screened the field of over 30 applicants and selected the nine most promising candidates. At a meeting in summer 2013 they presented themselves, and then the Group discussed the merits of the candidates in several hearings *in camera*. Interestingly enough, the WGB was able—without resorting to straw

84. OECD Rec. 2009.

85. Cf. Annex II to the OECD Rec. 2009.

86. Amendments adopted by Council 18 February 2010 to reflect the inclusion of Annex II, Good Practice Guidance on Internal Controls, Ethics and Compliance.

87. Cf. Low 2014, 611 et seq.; Urofsky and Moon 2014, 684 et seq., 712 et seq.

88. TI Business Principles 2009; Trace 2010; Vincke/Kassum 2013.

89. Cf. Pieth 2011.

polls— to openly address advantages and disadvantages of each candidate in several rounds until the group of candidates was down to three. And again, it was able to discuss the selection in an open and transparent manner until unanimity was reached on the new Chairman.

12. CONCLUSION

Overall, the WGB and its procedures have developed into probably the most effective international tool against (foreign) bribery. It could serve as a model for other regional or worldwide international bodies.

8

The UN Convention Against Corruption

FRITZ HEIMANN ■

1. GLOBAL SIGNIFICANCE

The UN Convention against Corruption (UNCAC) has worldwide membership and an extremely comprehensive scope, giving it the potential to become the pre-eminent instrument for combating global corruption. It has been ratified by more than 180 governments, over 90 percent of the members of the United Nations. Its membership is more than four times larger than that of the OECD Convention.

UNCAC's broad scope establishes a sound legal framework for combating corruption in the global economy of the twenty-first century. Unlike the OECD Convention, which deals only with bribery of foreign public officials, UNCAC covers a wide range of criminal offenses, domestic and foreign, public and private. It also provides extensive preventive measures, such as codes of conduct for public officials, rules on public procurement, management of public finances, independence of the judiciary, and prevention of money laundering. UNCAC also provides measures for international cooperation, including extradition, mutual legal assistance in investigations, prosecutions and judicial proceedings, asset recovery, and technical assistance.

UNCAC's worldwide participation and broad scope are great strengths. However, these same factors complicate its implementation. UNCAC's membership is very diverse, including different levels of economic development, and differing political institutions and legal systems. Ratifying UNCAC was

Confronting Corruption. Fritz Heimann and Mark Pieth.

a popular step in most countries; implementing its numerous provisions has been much more difficult. Follow-up monitoring was controversial at the outset and UNCAC was adopted in 2003 without providing for monitoring reviews. It required six years of struggle, in which Transparency International played an active role, before a review process was adopted at the Third Conference of States Parties in Doha in 2009.[1]

2. THE POLITICS OF UNCAC

Following customary UN practice, UNCAC decision-making requires consensus. This is determined informally, without vote-taking, and proceeds at two levels. There is a process of consultation in Vienna between UNODC and representatives of the parties. (UNODC, the UN Office of Drugs and Crimes, based in Vienna, acts as the Secretariat for the UN Convention.) The second level involves biennial Conferences of States Parties (COSP), as well as intervening meetings of the Implementation Review Group (IRG), in which all parties can participate.

From the time of the initial treaty negotiations in 2002–2003 in Geneva, the politics of UNCAC has been characterized by a split between countries that support a stronger Convention, with consistent and timely compliance, and those that favor a softer approach, with substantial national discretion over implementation. As a result some Convention provisions are mandatory ("the parties shall . . ."), whereas others are discretionary ("the parties may . . ."). The split also resulted in the stalemate over follow-up monitoring. The Implementation Review Mechanism agreed to at the Third COSP in Doha was a controversial compromise. It allows individual governments to prevent country visits by review teams, to restrict participation in reviews by nongovernmental organizations (NGOs), and to prohibit publication of the full text (as distinct from executive summaries) of country reports.

The group favoring national discretion in implementation is led by Russia, China, Iran, Pakistan, Venezuela, and Ecuador. These governments have been very outspoken in their opposition to a stronger Convention. They have had support from a number of other governments, primarily from developing countries. The number of supporters is uncertain because there are no

1. The review process began in 2010 and is scheduled to take ten years, with half of UNCAC's provisions reviewed in each of two five-year segments. Present indications are that implementation is quite uneven. Although the review process identifies deficiencies in implementation, the process to get governments to correct deficiencies is unclear.

votes. TI believes that a substantial majority of governments favor timely and consistent implementation. This majority has been much less vocal than the opponents of strict implementation. The reliance on consensus, and the inability to take votes, magnifies the power of the opponents over their actual number, giving a strong tactical advantage to even a small group of outspoken opponents.

Operating under the UNODC's consensus-based system is cumbersome and time-consuming. However, the experience of the past decade has shown that with careful leadership from UNODC considerable progress had been made. This was most clearly demonstrated by the 2009 agreement on the Implementation Review Mechanism. The compromises made, such as giving governments the right to avoid country visits and limit NGO participation in reviews, have not been widely exercised. A quiet consensus on acceptable practices appears to have emerged.

From a long-term perspective there are sound reasons for optimism. The rapid spread of digital communications and the continuing growth of globalization ensure that UNCAC is reinforced by the most fundamental megatrends of our time. Digital communications make it ever more difficult to keep corruption secret; once uncovered, bribery is instantly publicized worldwide. Ready use of public media has resulted in the overthrow of long-established corrupt governments. Increasing globalization means that the constituency supporting acceptable global standards continues to expand.[2] In sum, the goals of UNCAC are sound and achievable. To achieve these goals, it is essential that UNCAC's proponents must be realistic, patient, and persistent.

3. THE UNITED NATIONS CONVENTION AGAINST CORRUPTION: ANTICORRUPTION'S EXPANDING FRONTIER

The United Nations Convention against Corruption is of compelling interest for international business because it provides a global framework for combating corruption. This Convention has been ratified by 180 parties, including key players in international trade, such as China, India, and Indonesia, in addition to the OECD countries. The United Nations Convention also has a much broader scope than the OECD Convention. Thus, the United Nations Convention is capable of tackling many issues that cannot be effectively dealt with by the OECD or regional anticorruption conventions. The United

2. For an in-depth discussion of globalization and the digital revolution, see below, Chapter 22.

Nations Convention's broad scope and worldwide participation are its greatest strengths. However, they also present difficult challenges in moving from words to deeds.

This section is divided into four subsections. Subsection A provides an overview of the scope of the United Nations Convention and its potential effect on anticorruption laws. Subsection B deals with the Convention's provisions directly affecting international business. Subsection C considers the preventive measures designed to strengthen national integrity systems and finally, Subsection D describes the Convention's ongoing monitoring program.

a. Overview of the United Nations Convention against Corruption

The United Nations Convention against Corruption was adopted in 2003 and became effective in December 2005. The Convention's parties include industrialized, emerging, developing, and least-developed economies. By comparison, the OECD Convention includes only forty-one industrialized nations, whereas the regional conventions only cover countries in their regions.

The scope of the United Nations Convention is particularly ambitious. There are twenty-eight articles covering criminalization and law enforcement, including foreign and domestic corruption, extortion as well as bribery, corruption in the public sector and the private sector, embezzlement, illicit enrichment of public officials, abuse of functions, and trading in influence.

In addition, the United Nations Convention contains important preventive measures designed to strengthen the capability of states to fight corruption; provisions on international cooperation, including mutual legal assistance, extradition, and joint investigations; and groundbreaking provisions on asset recovery; as well as provisions on technical assistance and information exchanges.

Several examples can be used to illustrate the provisions of the United Nations Convention that are of particular relevance to multinational enterprises:

- The provisions for international corporations should substantially improve cooperation among national enforcement officials. There are detailed articles dealing with mutual legal assistance and extradition. These should expedite a prosecutor's ability to obtain evidence and witnesses located in other countries, thereby overcoming one of the biggest obstacles obstructing foreign bribery cases.

- The criminalization provisions break important new ground. Particularly noteworthy is the article on "compensation for damages," which provides for private rights of action to enable those damaged by acts of corruption to obtain compensation from those responsible for the damage. Also of interest is the article requiring governments to "address consequences of corruption," including annulling contracts and withdrawing concessions.
- The United Nations Convention includes innovative provisions on asset recovery designed to enable governments, most commonly in the global South, to recover funds deposited abroad by corrupt officials, often in the North, but increasingly elsewhere. In the past, asset recovery has been very difficult to pursue. The World Bank and the United Nations Office of Drugs and Crime have launched a Stolen Assets Recovery (StAR) initiative to increase and accelerate this process. Companies dealing with corrupt officials must exercise high levels of diligence to ensure that any assets that they may obtain as a result of dealings with corrupt officials, or other politically exposed persons (PEPs), cannot be frozen and confiscated in asset recovery proceedings.

The United Nations Convention's broad scope and worldwide participation provide unique potential for global progress against corruption. However, these same factors present difficulties and complexities in their implementation that will take time to overcome. The parties are at different levels of political, legal, and economic development. Most provisions of the Convention are not self-executing and require governments to pass new legislation, to build and strengthen organizations and provide them with adequate funding and staffing. Some of the United Nations Convention's provisions are mandatory ("governments shall adopt laws"); others are discretionary ("governments shall consider adopting laws"). Some are spelled out in great detail: the article on mutual legal assistance includes thirty sections; others are expressed only in broad generalities.

The rate at which the implementation of the United Nations Convention will progress is difficult to predict. That almost all the parties who have signed the Convention have also ratified it is a positive sign and means that governments recognize the need for comprehensive international action in the fight against corruption.

There is widespread recognition of two fundamental points: (1) globalization of economic life will continue to expand, and (2) corruption operates on a global scale and is continuing to grow. Therefore, there is a compelling need for the United Nations Convention to evolve into effective action programs.

b. Provisions Directly Affecting International Business

The provisions of most direct impact on international businesses are primarily in the Convention's Chapter on Criminalization and Law Enforcement.

The provision on "Bribery of national public officials" is mandatory and requires that governments criminalize domestic bribery (active corruption) and solicitation (passive corruption). The OEDC Convention only deals with bribery of foreign public officials. Bribery of national officials is prohibited by the criminal laws of most countries.

The provision on "Bribery of foreign public officials and officials of public international organizations" is also mandatory and requires that governments criminalize foreign bribery. However, the criminalization of solicitation by foreign public officials is left discretionary. The prohibition of solicitation applies whether the company solicited is domestic or foreign. The OECD Convention covers bribery of foreign public officials, but does not deal with solicitation.

United Nations Convention, Article 16

Bribery of foreign public officials and public international organizations

1. Each State Party shall adopt such legislative and other measures as may be necessary to establish as a criminal offence, when committed intentionally, the promise, offering or giving to a foreign public official or an official of public international organization, directly or indirectly, of an undue advantage, for their official himself or herself or another person or entity, in order that the official act or refrain from acting in the exercise of his or her official duties, in order to obtain or retain business or other undue advantage in relation to the conduct of international business.
2. Each State Party shall consider adopting such legislative and other measures as may be necessary to establish as a criminal offence, when committed intentionally, the solicitation or acceptance by a foreign public official or an official of a public international organization, directly or indirectly, of an undue advantage, for the official himself or herself or another person or entity, in order that the official act or refrain from acting in the exercise of his or her official duties.

The provisions on "Trading in influence," "Abuse of functions," and "Illicit Enrichment" are discretionary and have considerable potential for broadening the reach of criminal law beyond the traditional prohibitions of bribery and extortion. The provision on "Illicit Enrichment" is particularly important because it shifts the burden of proof on to public officials who get rich in office. All these provisions go beyond the OECD Convention. Companies need to consider whether to cover "Trading in influence" under their anti-bribery policies; this can raise the difficult issue of distinguishing between legitimate advocacy activities and improper trading in influence.

United Nations Convention, Articles 20 and 21

Illicit enrichment

"Subject to its constitution and the fundamental principles of its legal system, each State Party shall consider adopting such legislative and other measures as may be necessary to establish as a criminal offence, when committed intentionally, illicit enrichment, that is, a significant increase in assets of a public official that he or she cannot reasonably explain in relation to hire or her lawful income."

Bribery in the private sector

"Each State Party shall consider adopting such legislative and other measures as may be necessary to establish as criminal offences, when committed intentionally in the course of economic, financial or commercial activities: (a) The promise, offer or giving, directly or indirectly, of an undue advantage by any person who directs or works, in any capacity, for a private sector entity, for the person himself or herself or for another person, in order that he or she, in breach of his or her duties, act or refrain from acting; (b) The solicitation or acceptance, directly or indirectly, of an undue advantage by any person who directs or works, in any capacity, for a private sector entity, for the person himself or for another person in order that he or she, in breach of his or her duties, act or refrain from acting."

The implementation of these provisions is important because the line of division between the private sector and the public sector has become blurred with the private sector taking on traditional public functions. These provisions go beyond the OECD Convention.

The provision of "Laundering of proceeds of crime" is mandatory. It provides that the corruption offenses covered by the United Nations Convention shall be predicate offenses triggering the anti-money-laundering prohibitions. This provision goes beyond the OECD Convention, which makes foreign bribery a predicate offense only in countries where bribery of domestic officials is a predicate offense.

The article on "Liability of legal persons" is mandatory and calls for corporate liability for the offenses covered by the United Nations Convention. This is an important step because it should accelerate the abandonment of the antiquated concept that only individuals and not corporations shall be criminally liable for the offenses. This article provides that the liability of corporations may be criminal, civil, or administrative; thus, it does not require that corporations shall be criminally liable. Governments must provide that corporations are "subject to effective, proportionate and dissuasive criminal or non-criminal sanctions, including monetary sanctions." The treatment of corporate liability under the United Nations Convention is similar to that of the OECD Convention.

United Nations Convention, Article 26

Liability of legal persons

1. Each State Party shall adopt such measures as may be necessary, consistent with its legal principles, to establish the liability of legal persons for participation in the offences established in accordance with this Convention.
2. Subject to the legal principles of the State Party, the liability of legal persons may be criminal, civil or administrative.
3. Such liability shall be without prejudice to the criminal liability of the natural persons who have committed the offences.
4. Each State Party shall, in particular, ensure that legal persons held liable in accordance with this article are subject to effective, proportionate and dissuasive criminal or non-criminal sanctions, including monetary sanctions.

The provision of a "Statute of limitations" is mandatory and calls for long statutes of limitations for corruption offenses. It also provides for a longer limitations period or suspension of the statute where there is evasion by the offender. This provision is stronger than the OECD Convention.

The article on "Freezing, seizure and confiscation" is mandatory and calls for the confiscation of the proceeds of corruption and of property used in or destined for use in corruption. Bank and other financial records shall be made available and bank secrecy may not be asserted. The OECD Convention provides that bribes and the proceeds of bribery are subject to seizure and confiscation.

The provision on "Protection of reporting persons" is a discretionary one and aims at ensuring the protection of persons who report offenses under the

Convention to the competent authorities (whistle-blowers). This subject matter is not covered in the OECD Convention.

As already mentioned above, the United Nations Convention contains a provision on the "Consequences of acts of corruption." This provides for annulling or rescinding contracts or withdrawing concessions in case of corruption. This matter is also not covered in the OECD Convention.

Another important novelty is the article on "Compensation for damages," which contains a mandatory provision calling for measures to enable persons damaged by acts of corruption to obtain compensation from those responsible for such damages. This provision for private rights of action has far-reaching implications. Private suits could make up for the reluctance of public prosecutors to take action. The OECD Convention does not provide for private rights of action.

This provision is broadly worded. Its scope and effect will depend on implementing legislation and court decisions. Presumably, suits could be brought by unsuccessful competitors and by various other damaged parties. It will be interesting to see how broadly courts will construe the category of potential plaintiffs: "entities and persons who have suffered damage as a result of an act of corruption." Similar questions are raised regarding the category of potential defendants: "those responsible for that damage." Presumably suits could be brought against corrupt companies and against corrupt officials. Could suits also be brought against governments that maintain corrupt procurement systems?

The article on "Cooperation with law enforcement authorities" provides that governments may mitigate punishment or grant immunity to persons cooperating in investigations and prosecutions of corruption. This is not covered by the OECD Convention.

The Convention's Chapter IV on "International Cooperation" includes provisions on mutual legal assistance, law enforcement cooperation, joint investigations, and special investigative techniques. There are important to international business because they should speed up the traditionally cumbersome and time-consuming procedures for dealing with international corruption.

As already mentioned above, Chapter V on "Asset Recovery" is of principal benefit to countries whose corrupt officials have deposited stolen assets in foreign countries. Companies making foreign acquisitions need to assess, as part of their due diligence reviews, whether properties to be acquired could be subjected to seizure and confiscation because of corruption by prior owners.

The successful implementation of the asset recovery chapter of the United Nations Convention is of far-reaching importance, because the attractiveness of corruption will be sharply reduced if corrupt leaders can no longer count on safely depositing the proceeds of corruption in foreign banks. In addition, recovery of stolen assets would contribute greatly to international development because a large share of the estimated billions of dollars of such assets originates from the poorest countries in the world.

c. Strengthening National Integrity Systems

The Convention's provisions on "Preventive Measures" are important because they will strengthen integrity and accountability, thereby curtailing corruption and improving conditions for doing business more broadly. The OECD Convention does not include preventive measures.

The article on "Preventive anti-corruption policies and practices" requires governments to develop anticorruption policies that reflect the rule of law, integrity, transparency, and accountability. Periodic evaluations are called for to determine the adequacy of anticorruption measures. This article should provide a useful advocacy tool for private sector and civil society groups.

The provision on "Preventive anti-corruption bodies" requires governments to establish organizations to implement the policies referred to in the preceding paragraph. Such bodies shall be granted the necessary independence to enable them to carry out their functions, as well as the necessary material resources and specialized staff.

The article on "Code of conduct for public officials" requires governments to promote integrity, honesty, and responsibility among its public officials by means of codes of conduct. Such codes should encourage reporting of violations. Also called for are declarations by public officials of outside activities, investments, assets, and substantial gifts from which a conflict of interest may result.

The provision on "Public procurement and management of public finances" addresses two areas of government activity long subject to widespread corruption. Governments are required to establish public procurement systems based on transparency, competition, and objective criteria in decision-making, including effective systems of appeal. They shall also promote transparency and accountability in the management of public finances, encompassing procedures for the adoption of the national budget, timely reporting on revenue and expenditure, accounting and auditing standards, and risk management and internal control. Improvements in these areas would be of great benefit to business.

United Nations Convention, Articles 9 (excerpted) and 10

Article 9—Public procurement and management of public finances
Each State Party shall, in accordance with the fundamental principles of its legal system, take the necessary steps to establish appropriate systems of procurement, based on transparency, competition and objective criteria in decision-making that are effective, inter alia, in preventing corruption [. . .]".

Article 10—Public Reporting
Taking into account the need to combat corruption, each State Party shall, in accordance with the fundamental principles of its domestic law, take such measures as may be necessary to enhance transparency in its public administration, including with regard to its organization, functioning and decision-making processes, where appropriate. Such measures may include, inter alia:

a. Adopting procedures or regulations allowing members of the general public to obtain, where appropriate, information on the organization, functioning and decision-making processes of its public administration and, with due regard for the protection of privacy and personal data, on decisions and legal acts that concern members of the public;
b. Simplifying administrative procedures, where appropriate, in order to facilitate public access to the competent decision-making authorities; and
c. Publishing information, which may include periodic reports of corruption in its public administration.

An article on "Public reporting" provides for public access to decision-making authorities and periodic reports on the risks of corruption in public administration.

A provision on the "Private sector" calls for governments to take measures to prevent corruption in the private sector, including enhanced accounting and auditing standards, codes of conduct, prevention of conflicts of interest, restrictions on employment of former public officials, internal controls, prohibitions of off-the-books transactions, and disallowance of tax-deductibility of bribes.

United Nations Convention, Article 12 (excerpted)

Private sector

"Each State Party shall take measures, in accordance with the fundamental principles of its domestic law, to prevent corruption involving the private sector, enhance accounting and auditing standards in the private sector and, where appropriate, provide effective, proportionate and dissuasive civil, administrative or criminal penalties for failure to comply with such measures. [. . .]

In order to prevent corruption, each State Party shall take such measures as may be necessary, in accordance with its domestic laws and regulations regarding the maintenance of books and records, financial statement disclosures and accounting and auditing standards, to prohibit the following acts carried out for the purpose of committing any of the offences established in accordance with this Convention:

a. The establishment of off-the-books accounts;
b. The making of off-the-books or inadequately identified transactions;
c. The recording on non-existent expenditure;
d. The entry of liabilities with incorrect identification of their objects;
e. The use of false documents; and
f. The intentional destruction of bookkeeping documents earlier than foreseen by the law

Each State Party shall disallow the tax deductibility of expenses that constitute bribes, the latter being one of the constituent elements of the offences established in accordance with articles 15 and 16 of this Convention and, where appropriate, other expenses incurred in furtherance of corrupt conduct."

The provision in the convention on "Participation of society" requires governments to promote active participation of individuals and groups outside the public sector in the fight against corruption. This includes business as well as NGOs. Another calls for ensuring that the public has effective access to information and protects the freedom to publish and disseminate information concerning corruption. Anticorruption bodies are required to provide access for reporting, including anonymously, of corruption offenses.

The provision on "Measures to prevent money laundering" calls for a comprehensive regulatory and supervisory regime for banks and other financial institutions to deter and detect all forms of money laundering.

The foregoing preventive measures provide an invaluable foundation for strengthening government capability to combat corruption, strengthening private participation, and enhancing corporate integrity programs.

d. The Implementation Review Mechanism

Experience has shown that follow-up monitoring is essential to make anti-corruption conventions work. It is particularly important for a convention as complex and with as many parties as the United Nations Convention against Corruption.

The need for monitoring was debated during the 2002–2003 Vienna negotiations that led to the adoption of the Convention. When it proved impossible to reach agreement on monitoring, the Convention was adopted with a decision on monitoring deferred for future action. It took six years, until the Third Conference of States Parties in Doha, Qatar, before an agreement on an "Implementation Review Mechanism" could be reached. The International Chamber of Commerce, as well as the World Economic Forum and Transparency International, played an active role in advocating for an effective monitoring mechanism.

The Review Mechanism got started in July 2010. The initial five-year cycle of country reviews covers the Convention's chapters on criminalization and international cooperation. The second five-year cycle will cover preventive measures and asset recovery. Each year about forty countries will be reviewed, an extremely ambitious undertaking.

The experience of the first five years indicates that completing country reviews on schedule is difficult. There are also challenging issues regarding the quality of reviews, including the need for adequate visits to countries being reviewed, the participation in country reviews by the private sector and civil society, and the transparency of the government reports to the reviewers as well as of the reports and recommendations made by the reviewers.

Keeping a review process involving over 180 countries moving on schedule is a formidable challenge. However, the quality of the reviews must not be compromised. The private sector can play an important role in the conduct of the individual country reviews and in pressing for adequate funding for the review process.

A rigorous review process is crucial for the success of the United Nations Convention. Implementation must be consistent between countries and for the different Convention provisions. The United Nations Convention must not be allowed to become an erratic patchwork quilt, with governments picking and choosing provisions that are easy to implement and ignoring the rest. Unless there is consistent global implementation, the United Nations Convention against Corruption cannot achieve its objectives. For example, asset recovery can be circumvented as long as some banking centers fail to implement the Convention's asset recovery provisions. Stolen funds will flow to countries with little or no implementation, particularly those that retain banking secrecy laws.

PART THREE

Pervasive Trouble Spots

Corruption comes in many ways (above Chapter 2), and overcoming corruption meets diverging problems according to the governance of the country one is talking about (below Chapter 23). However, corruption also depends upon specific activities or the problems of industries. The following Part of the book focuses on challenges encountered in several concrete "continuing trouble spots." Turning to the state of anticorruption at present, this Part entails analyses of the most corruption-prone industries. Apart from a discussion of sector-specific risks and initiatives, the reader also benefits from the hands-on personal experiences of the authors.

9

Finance and the "Shadow Economy"

MARK PIETH ■

1. GRAND CORRUPTION AND MONEY FLOWS

The financial sector plays a key role in corruption: both as part of the problem and as a key to resolve it. Corruption, especially so-called "grand corruption," typically involves the use of the financial system. This can be observed in large payments in commercial corruption. It is true in a far more pronounced way where a corrupt regime is systemically on the take: detailed studies of how Angola has transformed from a war economy into a kleptocracy demonstrate the fundamental role of offshore centers and the banking industry. Already in a documentation published in 2004[1] the nongovernmental organization (NGO) Global Witness reported that for years, billions of US dollars (between 10 and 40 percent of the annual gross domestic product (GDP)) had miraculously disappeared, mostly into the offshore accounts of President dos Santos and his cronies. Whereas the leaders of this oil-rich country have become very rich since the end of the civil war in 2003, the population at large has remained amongst the poorest in the world. Child mortality is high, malnutrition still widespread.

Why would a country whose leadership is now heavily investing in its former colony (Portugal) still be so dependent on foreign aid? The answer is to be found in a web of organized graft. Banks at offshore centers, but also the

1. Global Witness 2004, 36 et seq. (chapter on Angola).

major financial centers of the world have played a crucial role in this organized theft. The documents published demonstrate that frequently banks know far more about the concrete transactions and their risks than they would publicly admit.

When we look at corrupt activities chronologically, they may start with the creation of a "slush fund." Typically, so-called "slush funds" are off the accounts books of a company. They will be held in the name of shell corporations in offshore financial centers to be used for all sorts of clandestine payments, especially for corruption in order to obtain contracts. The Siemens case is famous for a huge "slush fund" of well over a billion euros ready to be used to grease any kind of future contracts.[2] The funds were brought to Liechtenstein physically in suitcases by an especially trusted Siemens employee. In a further stage of the bribe process the actual payments will be made and if ever possible obscured.[3] Finally, the recipient of the bribe needs to launder the profits. Typically, a combination of shell corporations incorporated at locations with company registers merely containing information on stooges and the like and bank accounts at places with strong bank secrecy and little likelihood of cooperation coupled with professional secrecy (such as attorney-client privilege) will be used.[4]

Many cases of corruption-related money laundering are known. A particularly difficult case was the Swiss Bhutto investigation, which had to be abandoned after eleven years for lack of cooperation by Pakistan and for political reasons. Jeremy Carver in Transparency International's "Global Corruption Report 2004" gives a lively description of the challenges involved.[5]

The hunt for Looted State Assets: the Case of Benazir Bhutto

Benazir Bhutto served twice as prime minister of Pakistan, and was twice removed for widespread abuse of public office. Pakistani authorities were fortunate to obtain early hard evidence implicating Bhutto and her family.

Key documents copied from the files of her lawyer in Switzerland revealed that significant commissions were paid by contractors in a series of deals

2. On the Siemens case cf. Weidenfeld 2011; PBS Frontline documentary, April 7, 2009: "Interview with the Prime Minister in 'Black Money.'"

3. Pieth 2014a, 425 et seq.

4. Pieth 2014a, 427 et seq.

5. Carver 2004, 102 et seq.; see also Asif Ali Zardari and Benazir Bhutto (SGS-Cotecna), Case Control Number 143 (http://star.worldbank.org/corruption-cases/node/18497) (last visited March 6, 2017).

between shell offshore companies and foreign corporations contracted by the government of Pakistan. In all cases, the beneficial owners of the various companies were Bhutto family members, usually Asif Ali Zardari, Bhutto's husband, commonly known as "Mr Ten Per Cent" during his wife's first term—and "Mr Forty Per Cent" after he assumed the post of minister of investment during her second.

In late 1997, Pakistan's attorney general promptly sent requests for assistance to his opposite numbers in Switzerland, Britain and the United States, three of the many countries identified as having some connection with these commission contracts. Only Switzerland provided swift and effective responses. The then Swiss attorney general, Carla del Ponte, instructed the federal police in Berne to cooperate with the Pakistani authorities and appointed judge Daniel Devaud in Geneva to take charge of judicial aspects of the investigation.

There were several strands to the initial evidence, implicating different companies in public contracts with Pakistan, each with a subset of offshore companies controlled by Jens Schlegelmilch, the Bhutto family lawyer in Geneva. One of the earliest steps taken was to identify Swiss bank accounts in the names of the Bhutto family, their front companies and known associates, and to freeze any balances in them. The order resulted in the freezing of no fewer than 500 separate accounts containing in excess of US $80 million, funds that remain frozen to this day.

The gap between freezing funds and repatriating them to another country is formidable, as Pakistan was just starting to discover.

For Switzerland to transfer the blocked funds to Pakistan required a conviction in Pakistan against Bhutto, her husband and possibly others for an offence that would allow judge Devaud to order the transfer. Alternatively, Bhutto would have had to be convicted in Switzerland for an offence giving rise to similar powers.

In July 2003, after more than five years, Devaud convicted Bhutto and her husband of money laundering, sentencing them to six months' imprisonment suspended for three years, and ordered the transfer to Pakistan of some US $12 million.[1] His decisions are now under appeal, and may take another year to resolve.

Examining why it took so long to arrive at this still-not-final result sheds light on what obstacles could be encountered in similar situations.

From the half a dozen offences disclosed by the initial documents, Devaud deliberately selected one in which those paying the commissions were Swiss companies. This tactic enabled him to investigate and seize within

Switzerland documents covering all aspects of the offence, whether from the companies or from Bhutto's lawyer. In this way, he did not need to rely on assistance from other countries.

Corruption was not a criminal offence in Switzerland until 2001, long after the frozen accounts had been filled with cash. But money laundering was an offence. Provided that Bhutto and Zardari could be prosecuted in Pakistan, anyone dealing with the corrupt proceeds could be indicted in Switzerland. Accordingly, Devaud issued indictments against five parties: Bhutto and Zardari outside Switzerland, and Schlegelmilch and the responsible executives of two Swiss companies within his own jurisdiction. Backed with the indictments, he ordered the seizure of documents and sought to interrogate the accused as investigating magistrate.

At an early date, he ordered that Pakistan be a "civil party" to the proceedings, as the victim of the alleged criminal activity. The commissions paid as bribes for the benefit of Bhutto, her husband and mother should have been accounted to the Republic of Pakistan, whose interests Bhutto had been bound to protect. As a civil party, the Pakistani authorities would have access to the entire file of the proceedings, and could be compensated for any losses established.

Devaud's judgments on what became known as the SGS-Cotecna case disclose that, during Bhutto's first term of office, the Swiss company Cotecna was awarded a contract by Pakistan's ministry of finance to take over preshipment inspection of goods entering Karachi port. Cotecna had agreed to pay a commission of 6 percent of the contract receipts to Mariston Securities Inc., an offshore company formed by Schlegelmilch and beneficially owned by Bhutto's mother. Mariston received US $1.2 million before the contract was terminated after Bhutto was first ejected from office.[2]

On her return in 1993, Bhutto appointed herself minister of finance. A contract with similar terms was awarded to SGS, a Swiss inspection company that owned much of Cotecna and had agreed to share both the revenue—and the obligation to pay bribes.

Schlegelmilch created a new offshore company, Bomer Finance Inc., whose beneficial owner was Zardari, though Bhutto controlled its assets. Two other companies were involved: Mariston and Nassam Overseas Inc., a company beneficially owned by Bhutto's then brother-in-law. The commission between them rose to 9 percent. Additionally, Schlegelmilch himself was to receive a commission of 1.25 percent of contract receipts. The SGS–Cotecna contract took effect from 1 January 1995, and large sums were paid to both companies over the next two years. Schlegelmilch made sure that the commissions were duly paid to the various Bhutto front companies, aggregating US $12 million. All the payments—including date, amount, payer and payee—are set out in Devaud's decisions. More than US $5 million was transferred to another front company, Hospital of the Middle East Inc. With access to bank records, Devaud was able to freeze the accounts and trap nearly all the money paid by the Swiss companies. But the final nail in the Bhutto coffin was the purchase of a diamond necklace worth £117,000 (US $195 000) from David Morris, a leading London jeweller. To pay for it, Bhutto had drawn £90 000 (US $150 000) from Bomer Finance's bank account[3].

The six-month suspended sentence against Bhutto and her husband may seem light for such serious offences, but they were the maximum Devaud could exact. With the appeals now filed, the superior court can impose much tougher sanctions.

Devaud also ordered Bhutto and her husband to pay Pakistan the aggregate of the bribes they had received. He further ordered forfeiture of all the remaining funds of the companies and the transfer of the diamond necklace to Pakistan. By his calculation, this left Pakistan short by US $250 000, which the two were ordered to pay forthwith. When these funds reach Pakistan, they will constitute a first in terms of a state directly recovering sums paid by way of bribes to responsible politicians.

The bribes paid in the SGS–Cotecna case are large, but they pale into insignificance against the harm suffered by Pakistan as a direct result of these corrupt contracts. Pakistan is estimated to have lost more than US $2 billion in tariff revenues as a consequence of the greed of Bhutto and her family.

Jeremy Carver (Clifford Chance law firm, Britain)

Notes

1. Devaud similarly convicted Schlegelmilch with a four-month term of imprisonment, but he was unable to forfeit the proceeds from the corrupt contracts because corruption was not then a criminal offence in Switzerland, as it was in Pakistan. An unofficial translation of Devaud's three decisions can be found on the website of Pakistan's National Accountability Bureau: www.nab.gov.pk

2. The Cotecna contract with Pakistan created a public scandal because of appalling performance by Cotecna. Tariff receipts by the ministry of finance dropped alarmingly. A public investigation blamed Cotecna for the loss of more than US $1 billion of revenue.

3. Through her spokespeople, Bhutto has denied involvement in the purchased necklace, indeed in all the facts uncovered by Devaud. But she steadfastly refuses to participate in the proceedings, save through the press, claiming that Devaud is politically motivated.

2. A NEW TOPIC ALTOGETHER

Money laundering is a fairly new topic. It was a concept invented first in a very focused way to combat illicit trafficking in drugs. After the Vietnam War, the United States and later on also Europe were swamped with drugs, first heroin and cannabis, later with cocaine. The traditional means applied in the "war on drugs" called by Lyndon Johnson[6] were, however, not really successful: moving up the supply chain from the street merchant to the organized criminal rarely worked. Rather a new policy went for the soft spot of organized crime directly, by freezing and confiscating the benefits of crime.[7] The aim was to deprive the drug barons of their ill-gotten gains. This approach developed in the United States and in the United Kingdom around the mid-1980s was included in the 1988 United Nations Convention against Illicit Traffic in Narcotic Drugs and Psychotropic Substances.[8] The rules on confiscation were extended to criminalize those impeding confiscation by obscuring ill-gotten gains, that is to "money laundering." Again, typically for common law countries the concept was originally limited to a specific type of crime, to illicit trafficking in drugs, and was at first not at all directed at corruption.

In order to be as effective as possible and to involve the financial sector from the outset, the international community insisted that the "gatekeepers" to licit and illicit activities be involved. The Group of 7 (G7) decided to create a Task Force, a soft law body to promote anti-money-laundering policies.[9]

THE FINANCIAL ACTION TASK FORCE ON MONEY LAUNDERING (FATF)

The concrete history of the FATF can once again only be understood through a sequence of anecdotes:

As Michel Camdessus, former president of the IMF, told me at a dinner in Paris, the French president Mitterrand had asked him in 1988, what could be a topic worthy of the inauguration of the new building in the honor of President Mitterrand, the "Arche de la Défence." M. Camdessus suggested "fiscal paradises" as the topic of a high-level conference termed "le Sommet

6. President Lyndon Johnson named Joseph Anthony Califano Jr. the first "anti-drug-Czar of the US."

7. President's Commission on Organized Crime from 1984: "Money Laundering is a process by which one conceals the existence, illegal source or illegal application of income, and then disguises that income to make it appear legitimate."

8. UN 1988, Article 3 (1) (b) and (c) as well as Articles 4 and 5.

9. Pieth 2013b, Vor Art. 305[bis] N 14.

de l'Arche." The United States agreed in principle, but insisted that it be drug-money laundering. President Mitterrand did not mind, as long as the new group was chaired by his finance minister and was initiated in Paris.

Seated around the table were the G7 countries and a series of financial centers of which one did not really know whether they were here to discuss or to be accused of participating in money laundering (like Luxemburg or Switzerland, my own country: I was part of a team of three—together with Alexis Lautenberg, the diplomat, and Daniel Zuberbühler, the director of the Secretariat of the Swiss Bank Supervisory Authority—myself representing the Swiss Office of Justice). Amongst the original group of twelve participant countries everyone threw their hobby horse into the discussion: the United States suggested cash controls, the UK notification of suspicious transactions, and the Swiss wanted their newly invented concept of identification of customers to be internationalized. Overall, the elements were stitched together in the so-called "40 Recommendations"[10] and frankly—at the time (in 1989)—no one believed they would survive the next three months. Now, in 2012 the same basic concepts have just been updated for the fourth time.[11]

Whereas the obligation to criminalize drug-related money laundering was contained in the 1988 UN Convention and later expanded to further crimes in other hard law instruments, such as the Council of Europe Conventions of 1990[12] and 2005,[13] the FATF continued to work with "soft law": the 40 Recommendations were routinely updated, roughly every five years, and the Member States were subjected to various monitoring rounds. In each of these rounds the FATF directed recommendations at the specific country and assessed its compliance with the "Recommendations". Follow-up mechanisms allowed to the public exposure of countries in a similar way as the instruments on corruption (the peer process discussed above in Chapter 7). In extreme cases of so-called "Non-Cooperative Countries and Territories" (NCCTs) the FATF even threatened harsh trade sanctions against noncompliant financial centers, in particular nonmembers:[14] to be cut off from the electronic transfer or the correspondent banking systems could be lethal for a financial center.

10. The first edition was enacted in February 1990: FATF 40/1990.

11. FATF 40/2012.

12. CoE 1990.

13. CoE 2005.

14. FATF NCCT Report 2000, Annex (criteria defining NCCTs).

How Do Myths Develop?

In the run-up to the work of the FATF in 1989, the US Treasury submitted a short paper in which it described how funds stemming from drug dealing (in particular using the example of Miami) were laundered. This is the document that speaks for the first time of three consecutive stages and identifies them as **"placement,"** **"layering,"** and **"integration."** It gives the following explanation:

1. **Placement**—the physical disposal of bulk cash proceeds. Recognizing that large volumes of cash may draw immediate attention to their illegal source, criminals often physically remove the bulk cash from the location of its acquisition. In a known narcotics trafficking section of a large city, let alone in a small town, disposing of bulk cash would likely draw law enforcement attention. Thus, criminal organizations are driven to coalesce these proceeds in areas where they are more easily disguised or misrepresented, and less easily recognized for what they actually are. Although physical separation from the location of the acquisition may have occurred, the placement of the bulk cash proceeds by any number of means into (a) traditional or (b) non-traditional financial institutions, (c) into the retail economy, or (d) out of the U.S. entirely, is the initial step to legitimize illegal proceeds.
2. **Layering**—separating illicit proceeds from their source by creating complex layers of financial transactions designed to disguise the audit trail of the illicit proceeds. If the placement of the bulk cash has been successful (i.e., undetected), the money launderers' activities become increasingly more difficult to uncover. The confusing and complicated ways in which layer after layer of activities and transactions are piled on one another are intended to make the traceability of the illegal, and thus seizable, proceeds extremely difficult for law enforcement.
3. **Integration**—the provision of apparent legitimacy to criminally derived wealth. Once the layering process has been accomplished, the money launderer needs to provide a legitimate looking explanation for his wealth. Integration schemes place the laundered proceeds back into the economy in such a way that it reenters the banking system appearing as normal business earnings. Unless the

> traceability of illicit proceeds has been established during the bulk cash placement or layering stages, it becomes extremely difficult to distinguish between legitimate and illegitimate wealth. Detection and identification of laundered funds at the Integration Phase is normally possible only through undercover infiltration or violator assistance.[15]

This original document, intended as a provisory contribution to a concrete session, has become so engrained in the AML discourse, that it is now standard text book knowledge and part of a student's examination knowhow.

3. EXPANSION

Rapidly the FATF expanded beyond the original group of members; it now includes all relevant *financial centers*. Furthermore, it created regional "satellites," groups working with the same methods (such as the Caribbean Financial Action Task Force (CFATF), Financial Action Task Force of Latin America (GAFILAT),[16] or Middle East and North Africa Financial Action Task Force (MENAFATF)).

Furthermore, it extended its reach beyond the traditional financial *professions* (banks, insurance companies, brokers, etc.) to capture so-called Non-Bank Financial Institutions (NBFIs), such as fiduciaries, casinos, precious metal dealers, and ultimately to include a further essential group of "gatekeepers": the lawyers and notaries, when acting as financial operators.[17] The rationale of these extensions was to be found in the methodology of money laundering, frequently involving offshore corporations and trusts, bank secrecy at uncooperative financial centers, and the misuse of attorney-client-privilege to obscure traces of the funds.

From our perspective the most essential extension, however, was the expansion of the list of so-called predicate *offenses* (the offenses generating the illegal funds). Whereas some countries had earlier on included in their concept of money laundering all crime, others maintained a very restrictive list

15. Report of the US Department of the Treasury, US Customs Service to the Subgroup "Statistics and Methods" of the FATF, Typology of Money Laundering, October 6–8, 1989, 4, 7, and 8.

16. Formerly known as Financial Action Task Force of South America (GAFISUD).

17. List of "designated non-financial businesses and professions": FATF 40/2012, 113 et seq.

of predicate offenses (such as Luxemburg, concentrating originally on drug money). International rules, first in 1996 ("all serious crime") and then in 2003, became more and more specific: the inclusion of financing of terrorism in 2001 had a strong influence on this development. From 2003 on, a list of offenses included *corruption*. In the same year the FATF started follow-ups on corruption-related money laundering in its monitoring process.[18] If the international bodies were originally slow to connect the anticorruption and the anti-money-laundering agendas, this has now changed.

Concurrently, international anticorruption instruments included money laundering in their program: the OECD Convention of 1997 demanded in its Article 7 the criminalization of corruption-related money laundering.[19] Likewise, the United Nations Convention against Corruption (UNCAC) of 2003 extended its reach to corruption-related money laundering in Article 23. Monitoring efforts by all bodies regularly assess the awareness of financial institutions and the notifications to so-called financial intelligence units (FIUs) of corruption cases. It needs to be said, though, that the picture is uneven. Whereas the financial institutions of some countries have been identified as active notifiers of corruption, most others don't really seem to be aware of the problem.[20]

4. CURRENT STATUS OF RULES AGAINST CORRUPTION-MONEY LAUNDERING

With the extension of predicate offenses to all kinds of graft, the door has finally been pushed open to link the two topics.[21] It is actually rather astonishing that it took so much time, as it is obvious that both the briber needs to hide his true intensions and the bribee needs to launder her bounty.[22] In fact, as mentioned, there are three types of monetary operations banks need to be concerned about, relating to bribery: the bribe-giving, the laundering of the proceeds, and the creation of slush funds on behalf of a company.

18. FATF Reference Guide 2012, 2; Pieth 2014a, 430.

19. Pieth 2014a, 422 et seq., 436 et seq.

20. Pieth 2014a, 444 et seq.

21. FATF Report 2012; FATF Report 2011.

22. FATF Best Practices 2013, 5, para. 10.

Case of Diepreye Alamieyeseigha

In the case involving Diepreye Peter Solomon Alamieyeseigha, former governor of Bayelsa State, Nigeria, this jurisdiction was able to recover $17.7 million through domestic proceedings and through cooperation with authorities in South Africa and the United Kingdom.

In September 2005, Alamieyeseigha was first arrested at Heathrow Airport by the London Metropolitan Police on suspicion of money laundering. An investigation revealed that Alamieyeseigha had $2.7 million stashed in bank accounts and in his home in London, as well as London real estate worth an estimated $15 million. Alamieyeseigha was released on bail and subsequently left the jurisdiction in November 2005, returning to Nigeria.

In Nigeria he claimed immunity from prosecution. He was subsequently removed from office by Bayelsa State's lawmakers, and thereby lost his immunity. Later in November 2005, Nigeria's Economic and Financial Crimes Commission charged him with 40 counts of money laundering and corruption, and it secured a court order restraining assets held in Nigeria.

For assets in the United Kingdom, close cooperation between the Commission and the London Metropolitan Police's Proceeds of Corruption Unit was crucial. The $1.5 million in cash seized from Alamieyeseigha's London home was confiscated under the Proceeds of Crime Act on the basis of a court order that the assets represented proceeds of crime. In May 2006, the court ordered the funds to be repaid to Nigeria, and the transfer was made a few weeks later. For the bank accounts, the process was more challenging because assets and evidence were located in the Bahamas, the British Virgin Islands, the Seychelles, South Africa, and the United Kingdom. Nigerian authorities recognized that requesting assistance from these jurisdictions could take considerable time and that orders from Nigerian courts would not necessarily be executed. In addition, the pursuit of legal proceedings in each of these jurisdictions was a daunting prospect because the Nigerian authorities had little evidence linking Alamieyeseigha to these assets and linking the assets to acts of corruption.

As a result, Nigerian authorities decided to bring civil proceedings in the United Kingdom and simultaneously pursue criminal proceedings in Nigeria. To secure evidence, the Nigerian authorities obtained a disclosure order for the evidence compiled by the Metropolitan Police in the course of its investigation[1]. Nigeria was able to use this evidence together with Alamieyeseigha's income and asset declaration[2] to obtain a worldwide restraint order covering all assets owned directly or indirectly by Alamieyeseigha, and a disclosure order for documents held at banks and by Alamieyeseigha's associates.

In parallel with those proceedings, the South African Asset Forfeiture Unit initiated NCB confiscation proceedings against Alamieyeseigha's luxury penthouse. Funds were returned to Nigeria following the sale of the property in January 2007.

Before a Nigerian high court in July 2007, Alamieyeseigha pleaded guilty to six charges of making false declarations of assets and caused his companies to plead guilty to 23 charges of money laundering. He was sentenced to two years in prison, and the court ordered the confiscation of assets in Nigeria. Alamieyeseigha's guilty pleas effectively voided his defense in the civil proceedings in the London High Court; and, in December 2007, the Court issued a summary judgment confiscating property and a bank account in the United Kingdom. A judgment in July 2008 led to the confiscation of the remaining assets in Cyprus, Denmark, and the United Kingdom.

Notes:

1. The Nigerian application for disclosure was not contested by the Metropolitan Police. This departed from the usual practice: the police usually do not concede to providing evidence gathered through criminal investigations to assist private parties pursuing civil claims.

2. The declaration was filed in 1999 when Alamieyeseigha was first elected state governor. It indicated that he had assets amounting to just over half a million dollars and an annual income of $12 000.[23]

The new version of the Recommendations of the FATF of 2012 is a helpful tool to set out the rules to prevent bribery-related money laundering:

- They insist on **criminalizing** the laundering of funds of all serious crime including corruption and bribery.[24]
- They call on Member Countries to introduce independent, adequately resourced and trained **authorities**. Their supervisory authorities are tasked to ensure fit and proper conduct of responsible bank staff.
- They are obliged to see that the supervised financial institutions:
    - **Identify** customers and beneficial owners, be it individuals or companies, including international business corporations.[25]

23. Brun et al. 2011, 17 et seq.

24. FATF 40/2012, Rec. 3, 112 et seq. (General Glossary, Designated Categories of Offences).

25. FATF 40/2012, Rec. 10 and Interpretive Note to Rec. 10 (Customer Due Diligence), 59 et seq.; Wolfsberg Principles 2012, 2 et seq. (Section 1.2).

- Apply ongoing **due diligence** to all business relations, including applying risk profiles, understanding transactions, and identifying complex, unusually large transactions or unusual patterns in general.[26]
- **Notify** the responsible FIU if they detect suspicious client-behavior.[27]

- The Member State will see to it that funds are **frozen**, possibly **confiscated**[28] and **shared.**[29] Thereby they will mutually cooperate with foreign authorities.[30]

Applying the so-called **"risk based approach"** (RBA), financial institutions are now obliged to distinguish clients and their transactions according to their risk profile and level of risk. Whereas traditional high street banking (retail banking) poses minimal risks, other types of banking activities, such as private banking, pose higher risk. There is an extensive risk matrix specifically for corruption cases. It has been partly developed by the public sector and the FATF;[31] essential contributions have, however, been made by the private sector itself, especially by the so-called "Wolfsberg Group on Private Banking."[32] Their specific text on corruption-money laundering focuses on different risk categories:[33]

- Customer risk factors[34]

  Under this heading both the FATF and the Wolfsberg Group discuss:

  - The **PEP**-risk, the risk that a customer or beneficiary could be a foreign (or now also domestic) politically exposed person: special sign-off provisions and regular checks on sources apply,[35]

26. FATF 40/2012, Rec. 10 and Interpretive Note to Rec. 10 (Customer Due Diligence), 59 et seq.; Wolfsberg Principles 2012, 4 et seq. (Section 2).

27. FATF 40/2012, Rec. 20 and 21; Wolfsberg Principles 2012, 6 (Section 4).

28. FATF 40/2012, Rec. 4.

29. FATF 40/2012, Rec. 38.

30. FATF 40/2012, Rec. 36 et seq.

31. FATF 40/2012, 63 et seq.

32. Wolfsberg Principles 2012, 4 (Section 1.3); cf. also Wolfsberg Guidance 2011, No. 5; Pieth and Aiolfi 2003, 267 et seq.

33. Wolfsberg Statement 2006; Wolfsberg Guidance 2011, Appendix I.

34. Wolfsberg Guidance 2011, Appendix II.

35. PEPs: FATF 40/2012, Rec. 12 and Interpretive Note to Rec. 12 (Politically Exposed Persons), 67; FATF Guidance 2013; Wolfsberg Principles 2012, 2 et seq. (1.2.3).

- special rules for **legal persons,**[36]
- and for specific **sectors** (e.g., particularly exposed sectors such as defense, infrastructure, or mining).

- Country or geographic factors

  Especially corruption indices (such as the **Transparency International index**) are relevant here, and financial institutions are forced to apply special care in dealing with customers in certain areas of the world.[37]

- Product risk

  Certain areas of banking (such as private banking), anonymous banking, non-face-to-face business relationships, and certain types of transactions (back-to-back loans) warrant additional diligence.[38]

For all the efforts going into this risk mapping it is astonishing how few suspicious transactions reports relate to corruption cases.

5. ASSET RECOVERY

For years dictators and officials have been able to siphon off funds from their state budgets and to export them to safe havens, especially in times when financial centers offered numbered accounts and the like and were unlikely to grant other states mutual legal assistance. It took decades in those landmark cases, especially Marcos of the Philippines[39] and Duvalier of Haiti,[40] to repatriate (some of) the funds. So far only a few financial centers have developed the necessary legal framework (especially Switzerland and to some extent the United States and the United Kingdom) that would enable asset recovery to happen more efficiently.

36. FATF 40/2012, Interpretive Note to Rec. 10 (Customer Due Diligence), 60 et seq.

37. FATF 40/2012, Rec. 23 et seq.; Wolfsberg Guidance 2011, Appendix II, 2 (Country Risk).

38. FATF 40/2012, Rec. 33 et seq.; Wolfsberg Guidance 2011, Appendix II, 1 (Services Risk).

39. Marcelo 2008, 89 et seq.; Dannacher 2012, 13; Swiss Federal Supreme Court Decision, BGE 113 Ib 257, 1 July 1987; BGE 115 Ib 496, 2 November 1989; BGE 116 Ib 452, 21 December 1990; BGE 119 Ib 56, 8 March 1993; BGE 119 Ib 380, 23 June 1993; BGE 123 II 595, 10 December 1997; BGE. 125 II 411, 9 July 1999; BGE 126 II 425, 25 August 2000.

40. Pieth 2008, 3 et seq.; Dannacher 2012, 22 et seq.; Swiss Federal Supreme Court Decision, BGE 136 IV 4, 12 January 2010; 2nd Board of Appeals of the Federal Criminal Court, Decision No. RR.2004.94, 12 August 2009.

In the Legal Jungle: Jean-Claude "Baby Doc" Duvalier

"According to a (Swiss) Federal Administrative Court (FAC) press release, on 23 September 2013, the FAC ruled against Mr. Duvalier and co-complainants and upheld the freezing of their assets ordered by the Federal Council in 2002. In its decision of 24 September 2013, the FAC also upheld the asset forfeiture proceedings launched by the Federal Department of Finance (FDF) on behalf of the Swiss Confederation on 29 April 2011. The press release stated, "In its decision of 24 September 2013, the FAC confirmed that these asset forfeiture proceedings were valid because the assets in question had been obtained illicitly. Specifically, the FAC felt that Jean-Claude Duvalier and his entourage did not demonstrate that the increase in their assets had resulted from activities unrelated to their role as public officials. Moreover, the level of corruption of the Haitian state was notoriously high during the period in which they had held public office. It was therefore concluded that the conditions determining the illicit origin of the assets in question were met." These assets have been frozen since 2002. Both decisions may be subject to appeal before the Federal Supreme Court, but barring an appeal, the way is now clear for the restitution procedure of these seized assets to be launched ((Source: Federal Administrative Court press release, "FAC confirms freezing and forfeiture of Duvalier assets," September 25, 2013; see also text of decision: "Extrait de l'arrêt de la Cour III dans la cause Département fédéral des finances contre Fondation Brouilly, Jean-Claude Duvalier, hoirie de feue Simone Ovide Duvalier, composée de Jean-Claude Duvalier, Nicole Duvalier, Marie-Denise Duvalier et Simone Duvalier, et Michèle Benett-Duvalier C-2528/2011 du 24 septembre 2013," BVGE 2013/40).

According to the Swiss Federal Department of Foreign Affairs, the funds were frozen by a Federal Council decision of 2010, which followed the January 2010 judgment by the Federal Court "which put an end to the mutual legal assistance between Haiti and Switzerland, this freezing order has avoided a return of the assets to the Duvalier family. The freezing remained in force until the entry into force of the Act on the Restitution of Illicit Asset (RIAA). This law was accepted by Parliament in the autumn session 2010 and is entered into force on 1 February 2011. The Duvalier assets have then been frozen on the basis of article 14 RIAA. The Confederation took legal action before the Federal Administrative Court to enable frozen assets to be forfeited in April 2011, further to the decision of the Federal Council to ask the Federal Department of Finance (FDF) to initiate proceedings for the forfeiture of the Duvalier funds frozen in Switzerland."[41]

41. Swiss Federal Department of Foreign Affairs, "Illicit assets of politically exposed persons (PEPs)"; cf. also: StAR: "Jean Claude 'Baby Doc' Duvalier (Switzerland)" (http://star.worldbank.org/corruption-cases/node/18515) (last visited February 10, 2017).

In fighting corruption, the logic of going for the money would be at least as efficient as with organized crime and drugs, as part of the motivation to steal and to take bribes is simply greed.[42] This has finally been recognized on an international level by UNCAC, allotting an entire chapter of its Convention (V.) to this topic and thereby for the first time enshrining the recovery and return of stolen assets as a fundamental principle of international law. As per the Convention's Article 51, "The return of assets . . . is a fundamental principle of this Convention, and States Parties shall afford one another the widest measure of cooperation and assistance in this regard."

Since then a number of domestic and international efforts to recover and repatriate stolen assets have been underway, but unfortunately this has so far not generated much further practice, even if many important cases would await solution (e.g., the Arab Spring[43]). Challenges relate primarily to lack of technical capacity to trace stolen assets and to the complexity of international cooperation in legal matters.

To address these issues, two very different, specialized organizations have emerged since the entry into force of UNCAC. Both have importantly contributed either to promote practical asset recovery, which is expected to produce tangible results in the coming years (notably the International Centre for Asset Recovery at the Basel Institute on Governance, ICAR), or to strengthening the body of literature and promoting policy debate on asset recovery. The latter efforts are being led by the joint World Bank and UN Stolen Asset Recovery Initiative (StAR).

StAR

From the World Bank side the key concepts around asset recovery were discussed on a day in Washington in a small group with World Bank president Wolfowitz; other participants were the then-managing director Ngozi Nkonjo Iweala, Maître Enrico Monfrini of Geneva (who had recovered most of the Nigerian funds), and myself. We explored the political and technical problems both in financial centers and in developing countries as well as a possible structure of StAR.

StAR eventually emerged in 2007 as a cooperation between the World Bank and the UN. Its main focus has been on giving advice to "victim states" of graft in the global South by sending experts; it has also authored

42. FATF Reference Guide 2012, 6.

43. Hottinger 2013, 3 et seq.

as sequence of practical handbooks and has organized workshops and conferences at various places in the world. Over time it has become more and more operational in its approach. It is now the official first port of call for asset recovery.

ICAR

The International Centre for Asset Recovery (ICAR) was established in 2006 as a part of the Basel Institute on Governance and with the strong support from the governments of Liechtenstein, Switzerland, and the United Kingdom. As a not-for-profit organization, ICAR's main mission is to strengthen and support the capacities of developing and transition partner countries to recover stolen assets.

To this aim, ICAR's team of seasoned former prosecutors and investigators advises law enforcement agencies, anticorruption authorities, and prosecution services in relation to the investigation and prosecution of corruption and money laundering cases, and facilitates international judicial cooperation. Most recently, ICAR was mandated by the government of Ukraine to assist its prosecution services to recover assets stolen by former Ukraine president Yanukovych.

This case-specific assistance comes together with a range of training and IT tools that help to build sustainable capacity within concerned institutions and countries to recover stolen assets. ICAR has provided this type of assistance to more than forty countries from around the world since its establishment, and from the growth of its activities we can clearly read a rapidly growing demand for support in the area of asset recovery, indicating a possibly greater political will and awareness of asset recovery.

Finally, ICAR also actively contributes to the international policy debate on a number of key policy issues, such as the return of stolen assets, the role of nonstate actors in asset recovery, and recent efforts to develop guidelines in support of more effective asset recovery.

---

6. IS ASSET RECOVERY WORKING?

There is a sequence of cases that one should ultimately consider success stories even if they indicate one major problem: Asset recovery is very time-consuming (take the reclaiming of the funds in the cases of Marcos, Montesinos, and

Abacha).[44] Other cases are ongoing in various stages (e.g., relating to Egypt, Libya, Tunisia; to Ukraine; to the Ivory Coast; to Uganda, Tanzania, Kenia and yet further cases relating to Peru).

Challenges are either technical or political[45] and they could arise either in the "victim country" or in the financial center. These challenges are the reasons for drawn-out battles. Sometimes countries and offenders take a shortcut by settling a case (e.g., ultimately in the case of Sani Abacha and Nigeria[46]).

Occasionally, political turmoil inhibits repatriation of funds, as in Egypt, where the military (close to the ex-president Mubarak) ultimately took power. In Ukraine, it proves extremely challenging that former cronies of the old system are still in office.

However, there are success stories, and they should not be underrated (take Chiluba/United Kingdom, Montesinos/Luxemburg).

7. THE OVERARCHING THEME: OVERCOMING THE "SHADOW ECONOMY"

The Panama Papers[47] and other similar leaks (such as LuxLeaks, SwissLeaks, Bahamas Leaks, etc.) have demonstrated how widespread the use of offshore resorts, shell corporations, and the like is to generate intransparency. The purposes are widespread. If they are illegal, they range from straightforward money laundering for organized criminals (drug dealers, traffickers in human beings, child prostitution rings, etc.) to tax defrauders. Frequently, also multinational enterprises (MNEs) use opaque structures to "optimize taxes," thereby moving profits to the most beneficial (lowest tax) places, leaving the social and environmental cost at the places where the profits are created.[48]

Relating to corruption, offshore constructions serve all the purposes discussed above—to hold slush funds, to participate in the underlying crime, and to launder funds. The Panama Papers implicate heads of state or prime ministers of many states of trying to hide conflicts of interest, to obscure illegal campaign contributions or to secure embezzled funds from the state they are running.

44. Pieth 2008, 41 et seq.

45. Pieth 2008, 3 et seq.

46. Premium Times, May 15, 2015: "Abacha Loot: Inside the secret deal Jonathan authorized to shield ex-dictator's family from prosecution."

47. See above 7 et seq., 136.

48. For details, see Obermayer/Obermaier 2016.

A broad coalition of international organizations fighting money laundering (Financial Action Task Force), corruption (OECD Working Group on Bribery), and tax fraud (Global Forum) is coming together to develop effective preventive tools: it is generally recognized that asking financial institutions to identify the beneficial owners of accounts and corporate structures is helpful to tax authorities, law enforcement, and regulators alike.[49]

In a more recent development policy experts and agencies are demanding that publicly accessible registries contain the correct data and beneficial ownership.[50] Even if essential questions remain to be resolved (such as the threshold for stakeholders or control persons), the overall concept is gaining ground. The committees of the EU parliament have suggested upgrading its company registers and motivating nonmembers to follow suit (or be blacklisted).[51]

8. CONCLUSION

Overall the financial services industry carries a heavy responsibility for large-scale corruption. Financial intermediaries and banks are used typically in grand corruption schemes by corporations, let alone by kleptocratic regimes. Frequently, they are fully aware of what they are involved in. They face serious legal risks as accomplices to graft and as money launderers. To prevent them from being inadvertently used for such purposes, compliance systems need to be in place reacting to the specific risks related to graft and corruption by clients. The rules and concepts exist.[52] They need to be implemented and applied—sometimes a challenging task for an industry above all interested in making money.

Beyond immediate financial regulation, a general trend—following revelations through whistle-blowers—points toward open registries of beneficial owners of companies, trusts, and the like.

49. FATF (http://www.fatf-gafi.org/) (last visited March 17, 2017); OECD Working Group on Bribery (http://www.oecd.org/corruption/anti-bribery/anti-briberyconvention/oecdworkinggrouponbriberyininternationalbusinesstransactions.htm) (last visited March 17, 2017); Global Forum (http://www.oecd.org/tax/transparency/) (last visited March 17, 2017).

50. David Cameron, Anti-Corruption Summit: London 2016; Stiglitz/Pieth 2016.

51. E.g. the "Panama Papers Committee of Inquiry into tax evasion and money laundering" (PANA); see also: European Parliament, Press Release, 28 February 2017: "Citizens should get access to data on firm owners to fight money laundering."

52. Wolfsberg Guidance 2011.

10

Extractive Industries

MARK PIETH ■

1. THE "RESOURCE CURSE"

Extractive industries are amongst the business sectors most exposed to corruption. Typically, they are dependent on licenses by government agencies, frequently in states with little other income than royalties from mining or from the oil industry. Very frequently these states are located in the global South with weak government structures. It is a common feature in these states that a small elite rapidly becomes extraordinarily rich, while the population at large remains in deep poverty (fact already observed in the example of Angola[1]). It is popular to talk of the "resource curse," as the economies of these states rely next to totally on the income from natural resources, and the domestic industry hardly ever has a chance to develop.

Some of the worst examples of plundering of state assets are to be found in resource-rich states such as Angola, Republic of the Congo, Nigeria, and maybe Venezuela.

Oil and mining companies, traders, and the finance industries may not actually be in the driving seat, but they very frequently go along and participate in the organized plunder. They are regularly fully aware that the funds they pay to officials are going to be stolen.[2] Sometimes they actively engage in bribery to secure drilling or mining licenses. Other players, such as traders, indirectly

1. Cf. above 119.

2. Global Witness 2004; Global Witness 1999; BBC World News, January 7, 2015: "Shell agrees $84m deal over Niger Delta oil spill."

Confronting Corruption. Fritz Heimann and Mark Pieth.

profit from the systemic graft by elites.[3] As accessories and conspirators, they contribute to the plight of the populations affected.

2. PUBLISH WHAT YOU PAY

Nongovernmental organizations (NGOs) such as Global Witness and governments (in particular the United Kingdom and Norway) have demanded that companies declare comprehensively all payments to resource-rich countries and that these countries report comprehensively and publicly what they have received. This should foster sound public accounting and allow the civil society to keep track of revenues and expenditure. Global Witness campaigned intensely in the 1990s using several dramatic case studies (in particular on Angola, Congo Brazzaville, Equatorial Guinea, and Kazakhstan) to push for transparency. The adoption of the Extractive Industries Transparency Initiative (EITI) Principles at the first EITI Conference hosted by the United Kingdom[4] helped a great deal to further the agenda on transparency in the extractive industries. In the meantime, public bodies have added their voice, on the one hand the United States with their Dodd-Frank Act[5] and on the other hand the European Union.[6]

In a next step NGOs, especially the Swiss NGO "Public Eye," at the time known as "Berne Declaration," and its allies went on to extend transparency rules to traders. So far, the industry has been reluctant to follow suit and governments have—even if they acknowledge the problems—been hesitant to regulate.[7]

3. THE EXTRACTIVE INDUSTRIES TRANSPARENCY INITIATIVE

EITI was founded when the UK government invited a group of resource-rich countries to a conference in London. The conference drafted the twelve EITI

3. Cf. the recent book edited by the NGO Public Eye (formerly known as "Berne Declaration") 2012: "Commodities—Switzerland's Most Dangerous Business."

4. EITI Rules 2011, Preface by Peter Eigen, Chairman of the EITI Board.

5. The Dodd-Frank Wall Street Reform and Consumer Protection Act (Pub. L. 111–203, 21 July 2010).

6. See the transparency and bookkeeping Directives 2013/50/EU (OJ L 294/13, 6 November 2013) and 2013/34/EU (OJ L 182/19, 29 June 2013) of the EU Parliament and of the Council.

7. Cf. below 144.

Principles.[8] After a pilot phase the criteria for participation (the so-called EITI Criteria) were adopted in 2005. The EITI system differentiates between "candidate countries" and fully "compliant countries." Countries graduate into the status of full participants based on a third party "validation."[9] A complex procedure encourages countries to ameliorate and maintain their position.[10]

The system requires cooperation with a national multi-stakeholder group within the participant country. Full implementation is defined in a further set of rules, the EITI Requirements.[11] The relatively demanding mechanism is administered by an international secretariat, with the EITI Board overseeing the process.

The general idea behind the detailed rules is to ensure that countries publish all income from extractive industries and that this information is matched with the data provided by business. Cooperative countries are encouraged to oblige business to provide data to the international secretariat.

EITI has acquired a strong reputation over time. Many of the resource-rich countries are cooperating. Together with other multi-stakeholder initiatives, however, it remains a soft-law instrument. Its rules do not have legally binding force on an international scale.

4. THE STRUGGLE FOR REGULATION

a. United States: Section 1504 of the Dodd-Frank Act

It was considered a great success by the international NGO world when the US Congress adopted the "Dodd-Frank Wall Street Reform and Protection Act" on July 21, 2010. Section 1504 of the Dodd-Frank Act introduced a section 13(q) into the Securities Exchange Act of 1934, obliging "resource extraction issuers"—under the supervision of the Securities and Exchange Commission (SEC)—to report annually in a country-by-country manner to the Commission and the wider public all payments "made to further the commercial development of oil natural gas, or minerals".[12] The implementing "Final Rules," enacted by the SEC, demanded the reporting of all sorts of taxes and other payments based on

8. Cf. EITI Rules 2011, 11 and EITI Standard 2015, 9.

9. Cf. EITI Standard 2015, 35 et seq.

10. Cf. the graph in EITI Standard 2015, 16.

11. EITI Standard 2015, 10 et seq.

12. 15 U.S. Code § 78(m)(q) (2010), disclosure of payments by resource extraction issuers.

corporate profits to the United States or foreign governments. In the fine print, a threshold of $100,000 per project was foreseen and a certain leeway to define the individual project was accorded. However, a group of lobbyists under the leadership of the American Petroleum Institute, the Independent Petroleum Association of America, the US Chamber of Commerce, and the National Foreign Trade Council challenged the final rules with partial success.[13] The major points of contention were that there were no exemptions foreseen in the legislation for cases where an autocrat regime abroad prohibited the publication of the relevant data.[14] A lesser critique was the worry that the Act would put US issuers at a competitive disadvantage vis-à-vis foreign corporations. Whether the lack of a clear definition of the project is going to become a major problem is yet uncertain. Finally, a fourth problem was identified concerning public disclosure using the Electronic Data-Gathering, Analysis and Retrieval System (EDGAR). After a District Court decision, the final rules are currently under revision by the SEC.

b. EU: Revision of Its Transparency and Bookkeeping Directives

The European Commission allowed itself to be influenced by EITI and the US Congress when it demanded the modification of the 2004 Transparency Directive. The Commission suggested that Corporations listed at a European stock exchange should—on a country-by-country basis—report annually their payments to foreign states. The European Parliament adopted a revised Transparency Directive on June 12, 2013.[15] Furthermore, the Council and the European Parliament decided on a revision of the Bookkeeping Directives (78/660 and 83/349), including also large private companies based in the European Union. Both new Directives are now in force[16] and Member States have twenty-four months to implement them. The system is, on the one hand, heavily influenced by EITI; on the other hand the fine print reflects many of the traits of the Dodd-Frank Act. Again, there are no exceptions for those dealing with autocratic regimes. The Directives subject all extractive industries including the logging industry to the new system (a compromise found in the so-called "Trilog"-negotiations among the European Council, the European Commission, and the European Parliament).

13. *American Petroleum Institute v. SEC*, 953 F. Supp. 2d 5 (D.C. 2013) [a state case].

14. *American Petroleum Institute v. SEC*, 953 F. Supp. 2d 5 (D.C. 2013) [a state case].

15. EU Transparency Directive 2013/50/EU (OJ L 294/13, 6 November 2013), 13 et seq.

16. Including the EU Bookkeeping Directive 2013/34/EU (OJ L 182/19, 29 June 2013), 19 et seq.

One specialty, though, is the "review clause": after three years, the disclosure regime needs to be reviewed.

5. REGULATING TRADING?

EITI as well as the public sector standards enacted by the United States and the European Union (EU) focus on extraction. So far, trading in commodities and commodity finance has slipped under the radar. For commodity finance this became obvious in the course of the investigation into the UN's Oil-for-Food Program in Iraq,[17] where it was found that the same bank that was acting as the fiduciary bank for the entire program (with a turnover of $100 billion) opened roughly half the letters of credit on transactions in oil and humanitarian goods needed for the program. Thereby the bank must have been aware of a multitude of abuses, including organized sanctions busting.[18] Nevertheless, domestic regulators, in particular the Swiss banking supervisor, found nothing wrong.[19]

Trading houses are another part of the problem: they contribute to the opacity of the business, they help mining companies infringe on labor rules and on environmental standards and other human rights, and to escape responsibility. They are frequently part of the corruption and money laundering cycle. They manage to minimize taxes and royalties, in particular in places where commodities are extracted. So far, however, there has hardly been a discourse on regulating trading in commodities. Since the Financial Action Task Force on Money Laundering (FATF) has not been very insistent on commodity finance, domestic regulators, such as Switzerland, refused to subject commodity traders to clear anti-money-laundering rules.[20] Switzerland may serve as an example for the most recent developments: over the last decade its market share as a commodity trading place (in particular Zug and Geneva) has grown exponentially (both in minerals[21] and in nutritional products[22]).

17. Cf. below 186 et seq.

18. Cf. the Report by Volcker, Goldstone, and Pieth 2005c, 6 et seq.; cf. also below 193.

19. EBK-Report "Oil-for-Food" 2005, 6 et seq.

20. In fact, the Swiss federal ordinance (Article 5 (2) (b) VBF) of November 18, 2009, clearly goes against the letter of the anti-money-laundering law of 1997 (cf. Article 2 (3) (c) GwG).

21. Oil: 2012 the Swiss worldwide market share in trading in oil was 53 percent, in metals 60 percent.

22. The Swiss market share worldwide was 35 percent in grain, 50 percent in sugar, and 60 percent in coffee.

A coalition of NGOs led by the "Public Eye" has come out with a book[23] and a set of aggressive proposals.[24] They have in fact gone as far as to create a fake "Federal Commodity Supervisory Body."[25] The reaction of the Swiss government has been to write a report,[26] basically echoing the criticism of the NGOs in a first part, however, in a second part adding very soft conclusions, essentially calling for a level playing field amongst international trading places. Apart from a few—not very enlightening—meetings among government, business, and NGOs the issue has remained stuck for political reasons.

6. COLLECTIVE ACTION AS A WAY FORWARD?

Of course, national regulation, as demanded by local NGOs, could be a way forward. However, business and government have a point if they prefer internationally harmonized standards also for the regulation of commodity trading. So far, however, no one has volunteered to "jump into the pool": that is where facilitators come into play. Their primary task is to create a sufficient basis of trust to define a common denominator. This approach has worked in other areas, specifically regarding anti-money-laundering rules in the banking industry[27] or various collective actions on anticorruption.[28]

23. Public Eye 2012: "Commodities—Switzerland's Most Dangerous Business."

24. Public Eye 2012, 378 et seq.

25. See http://www.rohma.ch (March 13, 2017).

26. Federal Council background report on commodities of 27 March 2013 and the follow-up report of 26 March 2014.

27. See 225.

28. See 237.

11

Infrastructure and Construction

MARK PIETH ■

1. THE RISKS

According to a recently published OECD study of its cases collected over the last ten years of monitoring, the infrastructure and construction sector comes out as second-most exposed, just after extractive industries.[1] Again, the reasons are rather obvious: typically, underdeveloped areas are most in need of motorways, bridges, railway lines, ports, and airports. Almost always these projects are about big money. Competition is fierce amongst bidders and frequently government agencies in insufficiently governed states decide who gets the job. Even where multinational development banks (MDBs) are involved as loan providers, they may find it difficult to prevent extortion and bribery, as they are required to respect their client country's sovereignty.

Officials in the public works departments have been known to be particularly exposed, not only in the countries of the global South.[2] Frequently, construction companies have paid to obtain jobs. In some areas of the world they form part of a wider web of organized crime.[3] Beyond the actual construction companies, consulting engineers are particularly vulnerable, as they have an enormous decision power, often totally disproportionate to their actual manpower:[4] they decide on the detail of the construction and, in the aftermath, whether an

1. OECD Foreign Bribery Report 2014, 21 et seq. (chart 9).

2. Cf. the examples of the Hungarian motorway: Higher Regional Court (Oberlandesgericht) Vienna, Decision No. 23 Bs 43/12k; see above Chapter 11.

3. Cf. in Sicily: with construction being one of the traditional Mafia-controlled sectors.

4. Cf. the International Federation of Consulting Engineers (FIDIC), Policy Statement, 1.

infrastructure construction has actually been completed according to specification and whether the payment is due. All these are highly sensitive decisions. Many case examples of bribe-affected constructions are known. The project to build a bridge in Bangladesh is a particularly significant example:

The Padma Multipurpose Bridge Project

In a rare case the World Bank's investigative arm (the Integrity Vice Presidency, INT) was informed prior to the actual payment of a bribe that high-ranking public officials, including a minister of Bangladesh, had been promised bribes by employees of the Canadian engineering company SNC Lavelin (with a senior vice president of the company present at the bribe-negotiations). As a consequence, the Bangladeshi officials shifted the company to the top of the shortlist and informed the World Bank that they had an "issue" with the company so far listed first. In a preventive strike INT intervened, the World Bank put payments on hold, and informed Canadian and Bangladeshi authorities. As the reaction by authorities in Bangladesh was slow, the Bank struck an agreement with the government that they would speed up domestic investigations and allow an external panel of experts appointed by the World Bank to assess whether the investigations were full and fair, in order to allow to continue the funding of the project (the World Bank loan amounts to $1.2 billion). All observers agree that the project of a six-kilometer-long bridge connecting the underdeveloped Southwest Bangladesh with the capital and its port would be of fundamental value for the development of the country as a whole. The Royal Mounted Police (RMP) of Canada first investigated a number of employees (not, however, the senior vice president).[5] Two years later it laid charges against the company itself, including for corruption related to Libya, Mexico, and Bangladesh. Settlement negotiations seem to be underway currently.

Reactions by the new company management (the former chief executive officer had to step down over the accusations) replicated a corporate attitude observed in the United States and Europe roughly ten years ago: the problems of the company were attributed to former employees, and now that the company took a cooperative approach to the investigations, it expected a light touch by law enforcement in exchange; after all, 40,000 jobs were said to be on the line. In particular the company feared automatic debarment for ten years on federal contracts in Canada.[6]

5. The Globe and Mail, February 22, 2013; CBC News, September 18, 2013.

6. Huffington Post, April 22, 2015.

The external panel of experts of the World Bank came to the conclusion that the activities of the (Bangladeshi) Anti-Corruption Commission (ACC) did not "constitute a full and fair investigation,"[7] in particular because it refused to investigate the role of the former minister of communications of Bangladesh. The panel was unimpressed by the reasons given by domestic investigators, "that it would cause a political upheaval in Dhaka."[8] The World Bank had to terminate its loan on June 29, 2012.

2. WHAT NEEDS TO BE DONE?

The case study on Bangladesh indicates that there are lessons to be learned in three directions: first, many companies seem to give themselves state-of-the-art anticorruption-compliance programs, but at the same time having them coexist "with a confidential policy to offer bribes."[9] Similar double standards apply when their competitors deny having been solicited for bribes by officials, even though in confidence they acknowledged such requests.

The World Bank has sent a clear message to a country reluctant to seriously tackle the demand side of corruption as soon as important political figures were involved. On the preventive side the Task Team Leaders (TTLs) of MDBs could, however, do more to identify risks in their projects. Furthermore, the external panel of experts is correct in encouraging the World Bank (and other MDBs) to step up their internal decision processes.[10] High-risk projects need to be very closely supervised (ongoing monitoring was ordered by the World Bank for instance in a very difficult project in Kenya: the construction of a new highway between Nairobi and Mombasa, where various bidders had to be debarred for corrupt behavior[11]).

The CoST Initiative

Currently operating in fourteen different countries, the Construction Sector Transparency Initiative (CoST) is a multi-stakeholder governance initiative

7. World Bank External Panel 2013, 1.

8. The Globe and Mail, February 22, 2013, quoting a letter of the president of the Committee.

9. World Bank External Panel 2013, 6.

10. World Bank External Panel 2013, 10 et seq.

11. Independent Advisory Board (IAB), Annual Report 2009, 10.

designed to promote transparency and accountability in publicly financed construction. It acts jointly with government agencies to gather, verify, and disclose information to the public realm.

CoST further involves government procuring entities and oversight agencies, private sector consultants and contractors, and civil society groups. The ultimate goal is a new governance and accountability mechanism that builds on existing government institutions, regulations, and demand for increased transparency and better construction results.

The CoST program was launched in 2012 and is expected to run for ten to twenty years.[12]

---

12. CoSt-Factsheet, (http://www.constructiontransparency.org/the-initiative?forumboardid=1&forumtopicid=1) (last visited March 13, 2017).

12

Aeronautics and Defense

MARK PIETH ■

The defense industry is rivaling the extractive industries as well as construction and engineering for the first rank in corruption. Surveys currently consider it the second-biggest problem.[1] Obviously, defense and security are affected by many different ways of corruption, ranging from petty corruption to evade conscription to hefty bribes to high- ranking commanders in combat situations.[2] The major challenges, however, arise from defense procurement.

The high exposure has particular reasons: defense procurement is about huge sums of money (observers estimate global annual defense expenses at $1.4 trillion or 2.5 percent of the global gross domestic product).[3] On both sides of the equation lie highly concentrated actors: large multinational enterprises and governments. The technical details of the requirements are complex; the legal details of contracts are confusing. They usually have a long life span, typically longer than the lifetime of a government. Government officials and military officers dispose of a large leeway of discretion. These contracts are frequently covered by a cloak of secrecy (national security considerations). Sometimes procurement rules are circumvented by government-to-government contracts. The already complex contracts are typically further confused through offset agreements.

1. TI-UK 2010, 2.

2. TI-UK 2011, 12 et seq, 45.

3. TI-UK 2010, 7 referring to a study by Stockholm International Peace Research Institute (SIPRI).

Confronting Corruption. Fritz Heimann and Mark Pieth.

1. WHAT ARE THE PARTICULAR RISKS IN DEFENSE PROCUREMENT?

All phases of defense procurement are vulnerable to corruption: it starts with the question of why the equipment needs to be acquired at all; does exactly this equipment need to be acquired, and why now? In extreme cases of state capture, the entire acquisition will serve no other purpose than rent-seeking (the proverbial "white elephant"[4]), be it directly or through dubious offsets.[5] Furthermore, the procurement process may be distorted by unclear specifications or technical requirements favoring certain bidders. The evaluation criteria may favor particular bidders; the evaluation process may be unfair as such (e.g., affected by conflicts of interest). Manipulations are also possible in the contracting or then in the execution phase.

Procedures excluding foreign competitors or, in the extreme, so called "single source procurement" have to be regarded as particularly problematic. They require very close supervision indeed.[6]

2. THE KEY ROLE OF DEFENSE OFFSETS

"Defense offsets are arrangements between national government and a foreign military equipment supplier to direct some benefit of the contract back into the purchasing country's economy".[7] Offsets are industrial countertrade mechanisms; they are typically used to make large defense expenses more palatable to the wider public. They are supposed to level an otherwise negative trade balance, to (re-)vitalize business in the acquiring country, maybe also to secure technology transfers. Economic analysis has shown, however, that they rarely achieve any of these goals at all[8] and that ultimately the importing country will pay the considerable cost of offsets on top of the contract. It has been said that "governments engaging in offsets policies are essentially paying defense companies to deliver economic development

4. BBC, January 29, 2015: "Panama ex-leader Ricardo Martinelli faces corruption probe"; Business Insider, December 23, 2014: "Nicaragua's planned $50 billion canal is 'A gigantic white elephant.'"

5. TI-UK 2010, 17 et seq.

6. TI-UK 2011, 56.

7. TI-UK 2011, 62; TI-UK 2010, 2, 6.

8. Cf. the references in TI-UK 2010, 20 et seq.

projects"—at a cost hidden to the wider public[9] and frequently not fully completed.

There are different types of offsets. Countries with a highly sophisticated industry of their own may be able to provide direct defense-related offsets (assembly under license or providing parts for the manufacturing process of the supplier). Typically, however, a large part of the offsets is indirect, sometimes defense-related, frequently also civilian (e.g., the striking example of "chicken wings" as offsets for fire engines to Bangkok[10]).

The dimensions of the offsets asked for in defense contracts vary. The United States claims to have agreed to an average of 71 percent of their defense contract values between 1999 and 2008.[11] Apparently, European countries demand a higher offset quota of up to 100 percent and beyond of the main contract value.[12]

Especially offsets in the civilian area are an impediment to free trade, therefore the World Trade Organization,[13] the European Union,[14] and the United States[15] have made efforts to restrict them. However, countries have continuously used "national security exceptions" to demand offset arrangements. European countries have refused toughening law by circumventing even a new Directive.[16]

3. SPECIFIC CORRUPTION RISK RELATED TO OFFSETS

Offset arrangements are typically highly technical and complex. They are opaque, as they evade the heightened scrutiny of the main contract. They are not in the public domain, due diligence on the beneficiaries is often insufficient,

9. TI-UK 2010, 24.

10. Supreme Court of Thailand, Criminal Division for Holders of Political Positions, Decisions No. 5/2554 and 7/2556, 10 September 2013 (subject: malfeasance in office, violations of the 1999 Act Concerning Offences Relating to the Submission of Bids to Government Agencies).

11. US Department of Commerce, according to TI-UK 2010, 10.

12. TI-UK 2010, 9.

13. WTO Revised Agreement on Government Procurement, 30 March 2012.

14. Treaty on European Union, amended by the treaty of Lisbon of 13 December 2007 (2007/C 306/01), Article 346 (formerly Article 296).

15. US Department of Commerce 2009, i; cf. TI-UK 2010, 8.

16. EU Directive 2009/81/EC of the European Parliament and of the Council (OJ L 216/76, 13 July 2009); cf. also European Defense Agency (EDA), Code of Conduct on Offsets 2009.

and the monitoring of performance and audits on delivery are frequently inexistent.[17]

Transparency International UK in its detailed study of 2010 gives an overview of the methods used to subvert offset arrangements for the purposes of corruption. The study distinguishes among political, bureaucratic, and private sector corruption[18] and gives case examples.[19] A more recent example has led to law enforcement action in Vienna and Munich as well as a parliamentary investigation in Austria (the case is not yet concluded):

Eurofighter

The sale of fifteen Eurofighters for €1.63 billion to Austria by a consortium made up of the European Aeronautic Defence and Space Company (EADS) (now called Airbus), British Aerospace, and Finmeccanica was riddled with incoherencies: law enforcement action focused first on dubious payments to intermediaries and possibly from there on to decision-makers.[20] Furthermore, they have concentrated on offset agreements of overall 200 percent of the main contract sum (!), valued at €3.5 billion.[21] This unusually high quota was used as a major sales argument by the ruling party to seek acceptance of the high price of the aircraft. Payments of €71.5 million to "Vector Aerospace," a postbox company in London, allegedly acting as an offset broker, seemingly without visible work product, sparked the interest of prosecutors.[22] According to media reports about Italian law enforcement action against the founder of "Vector," "real business transactions were used to cover up possibly illegal payments."[23]

Interestingly, some of the purported offset contracts had nothing to do with the fighter deal. Media reported that the sale of 6,500 military transporters by MAN to the British armed forces to be sold at €700 million (roughly 20 percent of the offsets due), was totally unrelated to the EADS deal. According to company officials, Rheinmetall was going to produce

17. TI-UK 2011, 62 et seq.

18. TI-UK 2010, 18.

19. Cf. TI-UK 2010, 26 et seq. (on South Africa, Portugal and Greece).

20. Financial Times, November 7, 2012; Süddeutsche Zeitung, December 3, 2014; Süddeutsche Zeitung, February 20, 2014: "Eurofighter-Treffen in der Milchbar."

21. Spiegel Online, December 17, 2012.

22. Reuters, November 19, 2012; Spiegel Online, December 17, 2012.

23. Spiegel Online, December 17, 2012.

them in Vienna anyhow. No trade enhancement at all was expected from this so called "Counter Trade".[24]

The case study demonstrates that without very sound due diligence on offset brokers there is a real risk that offset arrangements are misused for corrupt purposes. Of course, the details of the case are still open, as it is still under investigation.

4. HOW TO PREVENT CORRUPTION IN THE DEFENSE INDUSTRIES?

It is, in theory at least, accepted that corruption in the defense sector is not just a waste of taxpayer money; it can be very dangerous, especially because it may hide behind purported "state security interest" and in the extreme, allow a corrupt elite to capture entire states.[25] Also on the side of the supplier, politics and business easily mix and frequently, interventions by government lead to impunity.[26]

Civil society[27] and the concerned business sector itself in collective actions (first the US Defense Industry Initiative[28] and then International Forum of Business Ethical Conduct (IFBEC)[29]) have decided to tackle the issue. They are finding together in somewhat uneasy multi-stakeholder formats.[30]

The NGO community has developed a series of key action points. They have invited governments:

- to develop an anticorruption action plan for the defense area
- to reduce secrecy to absolute minimum
- to involve civil society in procurement
- to, in particular, address procurement risks by ensuring that "procurement and policy decisions are open and based on published strategic needs"; they ask for fair competition in bidding

24. Spiegel Online, December 17, 2012.

25. E.g. the Anglo leasing case in Kenya, see below Chapter 16.

26. Already above we have given several such examples focusing on the UK, Finland, Sweden, and Austria.

27. TI-UK 2013: Government Defence Anti-Corruption Index 2013; TI-UK 2015: Defence Companies Anti-Corruption Index 2015.

28. US DII Principles 1997.

29. IFBEC Global Principles 2009.

30. Cf. TI-UK 2015: Cover and Mustafa 2014, 27 et seq.

Also,

- offsets contracts need to be public, subject to due diligence, and its outcomes need to be regularly assessed
- governments should ensure that bidding companies have compliance programs in place and that they extend the requirements to their subsidiaries and subcontractors[31]

Companies have mirrored these requirements in their collective actions; they reflect the current standards on compliance and require

- a clear commitment by senior management
- a code of conduct conveyed in company values
- a serious risk assessment (risk mapping)
- detailed rules to prevent illicit and unethical behavior
- training modules
- reporting mechanisms
- regular program assessment[32]

So far, the industry and NGOs have not yet seen eye to eye on the amount of information that needs to be published. The NGO surveys are primarily based on publicly available material with some additional based on questionnaires to companies.[33]

Who Is Going to Jump First?

Collective action is going to be discussed in Chapter 20. One personal experience needs to be shared here, however: US Defense Corporations had developed their Defense Industry Initiative (DII) as early as 1997. It would have made sense to widen it to a transatlantic or even a worldwide group as early as possible. In 1999, after initial successes in the financial sector, the Basel Institute on Governance launched a first attempt to create such a transatlantic group. Five US and four European defense corporations were invited and showed initial interest. However, they could not decide on the venue (!). Whereas the French company Thales, offered a château near Paris,

31. TI-UK 2013, 38 et seq.

32. Cf. US DII Principles 1997 and IFBEC Principles 2009.

33. TI-UK 2015.

Lockheed's Frank Menacker insisted that everybody come to his ranch in West Virginia. The compliance officers laughed and said it was like kids standing around the pool and no one daring to go first, but the consequences were serious: the Europeans decided to go on with it alone.

A second major setback came, when the BAE story (above Chapter 7) broke: I remember trying—unsuccessfully—to convince Michael Lester, the Group Legal Director[34] over a sumptuous lunch at l'Orangerie near Pall Mall to rejoin the Group. In vain. I had not yet read what *The Guardian* had written about him and his company that very morning.

The process reminds one somewhat of Agatha Christie's famous novel: now there were three companies left (EADS, Thales, and Dassault). The Group from now on met in Paris at the restaurant Clovis. No one would have doubted the motives of the Group when it signed a compact under the heading of the "Clovis Principles."[35] Only if you knew that Clovis is the name of the first king of a united strong "France" (Frankish Empire).

But things ultimately turned for the better after the BAE story had ended. Now IFBEC, a genuinely international group of defense companies especially focusing on aeronautics, emerged and rapidly grew into the worldwide integrity initiative in defense.

---

34. Cf. above 89.

35. The Clovis Principles for the Defence Industry, Paris 2007.

13

The Art Market

MARK PIETH ■

1. CHALLENGES

The worldwide art markets have experienced a dramatic surge over the last decade: according to the European Fine Art Foundation the worldwide annual turnover of art has grown from €18 billion in 2003 to about €47 billion in 2013.[1] The reasons given for this extraordinary growth rate are, on the one hand, the low return on classic investments or investment tools since the crisis of 2008, and on the other hand, the regulatory pressure on the banking system.[2] Now, if art is not high on the corruption statistics, this does not mean that this industry is immune to abuses. On the contrary, it is merely more diversified: problematic transactions include trading in looted objects (be it looted by the Nazis or items from illegal digging in Tuscany, or more recently even the systemic exploitation of antiquities by the "Islamic State" to fund their war effort), professional counterfeiting and fake or incorrect certificates (see the infamous Jäger/Beltracchi-Case[3]), or the sale of art for the purpose of money laundering.[4] Of course, here all sorts of graft and illicit enrichment (e.g. by heads of state, ministers, or other officials) come into play.[5]

1. Financial Times, April 7, 2015.

2. Swiss Info, June 1, 2015, 2.

3. Basel Art Trade Guidelines 2012, 23.

4. Swiss Info, June 1, 2015.

5. Cf. the amazing art collection of the former Ukrainian President Yanukovych.

The definitions of the collected items found in international instruments are deliberately broad:[6] they include archeological, prehistorical, historical, literary objects, objects of art and science, and further collectable items. They also include such delicate items as conflict diamonds.[7] Players involved in trading on the art markets include auction houses, galleries, organizers of art fairs, experts, insurers, curators, restorers, private collectors, and museums.[8] The art trade is particularly vulnerable to illegal practices because it is so opaque.[9] Frequently, both the vendor and the purchaser are interested in confidentiality. As art has become a fashionable object of investment, the art trade has a heightened interest in establishing the provenance of the object and the provenance of the funds taken in exchange for the object. Regulation will be needed to bridge this gap.

Traditionally, though, public interest in the art markets has remained low. It is "normal" to acquire pieces of art with high sums of cash. Even if the traditional auction houses, galleries, and museums have given themselves guidelines and in-house rules, standards are uneven and confusing. Public regulation and international treaties are slow to be implemented.[10]

Additional practices add to the lack of transparency: it has become fashionable to store pieces of art "offshore," in tax-free storage centers with all necessary amenities to safeguard, store, and sell art (such "freeports" are to be found namely in Geneva, Singapore, Luxemburg, and recently also in Shanghai and Beijing). According to media reports up to 40 percent of the value of goods in Swiss freeports is made up of pieces of art. They claim that in Switzerland alone CHF100 billion of such goods are stored in freeports.[11] Finally, art has become attractive for illegal trade because prices paid are quite irrational and beyond control (for some objects of art hundreds of millions of dollars/euros have been paid recently: one such example is the acquisition of a Gauguin from the Staehelin family in Basel for CHF300 million by a Qatari customer).

In short, the art markets are increasingly vulnerable to money laundering (and related graft), and yet, antiquities and art traders are not subject to money laundering controls as such in most countries.[12]

6. Cf. UNIDROIT 1995: Convention on Stolen or Illegally Exported Cultural Objects; UNESCO 1999: International Code of Ethics for Dealers in Cultural Property.

7. Global Witness 2004.

8. Basel Art Trade Guidelines 2012, 10 (cf. definition in Article 1 and 2).

9. Basel Art Trade Guidelines 2012, 9.

10. Basel Art Trade Guidelines 2012, 6 et seq.

11. Swiss Info, June 1, 2015, 4.

12. Crit. Roth 2015, 35 et seq.

Modigliani or Rothko?

The Russian Dmitry Rybolovlev earned billions in potash mining. He founded a family trust and decided to collect art, grand style: with the help of a Geneva-based logistics specialist and freeport owner turning art dealer, Yves Bouvier, he systematically bought masterpieces, thought to be worth $2 billion in all. When he realized that the art dealer was probably overcharging him, Rybolovlev had him arrested in Monaco for "price fixing and money laundering." The local authorities obliged. After all, Rybolovlev was the owner of the AS Monaco football club.[13]

But, is "overcharging" really criminal on a market where prices are as volatile? Isn't Bouvier right in his defense, claiming that where there is a buyer, there is a price? Or does a market aiming to replace private banking not depend on secure return on investment?[14]

It is highly probable that in the Bouvier cases political issues and a complex marital settlement play a crucial role.

2. SELF-REGULATION?

The art market is inherently nontransparent. The multitude of legal risks confronting market participants has led some market leaders to develop comprehensive in-house compliance programs and departments (especially big auction houses). In the wake of a series of scandals, various trade associations and organizations of museums have gone on to give themselves guidelines and codes of ethics.[15] However, the world of self-regulation remains extremely touchy, and above all it does not aggressively address the main challenges.

As a follow-up to a worldwide conference[16] the Basel Institute on Governance initiated a process leading to the **Basel Art Trade Guidelines (BAT)**. Originally, the large auction houses and leading trade associations, such as the European Fine Art Foundation (TEFAF), participated. The text aims to address the two sides of the main problem: to establish the "provenance of the object" and

13. Financial Times, April 7, 2015; Swiss Info, June 1, 2015, 4.

14. Gabus and Bandle 2014.

15. For a comprehensive list cf. Basel Art Trade Guidelines 2012, 6 et seq.

16. Basel Art Trade Guidelines 2012, 3.

the "provenance of the funds".[17] The draft Guidelines go into some detail on what traders should do to identify the seller and the buyer as well as possible beneficial owners of object and funds.[18] Discretion does not pose a major problem as long as the trader seeks to identify the parties. However, the real problems arise where disclosure to the buyer or to third parties is an issue.[19] Obviously, due diligence reduces risk for the art market operator. Where the seller seeks to withhold disclosure of his identity or of the beneficiary of the object to the buyer or even to a justified third party (with a legitimate interest), the BAT try to strike a compromise between confidentiality and the legitimate interest of disclosure. They try to bridge the gap by imposing "enhanced due diligence" obligations on the trader and by asking him to provide a "purchase back guarantee" to the buyer. The Guidelines go on to suggest a conflict resolution mechanism[20] and a monitoring process by an advisory body made up of the parties to the instrument.[21] The Guidelines add some delicate rules on determining the provenance of the funds, clearly influenced by international anti-money- laundering standards. Probably the most delicate is the obligation to notify law enforcement of a doubtful provenance of objects or the suspicion of money laundering.[22] What would go down under public regulation is a big leap in a self-regulatory context.

What did the art dealers oppose?

The feedback received by art dealers so far indicates that:

- they are particularly unhappy about the rules curtailing confidentiality,
- they do not necessarily see the need for increased due diligence before sale,
- particularly the "provenance of funds" is not yet an accepted topic in the sector,
- they do not see the need for an advisory board and are satisfied with existing conflict resolution mechanisms.

17. Basel Art Trade Guidelines 2012, 5.

18. Basel Art Trade Guidelines 2012, 11 et seq.

19. Basel Art Trade Guidelines 2012, 11 et seq.

20. Basel Art Trade Guidelines 2012, 15 (Article 7).

21. Basel Art Trade Guidelines 2012, 17 (Article 9.2.).

22. Basel Art Trade Guidelines 2012, 14 et seq. (Article 4.4.2.2. and 5.3.).

It is therefore understandable that the facilitators of the process concluded in 2012 that the business did not yet seem ready for comprehensive self-regulation.[23]

3. INTERNATIONAL LAW?

There is a series of international public instruments aiming to regulate the art trade and in particular to prevent trading in looted, stolen, and illegally exported or fake art.[24] But so far, countries have been reticent to join, as they have feared for the competitiveness of their respective market places (in particular vis-à-vis the UNIDROIT[25] Convention).

Maybe this is too big a bite. However, faced with the growth of the market and the new risks of money laundering,[26] it would make sense if the Financial Action Task Force on Money Laundering gave the art trade closer attention. Even if it is maybe understandable that the members of the industry do not want to self-impose banking-style anti-money-laundering rules, a competition-neutral international public standard needs to be enacted. All "art market operators" would be treated as financial intermediaries and be subjected to identification of their clients, to risk assessment rules, and to notification obligations for suspicious transactions, unless they left the client due diligence entirely to the banking sector (this means no dealing in cash!).

It is indeed up to the sector if it gets its act together or if it needs to be obligated to do so by law.

23. Basel Art Trade Guidelines 2012, 23 et seq.; cf. also Financial Times, April 7, 2015.

24. UNESCO 1970: Convention on the Means of Prohibiting and Preventing the Illicit Import, Export and Transfer of Ownership of Cultural Property 1970; UNIDROIT 1995; European Council Directive 93/7/EEC on the return of cultural objects unlawfully removed from the territory of a Member State (OJ L 074, 15 March 1993).

25. The International Institute for the Unification of Private Law (UNIDROIT).

26. According to *Financial Times*, April 7, 2015, at the "FT Panel" in Davos in January 2015 the expert Roubini claimed that "[p]lenty of people are using it for laundering."

14

The Pharmaceutical Industry

MARK PIETH ■

1. CHALLENGES

Roughly a decade ago, at a meeting of compliance officers of the pharmaceutical industry, representatives of large multinationals assured: "we do not have a problem." They insisted that as the object of their trade needed to be clean, they could not let their image be tarnished by rumors of corruption. And the large trade associations, especially the International Federation of Pharmaceutical Manufacturers and of Association (IFPMA),[1] have made efforts to regulate adequate expenses on "continuing medical education" (CME) and similar marketing tools. Although there was no problem in covering necessary expenses for educational conferences, self-regulatory tools, such as the "pharma codex",[2] have defined what is acceptable beyond this minimum. In developed countries, also some national regulators have become active and have sanctioned companies for overstepping acceptable marketing standards. However, these rules have in practice not been applied universally.

What seems to have eluded the compliance officers in those early days is that the pharmaceutical industry faces some very straightforward corruption risks, just as real as any other sector. Their sales force has been buying prescriptions, and bribing practitioners and hospital staff to buy their produce; sometimes

1. IFPMA Code of Practice 2012.

2. IFPMA Code of Practice 2012 and the EFPIA-Code on disclosure of transfers of value from pharmaceutical companies to healthcare professionals and healthcare organisations, 6 June 2014.

they have been caught using more indirect means, such as fake follow-up research programs (so-called "patient experience surveys").[3]

The real wake-up call, however, came when China, under its new leadership, cracked down systematically on the pharmaceutical industry. Not only did the industry have to accept that it had a systemic problem in its biggest growth market, it (and maybe other sectors) was confronted with a new legal front: beyond the Foreign Corrupt Practices Act (FCPA) and the UK Bribery Act one of the biggest victim countries took action (or in the words of Xi Jinping, the new leadership spoke of "baring the sword"[4]) and did not just target ethnic Chinese managers this time.

GSK and Others in China

Chinese law enforcement first cracked down on GlaxoSmithKline (GSK) in 2013 for having paid bribes to doctors, hospital managers, and public officials of up to $500 million. Apparently, the local subsidiary had—in this growth market—kept raising the sales targets for its sales force.[5] Local commercial staff had routinely siphoned off funds with the use of hotels and travel agencies and fake invoices.[6] Now, China has a serious corruption problem. This is well known. Many officials and also doctors top up their meager salaries with bribes. In fact, it is hard to believe that in an otherwise centralized state these practices went unnoticed by the government. On the other hand, it is just as unlikely that the local board of directors of the pharmaceutical companies and, in the case of GSK, considering the size of the alleged payments, the head office did not notice that something was amiss.[7]

Of course, in a world where false and falsified invoices can be bought on the road,[8] it is easy to trick not overzealous internal auditors or external auditors relying primarily on complicit local staff.[9] Nevertheless, the assumption that the companies in question had been caught totally off-guard puts the seriousness of the implementation of their compliance programs in question.

3. Reuters, September 17, 2013: "Novartis to investigate bribery claims at Alcon unit in China."

4. China Copyright and Media, November 12, 2013: "Xi Jinping's 19 August speech revealed? (Translation)."

5. Shanghai Daily, August 14, 2013.

6. The Financial Times, April 3, 2014; The Guardian, May 28, 2014.

7. Fox 2013, Chapter IX.

8. In detail cf. Fox 2013, Chapter V.

9. Fox 2013, Chapter IX.

One might add as a further peculiarity that GSK, after having received the first whistle-blower information, initiated internal investigations that apparently found nothing wrong[10]—only to hear Chinese authorities shortly afterward come out with the $500 million allegations. They were feeling like "Alice in Wonderland" in an environment that was in reality highly treacherous. They must have been blinded by the phenomenal annual growth rates, and of course there might have been a political component behind the decision to crack down on the industry at this specific moment in time: Was the medication simply becoming too expensive?[11]

Shortly after the crackdown on GSK, other companies in China also came under scrutiny, amongst them AstraZeneca, Eli Lilly, Novartis, Novo Nordisk, Roche, and Sanofi.[12]

There are ways out of the dilemma, though. It is clear that the sales target approach needs to be reconsidered and that due diligence, monitoring, and auditing need to be stepped up dramatically in China.[13]

If we go beyond the China example, the pharmaceutical industry does indeed have a problem and maybe it has just been able to ignore it for so long because the enormous gains have left companies unaffected by amazingly high fines. One would need to remind oneself that GSK had already in July 2012 just pled guilty to the US Department of Justice to resolve allegations of fraud and failure to report safety data, and paid $3 billion (!).[14] Now, after the China case was resolved with another fine of £297 million,[15] a case is still ongoing in the same and similar matters with the Serious Fraud Office (SFO) in the United Kingdom.[16] Interestingly enough, all this flack has so far not undermined the position of GSK's leadership.

10. As reported by The Guardian, May 14, 2014.

11. For critique: Reuters, July 26, 2013: "Why China pays too much for medicines."

12. Cf. also Frankfurter Allgemeine Zeitung, August 23, 2013; NZZ, May 23, 2014, 27.

13. Fox 2013, Chapter IX.

14. For details: Fox 2013, Chapter II.

15. The Telegraph, September 19, 2014: "China fines Glaxo £297m for bribery, Mark Reilly sentenced."

16. The Guardian, May 28, 2014: "GlacoSmithKline faces criminal investigation by Serious Fraud Office."

The relaxed approach in official statements of companies ("AstraZeneca China cooperates with various Chinese authorities on a regular basis across a wide range of interactions and is committed to acting with integrity at all times, in all of our operations and customer interactions"[17]) is in stark contrast with the shock waves the Chinese crackdown sent through the industry and beyond.[18]

2. WHAT NEEDS TO BE DONE?

The worldwide pharmaceutical market is dominated by few very big companies. Of course, there are also many smaller companies with a far smaller market share, though. The major suppliers all have state-of-the-art compliance programs and they are spending considerable amounts of money on compliance practice. Nevertheless, examples such as the China experience of the pharmaceutical industry demonstrate that goodwill alone does not change attitudes: very serious efforts in the selection of employees, in training, in monitoring, and in auditing are necessary. Compliance is not just a "nice to have" or a "necessary evil"—it is fundamental to the protection of the company's interests. And, even in the biggest multinational enterprises this message is not always fully understood.

17. The Guardian, May 28, 2014.

18. Financial Times, April 3, 2014, 17.

15

Sports Governing Bodies

The FIFA Experience

MARK PIETH ■

1. EMOTIONS AND BIG BUSINESS

Sports are big business, but they are also a highly emotional matter, in particular with fans drawing their self-esteem from the performance of "their" club. No wonder that fans take manipulations and graft in sports as a personal offense. The United Kingdom's Justice Cooke said in his sentencing remarks in a recent match-fixing case:

> "The image and the integrity of what was once a game but is now a business is damaged in the eyes of all, including the many youngsters who regarded you as heroes and would have given their eye teeth to play at the levels and with the skills that you had."[1]

Sports governing bodies have a particularly bad reputation for governance. Sports have traditionally been treated as a private activity. States have abstained from regulating sports. They have also held back on defining standards for sports regulators.

1. BBC, November 3, 2011: "Salman Butt and Pakistan bowlers jailed for no-ball plot."

Confronting Corruption. Fritz Heimann and Mark Pieth.

Until recently most sports were governed by "gentlemen's clubs" and lucky to financially survive the next major tournament.[2] With the new media and the marketing methods especially soccer and athletics started to generate enormous amounts of money. Now, a soccer World Cup is worth $5 billion to the International Federation of Association Football (FIFA). The Olympics generate similar amounts for the International Olympic Committee (IOC).[3]

It is crucial for these governing bodies that they are allowed to run a monopoly. No one wants to be world champion of one association next to others; everybody wants to be *the* world champion.

Match-Fixing in Cricket

Considering the facts, the case seems relatively harmless: in a sting operation by an investigative journalist, a UK-based sports agent was filmed receiving £150,000 "after boasting how he could arrange for Pakistan cricketers to rig games for money."[4] The agent promised the reporter that two bowlers would deliver three so-called "no-balls" at specific moments during the Lord's Test between Pakistan and England from August 26 to 29 in 2010. The "no-balls" were bowled exactly as promised. They are not in themselves hugely damaging. The specifics of such a manipulation, however, allow insiders to bet at terrific odds (here at a probability of 1.5 million to one). So the actual damage caused is directed at defrauding bookmakers and betters.

This is one aspect leading to harsh sentences: the fixer of the scam was sentenced to thirty-two months, the team captain to thirty months, and one bowler to one year and the other to six months of imprisonment, with parole possible at the earliest after having served half of their sentences. The verdicts were handed down for "conspiracy for accepting corrupt payments" and "to help others cheat at gambling."[5]

2. Governing FIFA, Concept Paper and Report, September 19, 2011, printed in Pieth 2014b, 127 et seq. (133, 136 et seq.).

3. IOC 2014.

4. Mail Online, November 2, 2011: "The men who cheated cricket: Pakistan trio guilty of match-fixing."

5. BBC, November 3, 2011: "Salman Butt and Pakistan bowlers jailed for no-ball plot"; The Guardian, November 3, 2011: "Pakistan spot-fixing players and agent sentenced to lengthy jail terms."

The rhetoric of judges and sports officials, however, goes well beyond denouncing fraud. They refer to the impact on those for whom the players are folk heroes:

> *Now, whenever people look back on a surprising event in a game or a surprising result or whenever in the future there are surprising events or results," said the judge, "followers of the game who have paid good money to watch it live or to watch it on TV will be led to wonder whether there has been a fix and whether what they have been watching is a genuine contest between bat and ball. What ought to be honest sporting competition may not be such at all.*[6]

The players have additionally been banned by the International Cricket Council (ICC) for five years.

2. MULTINATIONAL ENTERPRISES AND QUASI-INTERGOVERNMENTAL ORGANIZATIONS

Now, governance structures have not kept up with the rapid transformation of the sports governing bodies into multinational enterprises.[7] Virtually all the oversight measures of large businesses were missing until very recently: sound bookkeeping and auditing, external financial controls, compliance systems, due diligence checks on key officials, etc.

Concurrently, it became more and more obvious that sporting events (such as the Soccer World Championship, the Olympics, and the Commonwealth Games) were no longer simply the private activity of a club. Competitions and more so the honor to host them got increasingly politicized.[8] Individuals are highly emotional about the performance of "their" club or their country. Heads of state make it their affair to win the hosting decision. They participate in the Assemblies of FIFA or the IOC and they receive soccer officials with the diplomatic honors of fellow heads of government or state. Governing sports has

6. The Guardian, November 3, 2011: "Pakistan spot-fixing players and agent sentenced to lengthy jail terms."

7. Governing FIFA, Concept Paper and Report, September 19, 2011, printed in Pieth 2014b, 127 et seq. (144, 146 et seq.).

8. Cf. the "Nice Declaration" on the Specific Characteristics of Sport, Annex IV of the Presidency Conclusions for the Nice European Council, 7–10 December 2000, para. 3; The Council of Europe Resolution on "Principles of Good Governance in Sport," adopted in Budapest on 14/15 October 2004.

become the activity of quasi-international organizations.[9] This adds to the challenges, as the governance structure is far from the democratic accountability one would expect from an international public body.

3. OLD BOYS SUDDENLY BECOMING RICH

Typically, the sports governing bodies, about sixty of which are based in Switzerland,[10] are incorporated in the simplest of legal forms, as associations, allowing them to choose their structure virtually freely. And yet they are traditionally nonprofit organizations benefiting from tax privileges, both at their headquarters and in the host states of tournaments. The first impulse of the "old boys," suddenly becoming rich, was to distribute the new wealth amongst themselves.[11] FIFA is made up of 209 Member Territories representing the entire world (in a more complete way than the United Nations, with all its problems, including corruption). On top of these "inherited" problems, FIFA has evolved into a patronage structure of a small group of predominantly long-time representatives (some have had a term of office of thirty years). They are the perfect illustration of what Bueno de Mesquita and Smith mean by "a small group of essentials."[12] Football (soccer) is by far not the only problem case; the challenges faced are systemic, and they can be found just as much in the IOC,[13] in handball,[14] volleyball,[15] cricket,[16] or car racing.[17]

4. FIFA: A COMPANY IN TROUBLE OR A CRIMINAL ORGANIZATION?

To stay with the example of FIFA, simply because it has recently been in the media so much: the lack of governance has allowed a vast graft and corruption

9. Governing FIFA, Concept Paper and Report, September 19, 2011, printed in Pieth, 127 et seq. (144 et seq., 156 et seq.).

10. Pieth 2014b, 24.

11. Pieth 2014b, 8.

12. Bueno de Mesquita and Smith 2011, 142, 146 et seq.

13. Cf. Jennings and Sambrook 2000.

14. Stern, 24 March 2009: "Korruption im Handball: Der Aufstieg des Manipulators."

15. Cf. Goijman, 94 et seq.

16. See box above 168 et seq.

17. The Guardian, August 5, 2014: "F1 boss Bernie Ecclestone to pay £60m to end German bribery trial."

network to evolve. However, it should be noted that we are not talking of public corruption, and that it is not easy to make out who the actual victim is. If an association decides to distribute its funds amongst its members, this is hardly a crime—even if the stakeholders, who have an interest in the sports they govern, may be aggrieved. Matters are obviously different where officials of the association secretly siphon off funds of the association into their private pockets (this is called embezzlement) or where event organizers are solicited for private bribes by game regulators. This could pose a problem in countries where private bribery is an offense.[18]

Over the last decade media have been very critical of FIFA, but until recently they have not really made a difference, not until an independent investigatory body was created for FIFA[19] and the results of an extensive investigation[20] were passed on to law enforcement agencies in the United States and in Switzerland. Two stories are symptomatic:

Payoffs for Senior Officials: The ISMM/ISL Case

The companies International Sports Media & Marketing (ISMM) and its subsidiary International Sport and Leisure (ISL) were the major media and marketing tools used by FIFA in its major financial growth period. Due to an overexpansion of its activities, ISMM and ISL went bankrupt on May 21, 2001. Allegations of bribery surfaced rapidly; however, both the bankruptcy and the relating criminal investigation dragged on. FIFA—even though one of the major victims of the bankruptcy case—was not overly eager to have the facts made known.[21] It emerged that part of ISMM/ISL's difficulties were linked to excessive "commissions" paid to senior FIFA officials and others in deviation from the official contract with FIFA.

> *From money that passed through the ISMM/ISL Group, it is certain that not inconsiderable amounts were channeled to former FIFA President Havelange and to his son-in-law Ricardo Teixeira as well as to Dr. Nicolás Leoz, whereby there is no indication that any form of service was given in return by them. These payments were apparently made via front*

18. E.g. the United States had opposed in the OECD the enlargement of the Convention to cover private commercial bribery, because it is a crime in the United States merely on the state level.

19. Cf. below 177.

20. Cf. below 3, 172 et seq.

21. Final Report by the Independent Governance Committee to the Executive Committee of FIFA, April 22, 2014, printed in Pieth 2014b, 71 et seq. (74 et seq.).

> *companies in order to cover up the true recipient and are to be qualified as "commissions", known today as "bribes."*[22]

Both in the criminal investigation in Switzerland and in the examination by FIFA's international Ethics Committee the most delicate issue, however, remained the role of President Blatter, who had been secretary general at the time of some of the transactions in question. The report of the Ethics Committee says, based on the so-called Order on the Dismissal of the Criminal Proceedings (ODCP) of the Public Prosecutor of the Canton of Zug in Switzerland:

> *According to the ODCP, there are no indications that President Blatter received any commission payments from ISL, its former Chief Executive Officer Jean-Marie Weber, or others.*
>
> *There are also no indications whatsoever that President Blatter was responsible for a cash flow to Havelange, Teixeira or Leoz, or that he himself received any payments from the ISL Group, even in form of hidden kickback payments.*[23]

CONCACAF, A RICO CONSPIRACY?

On Wednesday, May 27, 2015, two days prior to the (re-)election of the FIFA president, US and Swiss law enforcement agencies stepped in: in Zurich, where the FIFA Congress was to be held that week, seven of FIFA's officials were arrested upon extradition requests by the US Department of Justice. The Swiss authorities independently raided FIFA's head offices and took millions of documents with them to investigate the World Cup hosting decisions for 2018 (Russia) and 2022 (Qatar).[24]

In the indictment published by the US Department of Justice (DOJ) on the same day[25] the fourteen defendants are accused of fraud, bribery, and money

22. Statement of the Chairman of the FIFA Adjudicatory Chamber, Hans-Joachim Eckert, on the examination of the ISL case, 29 April 2013, 3.

23. Statement of the Chairman of the FIFA Adjudicatory Chamber, Hans-Joachim Eckert, on the examination of the ISL case, 29 April 2013, 4 et seq.

24. Press release of the Swiss Attorney's Office: news.admin.ch, May 27, 2015: "Bundesanwaltschaft stellt Dokumente bei FIFA sicher."

25. Press release: DOJ, May 27, 2015: "Nine FIFA officials and five corporate executives indicted for racketeering conspiracy and corruption."

laundering. The US authorities used their Racketeer Influenced and Corrupt Organizations Act (RICO) and are talking of conspiracy and racketeering. It seems that marketing executives and intermediaries are accused of having paid off soccer officials in order to obtain media and marketing rights to international soccer tournaments. The exact legal basis of the indictment is not obvious[26] and the defense will have a lot of ammunition for a protracted fight. However, the indictments and the then-US attorney general Loretta Lynch, appearing before the press using strong words, had to prove their case:

> *The indictment alleges corruption that is rampant, systemic, and deep-rooted both abroad and here in the United States . . . It spans at least two generations of soccer officials who, as alleged, have abused their positions of trust to acquire millions of dollars in bribes and kickbacks. And it has profoundly harmed a multitude of victims, from the youth leagues and developing countries that should benefit from the revenue generated by the commercial rights these organizations hold, to the fans at home and throughout the world whose support for the game makes those rights valuable. Today's action makes clear that this Department of Justice intends to end any such corrupt practices, to root out misconduct, and to bring wrongdoers to justice—and we look forward to continuing to work with other countries in this effort.*[27]

The effect of the coup could not have been more dramatic: three days after his re-election FIFA president Blatter resigned, and there is currently a worldwide debate whether or not just the continental soccer confederations CONCACAF (North, Central American and Caribbean Association Football) and maybe CONMEBOL (South American Football Confederation) are racketeering organizations, but whether FIFA itself falls into the box of "organized crime"—obviously, a very serious allegation that could easily lead to the end of the organization. One is reminded that critics had asked for a "New FIFA" altogether.

It will be challenging to decide whether the head office of a worldwide association with limited decision power over its member associations and no decision power over the continental organizations is a criminal organization, simply

26. *United States of America v. Jeffrey Webb et al.*, 15 CR 0252 (E.D.N.Y.) [indictment].

27. Press release: DOJ, 27 May 2015: "Nine FIFA officials and five corporate executives indicted for racketeering conspiracy and corruption."

because the representatives of those continental organizations are also delegates in the FIFA "government," the Executive Committee (ExCo)—however, without the organization FIFA electing them. Does this affect the entire organization? And if so, what is the difference between FIFA and Walmart, Siemens, Glaxo, and other multinational enterprises (MNEs) in difficulties mentioned earlier in this book. I do not think one could maintain that FIFA and even the continental confederations have been created for the purpose of serving as fronts for criminal activities, but their governance is so bad that they have permitted systematic misbehavior. Individuals, including the former FIFA president, are now under criminal investigation!

5. THE RESPONSIBILITY OF THE HOST COUNTRY

Whose task is it to clean up? Obviously, if these sports governing bodies are public, the host country has a responsibility to define a minimum standard of governance for sports governing bodies based in its territory.[28] It does not need to change its company law. It could reserve certain forms of incorporation for sports governing bodies or it could apply its charity-supervision to those bodies seeking nonprofit status.[29] It is rather astonishing, though, that for example in Switzerland a small nongovernmental organization (NGO) is subjected to far stricter controls than any of the sixty-odd sports governing bodies domiciled in this country. It seems that authorities were so flattered to be chosen as the host country that they were blind to risk. This is not an uncommon feature for Switzerland, a country that some have repeatedly compared to a pirate's den.[30] This assessment was valid up to the point when the Swiss Federal Attorneys Office, in cooperation with the US attorney general, opened a case against the top echelon of FIFA.

6. WHAT'S WRONG WITH SELF-REGULATION?

What remains is self-regulation. Obviously, self-regulation could work—it has worked in other fields. And there certainly is substantial public pressure on

28. Pieth 2014b, 23 et seq.

29. Pieth 2014b, 27.

30. Pieth 2014b, 24 et seq.

the sports governing bodies to reform.[31] However, they have so far been astonishingly resistant to change. It is basically the large traditional European soccer nations demanding reform, but, under the "one nation one vote" regime of FIFA they are outnumbered.

Both the IOC and FIFA have made efforts toward reform after major scandals.[32] Interestingly enough, the drive toward reform does not come bottom-up; rather, in the case of the IOC a new president and, in the case of FIFA the old president, whom many see as part of the problem, have decided to introduce a reform process. The advantage to this top-down approach is its rapid pace. However, the main challenge is that reform is not the result of a change of culture. Rather, it remains open if the technocratic changes will—in the long run—bring about a fundamental change of attitude.[33]

How to Become President of a Sports Governing Body

A sports governing body works like any other major organization: it is governed by the rules of politics. Candidates for the presidency have to campaign and rally for supporters. Considerable funds are necessary, in particular for outside candidates. Allegiances can be formed by different means, such as common interests, membership of the same regional organization (in soccer: "Confederation"), or—at least traditionally—by doling out presents and payoffs. The incumbent president has the advantage in that he can—not very different from any sitting head of government—distribute privileges and contributions to his allies (e.g., in the form of "development aid").

Apart from these established forms of political campaigning, sports governing bodies have a history of outright acquisition of votes for the presidential race or also in the context of hosting decisions: a private "sting" operation by a British newspaper demonstrated that members of FIFA's ExCo were

31. Hershman 2014, 17 et seq.; e.g. New York Times, December 2 2011: "Skeletons in Blatter's Closet Return to Haunt Him"; FIFA press release, 29 May 2011; INTERPOL press release, 9 May 2011; The Guardian, June 1, 2011: "Sepp Blatter allies dismiss Fifa corruption charges as 'English lies'"; Daily Mail, 1 May 2006, 68 et seq.

32. For the IOC reforms see Governing FIFA, Concept Paper and Report, September 19, 2011, printed in Pieth 2014b, 127 et seq. (164 et seq.); for the FIFA reforms see: Second Report by the Independent Governance Committee to the Executive Committee of FIFA, February 6, 2013, printed in Pieth 2014b, 91 et seq.

33. Goldsmith 2014, 3 et seq.; Pieth 2014b, 59 et seq.

ready to sell their votes at a time when the ExCo was still deciding over the future hosting of the World Cup.[34]

The former president of the Asian Football Confederation (AFC), member of the FIFA ExCo and presidential challenger, Mohamed bin Hammam of Qatar, faced (together with the president of the CONCACAF, Jack Warner) sanctions by FIFA's Ethics Committee for allegedly offering bribes in exchange for votes in the presidential election.[35]

A huge batch of emails leaked to the media and partially published by the *Sunday Times*[36] seems to demonstrate—if genuine—that many African soccer officials have received substantial sums from bin Hammam in exchange either for support of his presidential campaign or in support of the candidature of Qatar for the 2022 World Cup, or both. So far, the details remain unclear:

Several email-chains seem to demonstrate that officials asked bin Hammam for financial support. For example, the Zambian Association-President writes to the secretary of bin Hammam "[a]s per our conversation, please Mr President if you could assist me with about 50 thousand Dollars for my Football Association and personal expenditures. I hope to repay you in the near future, as the burden is a little bit too hard for me at the moment." Shortly afterward he receives a note indicating that $50,000 had been transferred to his account. Similarly, the president of the Football Association of São Tomé requested financial aid of $232,000 for eight soccer pitches and a further email by the secretary of bin Hammam indicates that $50,000 had been transferred to his account. It is obviously difficult to judge the authenticity of these emails, and their interpretation leaves questions open. Likewise, a spreadsheet indicates that guests of the Asian Football Confederation at a Kuala Lumpur meeting October 15–17, 2008, received beyond expenses an allowance of $5,000. A further email by the organizer (Vice-President of the Football Association of Ivory Coast) Idriss Diallo to the secretary of bin Hammam refers to several actions planned in order to support both bin Hammam and the bid of Qatar: "My President Jacques Anouma ask me to think about a strategy to help his very good friend President Bin Hammam. So if you can translate for him, I send you in this mail a proposal to push very hard the Bid of Qatar 2022. Thanks."

34. Cf. Final Report by the Independent Governance Committee to the Executive Committee of FIFA, 22 April 2014, printed in Pieth 2014b, 71 et seq. (75).

35. Final Report by the Independent Governance Committee to the Executive Committee of FIFA, April 22, 2014, printed in Pieth 2014b, 71 et seq. (75).

36. The Sunday Times, June 1, 2014.

It has been the task of FIFA's Ethics Committee to determine whether these payments were actually destined for the hosting decision or rather for the support of bin Hammam's presidential campaign. The Statement of the Chairman of the Adjudicatory Chamber of the FIFA Ethics Committee of November 13, 2014, claims that the evidence ". . . does not support the conclusion that the purpose of these payments was to promote the Qatar 2022 FIFA World Cup™ bid. Rather, the evidence before the Investigative Chamber strongly suggests that Mr. bin Hammam paid officials of the Confederation of African Football (CAF) to influence their votes in the June 2011 election for FIFA President where he was a candidate."[37]

Since September 2015, however, the Swiss law enforcement authorities are investigating Mr. Blatter personally in two cases of possible misappropriation of corporate funds.[38] The outcome of this procedure is yet unknown.

7. EXAMPLE FIFA

The reform process within FIFA has taken on a dual direction:[39]

Looking into the past, FIFA has created a new independent Ethics Committee with a professional investigator and his deputy and an equally independent judge and deputy. They decide autonomously from the FIFA administration which case to run, and FIFA is obliged to supply the necessary means. This Committee is currently involved in very challenging international investigations into past hosting decisions, especially the choice of Qatar for the World Cup 2022.

Looking ahead, FIFA has elected an equally independent Chair and a deputy to preside over its Audit and Compliance Committee. They are able to participate in all Committee Meetings of their choice; they also have full access to all documentation. It is their task to introduce all those safeguards that are common standards in a modern multinational enterprise (e.g., financial controls, compliance programs, conflict-of-interest policies, rational decisions on remuneration of top officials, etc.).

To date, not all the items on the reform list have been implemented. In particular introducing independent "directors" or members of the ExCo met

37. Statement of the Chairman of the Adjudicatory Chamber of the FIFA Ethics Committee on the Report on the Inquiry into the 2018/2022 FIFA World Cup™ Bidding Process prepared by the Investigatory Chamber of the FIFA Ethics Committee, 13 November 2014, 28.

38. News.admin.ch, September 25, 2015: "Strafverfahren gegen FIFA-Präsident eröffnet."

39. Final Report by the Independent Governance Committee to the Executive Committee of FIFA, April 22, 2014, printed in Pieth 2014b, 71 et seq.

resistance; likewise the age and term limits were not received favorably and so far, most senior officials have been reluctant to publish their annual remunerations. What is maybe the biggest challenge, though, in the long run, is a serious change of culture in the institution. Reform definitely has to last beyond the current change of presidency.[40]

The Investigation into the Russia and Qatar Hosting Decisions of FIFA

Unluckily with FIFA there is a tendency that every activity turns into a scandal: after the creation of a genuinely independent Ethics Committee and a real separation of powers between the Investigatory and the Adjudicatory Chambers one would have hoped that the new institutions would help change FIFA's reputation for the better. In several smaller cases they demonstrated that they could meet these expectations. However, when it came to assess the bidding procedures for the World Cup tournaments 2018 and 2022, the challenges were obviously too high for the newly created institutions.

Both investigator and judge demonstrated their independence; however, they acted more like "loose cannons": the judge delivered a public forty-page summary of the investigator's four hundred-page report, which was only published years after. The summary left crucial questions open. It seemed to let Russia get away with flimsy explanations and could not really explain why the money handed over to decision-makers did not implicate Qatar. Therefore, many observers and also insiders of FIFA demanded the publication of the so-called Garcia report (the four hundred pages).[41] It is still unknown why the judge was hesitant to allow its publication. He claimed the full publication of the Garcia report was not legally possible.[42] After a public outcry the ExCo decided, on the basis of a report by its Independence Chairman of the Audit and Compliance Committee, to publish the report with adequate redactions.[43] In the meantime, the investigator who had claimed the summary had distorted his report[44] stepped down.[45]

40. Pieth 2014b, 59 et seq.

41. NZZ, November 14, 2014; The Standard, September 26, 2014.

42. FIFA online, October 17, 2014.

43. Deutschlandfunk, December 21, 2014: 'Eine positive Entwicklung'.

44. Bloomberg, November 13, 2014.

45. The New York Times, December 18, 2014; FIFA online, December 17, 2014; Le Matin, December 18, 2014; AFP, December 17, 2014.

Overall, the chaotic management of the publication of the findings in such an essential investigation did not inspire trust in the newly created institutions. Furthermore, the investigation is of key interest to FIFA, as it has to make up its mind—as soon as possible—whether it can really go ahead with the World Cup events in Russia and Qatar. For the time being, FIFA has decided to stick to its original hosting decisions.[46]

8. INTERNATIONAL REGULATION

Several international public initiatives are underway in international organizations to define governance standards for sports governing bodies. This could have a decisive effect on host countries. However, it is an open question if the Council of Europe[47] is the right forum, simply because of its limited reach.

9. WHAT IS ON THE CURRENT REFORM LIST?

The resignation of the long-time President Blatter is obviously a chance for FIFA. It allows a far more fundamental reform if the organization makes use of its chance. The list of reform points brings us back to the dual references, FIFA as a quasi-MNE and as a quasi-international organization. As far as it is a business, it needs to adapt to the standard for *large international companies* and to introduce

- sound international accounting and auditing rules
- a compliance program
- conflict-of-interest rules
- integrity tests for new or re-elected candidates for office
- a serious whistleblower-hotline

As far as it resembles an *international organization* accountability and transparency are in the foreground. They translate into concrete requirements such as:

- rules for the election of the president
- rules for hosting decisions of events

46. FIFA online, November 13 and 19, 2014.

47. CoE 2014.

- rules on the selection of partners in marketing
- clear rules for foreign aid
- independent directors in the ExCo
- age limits and terms of office
- publication of salaries and bonuses of top officials and employees.

FIFA has nominally picked up many of these points but the organization has yet to change its culture dramatically.[48] Furthermore, these requirements go well beyond FIFA. FIFA has merely served as an example for the entire universe of sports governing bodies.

48. Pieth 2014b, 59 et seq.

16

Development Assistance

MARK PIETH

1. ITS LOGIC

Amongst the key players in combating corruption are the institutions promoting development, the International Financial Institutions (IFIs) (or multilateral development banks, (MDBs)) and the bilateral development aid agencies. At first sight the logic of development assistance seems obvious and simple. Whoever enters the main building of the World Bank is informed that this huge and powerful institution has one goal: "alleviating poverty." Its new president, Jim Yong Kim, has refocused the attention of the institution on exactly this goal. He has set a target: to reduce extreme poverty by 2030.[1]

A seminal speech of one of Kim's predecessors, James Wolfensohn, had in 1996 initiated a dramatic change of policy of the World Bank Group: for Wolfensohn, corruption was a major impediment to development and he recognized the responsibility of the World Bank to tackle corruption and to foster good governance.[2] This was a crucial step beyond the traditional approach of the Bank not to get involved in "political matter"—and corruption was considered a political issue.[3] What was first developed in the work of the analytical arm of the World Bank, the World Bank Institute,[4] was now introduced systematically in World Bank Operations: a comprehensive "Governance and

1. See World Bank 2013, 1 et seq.

2. Kunicová 2013, 41.

3. Cf. already above 12, 50.

4. Cf. World Bank online: "Six Questions on the Cost of Corruption with World Bank Institute Global Governance Director Daniel Kaufmann."

Confronting Corruption. Fritz Heimann and Mark Pieth.

Anti-Corruption" policy was developed (the GAC)[5] and its implementation continuously assessed.[6] The challenge was to mainstream governance strategies throughout the everyday lending operations of the Bank.

Concurrently, an Integrity Vice Presidency (INT) was created and upgraded systematically. After a political breakdown in the era of World Bank president Paul Wolfowitz, Paul Volcker was commissioned by Wolfowitz's successor, Bob Zoellick, to analyze the situation and make recommendations. Amongst them was the creation of an Independent Advisory Board to help keep INT out of trouble and to protect it from interventions by bank "operations."[7]

2. IS DEVELOPMENT ASSISTANCE EFFECTIVE?

Whoever doubts that development assistance can work will have to study the example of the Marshall Plan for Europe in the aftermath of World War II. Between 1946 and 1952 the United States dispensed over $182 billion into the destroyed economies of Western Europe.[8] Not only did the United States achieve their political goal in developing an alliance against communism, they laid the foundation of the postwar economic recovery of Europe.

Why then has development aid going to countries of the global South been so much less successful? In fact, critics maintain that the standard of living in many African countries is today lower than at the time they gained independence. Why is development assistance so much less effective than expected?[9]

The explanation has to take into account that the European states—for all the aggression that was unleashed in the first half of the twentieth century—were basically organized states with operating institutions. They had a judiciary, parliaments, and governments with a history. The more recent recipient states of aid, namely in Africa, had only just emerged from colonial rule; they were still in the process of developing democratic institutions and finding ways to implement the rule of law. Frequently, corporations based in developed states and corrupt elites conspired to appropriate the resources of the new states in the South.[10]

5. See Kunicová 2013, 41 et seq.; Recanatini 2013, 64 et seq.

6. Kunicová 2013, 43 et seq.

7. Cf. below 194 et seq.

8. Bueno de Mesquita and Smith 2011, 177.

9. Bueno de Mesquita and Smith 2011, 177; Moyo 2009, xviii.

10. Pieth 2008, 3 et seq.

In this context, a dangerous "conspiracy between unaccountable lending agencies and unaccountable borrowing governments"[11] was responsible for creating (and possibly recreating) a general debt crisis: governments liked to borrow, because new projects gave them control over money, opportunities for patronage, and graft. The MDB's "disbursement policy" evades public accountability and neither Bank staff nor government officials have to account for failed projects. And the rate of failure can be high: Brian Cooksey[12] refers to a report written by the World Bank's Operations Evaluation Department on agricultural projects in Tanzania, concluding that, between 1965 and 1997, 72 percent of projects representing lending of a half a billion USD had failed. His headline is damning: "Borrow from World Bank, Stay Indebted Forever."

3. DONOR INTEREST

The major problem is that aid is rarely given unconditionally. As in the example of the Marshall Plan, development aid typically pursues a specific political interest of the donor; the United States has in the past heavily invested in humanitarian relief and in military aid to countries where they had essential geopolitical interests: Egypt, Pakistan, Iraq, and Latin America.[13] It is sometimes hard to identify the predominant motivation, development or political alliance. And there can be an outright conflict of interest between the agendas.

4. TOLERATING EMBEZZLEMENT?

Many of the worst examples of failed development assistance are autocratic states. Frequently, at least part of the payments have been siphoned off by the ruling elites. This can happen very openly, by taxing development operations, by extorting relief convoys by military guerrilla organizations or in more subtle ways through budgetary manipulations: MDBs are fully aware that "money is fungible." It can be shifted from projects into private pockets. MDBs are frequently simply left to take care of the essential need of the population (healthcare, education, housing, food), whereas the rulers steal from the national budget (e.g., for "defense expenses," as in the Anglo-Leasing case in Kenya).

11. The East African, May 17–23, 1999, 12: "Borrow from World Bank, stay indebted forever."

12. The East African, May 17–23, 1999, 12: "Borrow from World Bank, stay indebted forever."

13. Bueno de Mesquita and Smith 2011, 161 et seq.

Anglo-Leasing

The "Anglo Leasing" scandal[14] is arguably one of Kenya's largest corruption scandals. The case came to light in 2004 following the release of a report by the then-permanent secretary in the Office of the President in charge of Governance and Ethics, John Githongo, who in the course of his work discovered a number of irregular government contracts. The case, which is still the subject of an ongoing, multi-jurisdictional investigation, involves eighteen government procurement contracts (with an overall worth of over $700 million) awarded to several different dubious entities, for the supply of different goods varying from weapons, to telecommunications systems, to a navy vessel.

Generally, each of these contracts was vastly overpriced and awarded on a single source basis, and in some cases goods were acquired that were not suitable or not actually needed by the government department they were being provided to. To add an extra device for the looting of funds, the contracts allegedly included clauses whereby the funds to pay for the goods were provided by a "financing company" chosen by the contracting companies. These financing companies, which are alleged to be owned by the same individuals as the contracting company, would then "lend" the required cost of the contract to the Kenyan government at an inflated interest rate, who would pay the "borrowed" money back over an extended period of time.

An example is the contract from which this scandal takes its name: the Kenyan government signed a heavily overinflated contract for the supply of a passport-issuing system with a company—Anglo Leasing and Finance Limited—who provided a fake registration address. It is alleged that even though the cost of the supply of goods was originally quoted as €6 million by a French firm, the contract was instead awarded to Anglo Leasing, who quoted the price of €31 million (and who would have actually subcontracted the work to the original French firm).

Although the case involves overall eighteen contracts, ranging from 1997 to 2004, these contracts are all lumped together as one scandal due to the fact that they all apply a similar technique to looting Kenyan government funds. Furthermore, the beneficial owners of the companies involved allegedly belong to one or the other of two important Kenyan families. Additionally, it has been suggested that each of the contracts, which could not have occurred without the collusion of public officials, were perpetrated by then government members to assist with party funding.

14. E.g. Wrong 2009, 206.

To date, almost no criminal judicial action has been taken in Kenya against either the contracted companies or the senior public officials involved in the procurement process.

The stories of embezzlement of foreign aid are manifold, and they testify to the amazing creativity of the corrupt elites. Creativity, if put to legitimate use, could lead to substantial economic success for those responsible.

Obviously, the question needs to be answered why donors accept that a substantial proportion of the funds is misallocated. The immediate explanation would be that cutting aid under the rules of conditionality would primarily hit the poorest and not those involved in rent-seeking. A less openly expressed explanation would have to admit that the hidden political agenda of (especially bilateral) development aid would be lost if aid was bound more directly to its declared goals.

5. IS THERE A WAY OUT OF THE DILEMMA?

Dambisa Moyo, in her award-winning book "Dead Aid",[15] has indicated a relatively obvious path: free trade instead of dependency through aid. In a similar way, Bueno de Mesquita and Smith ask whether foreign aid is "good for policy, or just good politics."[16] Using the example of Kenya, they suggest that "everyone should specialize in what they are relatively good at and then trade their goods and services": Kenya by exporting flowers to the North, Europe by exporting pharmaceuticals, machinery, and computer software (e.g. to Kenya).[17] This approach, however, requires the developed countries to open their borders for goods from the global South.

Obviously, no one will oppose the limited form of immediate hunger relief necessary to overcome an acute crisis and to prevent a population from starving. The challenge is rather how to prevent the next such crisis.[18] And yet even such immediate relief operations can go seriously wrong. The Oil-for-Food Programme of the UN in Iraq testifies to this risk.

15. Moyo 2009.

16. Bueno de Mesquita and Smith 2011, 181.

17. Bueno de Mesquita and Smith 2011, 184 et seq.

18. Moyo 2009, 144 et seq.

6. OIL-FOR-FOOD

a. The Official Programme

The Oil-for-Food Programme of the UN in Iraq is one of the most dramatic examples of a relief program that went seriously wrong: in the aftermath of the Gulf War in 1990 the UN Security Council declared its up to then most rigorous trade embargo ever.[19] Its consequences were severe, especially for the population of Iraq at large who were used as hostages by Saddam Hussein and his regime: malnutrition became general, child mortality skyrocketed nearly immediately. It soon became obvious that the world community would not be able to maintain the embargo much longer. Therefore, talks began in order to explore if the arms embargo could be maintained whilst allowing for a supervised regime of humanitarian relief goods to be brought into the country in exchange for the controlled sale of Iraqi oil. A complex mechanism involving the supervised sale of oil and acquisition of humanitarian goods was to be put in place. A fiduciary bank and two inspection companies were hired. The Programme was organized by a newly created unit in the UN Secretariat in cooperation with a working party of the Security Council (the 661 Committee, named after Security Council Resolution 661) and the relevant ministries of Iraq. Between 1996 and 2003 the Programme sold oil for $64.2 billion and acquired humanitarian goods for the sum of $37 billion. Thirty percent of the value of Iraq's oil exports went into a compensation fund for the damages caused to Kuwait in the course of the Gulf War.[20] That is, in short, the description of the official side of the Programme.

b. Planned Distribution of Oil Proceeds

Figure 16.1 below shows the planned modus operandi as envisioned by the UN.[21]

c. What Went Wrong?

The Iraq of Saddam Hussein managed to circumvent the embargo, basically using two avenues: on the one hand by smuggling and on the other hand by

19. Security Council Resolution 661 (6 August 1990, UN Doc. S/RES/661).

20. Volcker, Goldstone and Pieth 2005b, 15, 44; 2005c, 252.

21. Volcker, Goldstone, and Pieth 2005b, 13.

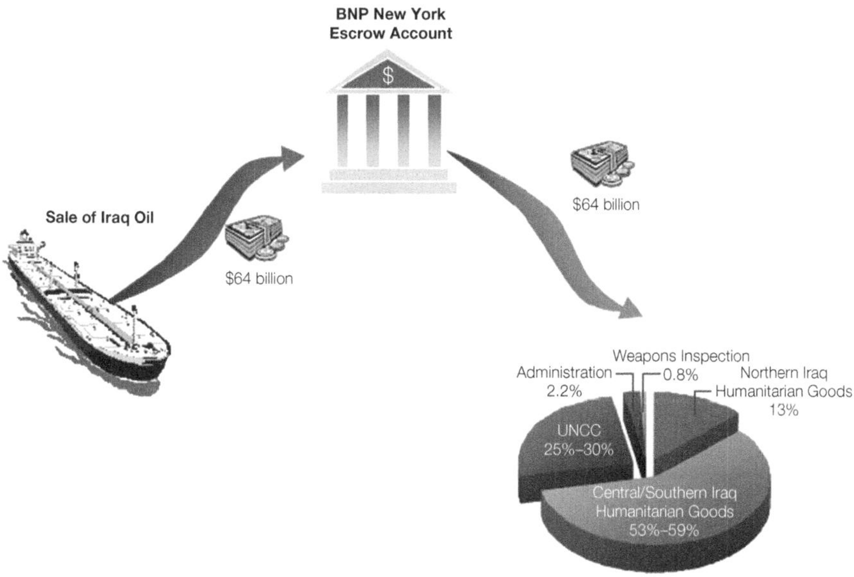

Figure 16.1 Planned Distribution of Oil Proceeds—BNP New York Escrow Account.
SOURCE: Volcker, Goldstone, and Pieth 2005b, 13.

manipulating the Oil-for-Food Programme of the UN. During the embargo, oil continued to leave Iraq unofficially and outside the Programme by pipelines and trucks. Iraq also kept acquiring arms. Estimates give figures close to $10.2 billion, generated with the means of smuggling.

For humanitarian relief experts it is, however, more relevant to study the manipulation of the Oil-for-Food Programme itself. For all the safeguards put in place, the administration of Saddam Hussein managed to illegally extract $229 million from oil sales and $1.59 billion by adding "after sales service fees" and "inland transportation fees" to the official and accepted prices. Overall, over two thousand companies were found to have paid so-called "surcharges" to Iraq beyond the official price. In many cases they actually agreed to these payments in written "side-letters," many of which have been found in the aftermath of the Saddam Hussein era.

d. Oil Surcharges—Flow of Funds

Figure 16.2 below depicts the flow of the surcharges from the oil buyers to the Iraqi regime.[22]

22. Volcker, Goldstone, and Pieth 2005b, 34.

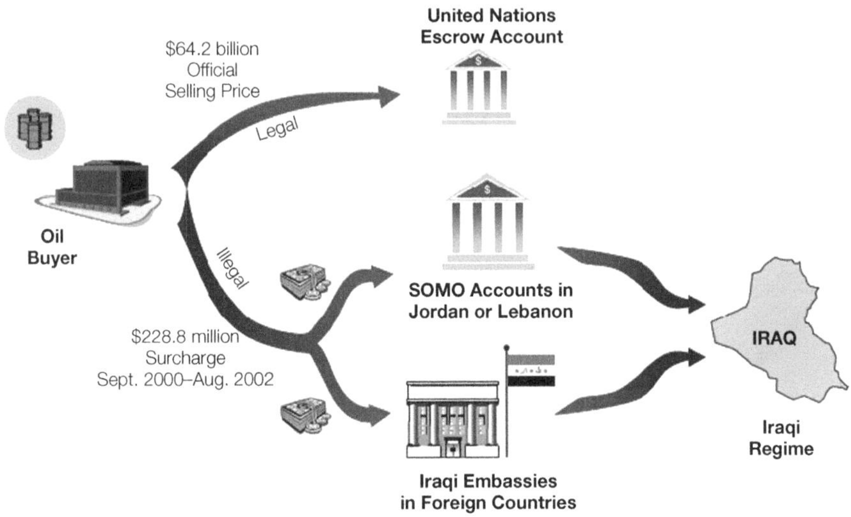

Figure 16.2 Oil Surcharges Flow of Funds—United Nations Escrow Account.
SOURCE: Volcker, Goldstone, and Pieth 2005b, 34.

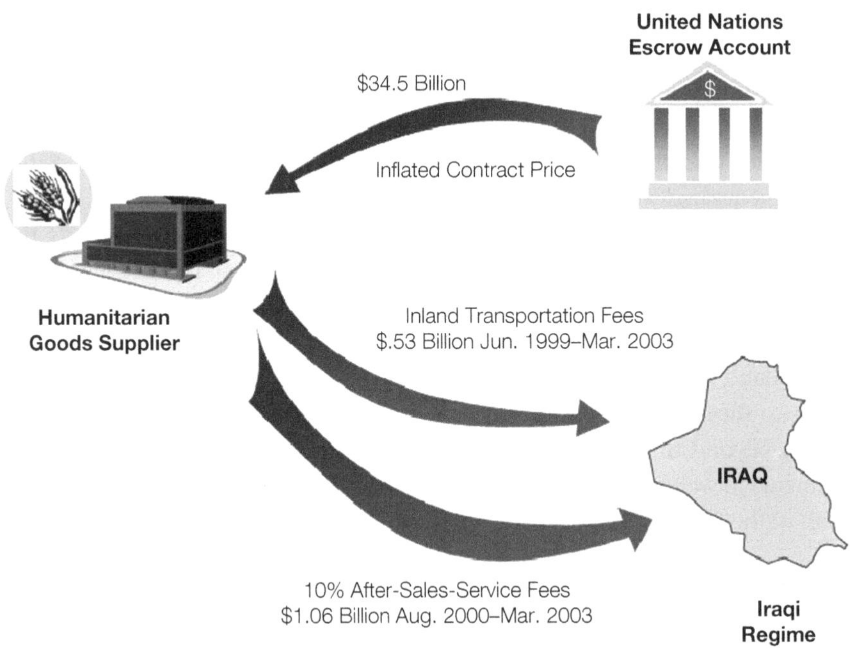

Figure 16.3 Humanitarian Contract Kickbacks—Flow of Funds—United Nations Escrow Account.
SOURCE: Volcker, Goldstone, and Pieth 2005b, 37.

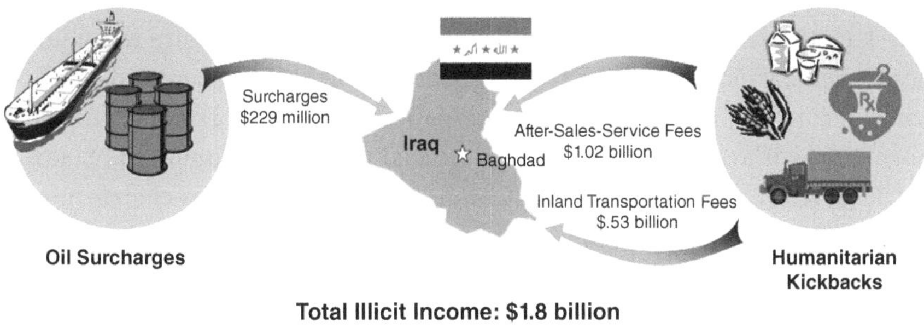

Figure 16.4 Illicit Income Received by Iraq under the Programme—Total Illicit Income: $1.8 billion.
SOURCE: Volcker, Goldstone, and Pieth 2005c, 1.

e. Humanitarian Contract Kickbacks—Flow of Funds

Figure 16.3 below shows the flow of kickbacks from humanitarian contracts to the Iraqi regime.[23]

f. Illicit Income Received by Iraq under the Programme

Figure 16.4 depicts an overview over the illicit income the Iraqi regime generated under the Oil-for-Food Programme[24]

"THE INDEPENDENT INQUIRY COMMITTEE—THE STORY"

From 2003 on, media and especially neoconservatives in the United States were mounting a campaign against the UN and the UN secretary-general Kofi Annan in particular. They felt entitled to this campaign since Kofi Annan had criticized the intervention in Iraq to depose of Saddam Hussein without the backing of the UN Security Council. The neoconservatives called the Oil-for-Food Programme—echoing Saddam's rhetoric—the "mother of corruption scandals." In order to defend the reputation of the UN and his personal integrity Kofi Annan called an independent inquiry into the Oil-for-Food Programme (the Independent Inquiry Committee (IIC)). A group of three commissioners lead by Paul Volcker, with Richard Goldstone and

23. Volcker, Goldstone, and Pieth 2005b, 37.

24. Volcker, Goldstone, and Pieth 2005c, 1.

Mark Pieth as members, was charged with the inquiry. The choice was politically well balanced: an American chairman of high stature and independence, a former prosecutor of the International Criminal Tribunal for the former Yugoslavia, who had played a crucial role in developing the South African Truth and Reconciliation Commission, and the Swiss chairman of the OECD Working Group on Bribery.

Obviously, Paul Volcker had done his due diligence on his colleagues, in my case with the secretary general of the OECD. Nevertheless, he was distrustful of the UN General Secretariat: had they introduced a defense attorney into his Committee? He called me one evening, before I had been officially approached by the UN, when I was having dinner in a restaurant with friends. Stepping out onto the road I heard him ask in his typical straightforward way: "Who the hell are you? Are you there to defend the Russians and the French?" It was the best possible introduction to a person with whom I should develop an intense working relationship carried by mutual respect over the next two years. Paul Volcker was the perfect choice as chair of the IIC with his standing in the United States and abroad, his access to a wide network of key players, and his independence.

Methodology and Challenges

Paul Volcker wisely asked for a Security Council Resolution early in our work to give us the necessary backing of the institution itself. We hired over seventy investigators who conducted extensive documentary analyses and interviews of witnesses within and outside the UN over a period of roughly two years. The report is made up of an extensive Final Report and three interim reports, thousands of pages in all.

The inquiry encountered several challenges: it had access to the UN documents; however when starting its work, it had to stop UN officials from shredding evidence. Furthermore, initially, the General Secretariat felt uneasy about investigators intending to image all the computer hard discs of the most senior staff of the organization. A compromise solution was found with the then-legal counsel, Professor Nicholas Michel: the sensitive material was read simultaneously by a member of the IIC and the legal team of the UN.

A major challenge was to trace the money flows into Iraq. Usually this requires tedious mutual legal assistance procedures with a plethora of appeal possibilities, sometimes taking years—time that the UN simply did not have. Paul Volcker obtained access to the Federal Reserve's dollar clearing data, online five years back: this is an investigatory means no law enforcement agency in the world has at its disposal. It makes "fishing expeditions" totally unnecessary. You know who has received which sum of money on which account from which account. Obviously, you don't know the background story, the reasons for the transaction, nor do you know the "beneficial owners," the persons behind the transaction. Therefore, we needed to persuade financial centers (with the help of the UN Resolution) to cooperate and let us have access to the relevant account files.

In a rather unusual approach to international cooperation we opened political channels first. A team made up of the former US assistant secretary of state Richard Murphy (who had a widespread network of acquaintances in the Middle East due to his earlier postings as ambassador), Gabriele Lechenauer, and myself visited Lebanon, Syria, and Jordan. The goal was to speak to the heads of state (in the case of Lebanon president Hariri), the ministers of finance, the heads of the Central Bank, of the Financial Intelligence Units, and of key commercial banks. Following up on this visit our investigators went to the countries in question with their data relating to concrete transactions and accounts. We obtained the necessary cooperation for all these states in a time frame of merely two months. In a similar way, we also obtained information about beneficial owners from Liechtenstein, data not contained in the company register (*Öffentlichkeitsregister*), and bank data from Monaco. In Switzerland, we hired specialized staff to collect hundreds of bank accounts and to conduct a daily exchange with the responsible officials on the one hand (Switzerland contributed information on roughly eight hundred bank accounts to the investigation) and the UN on the other hand.

Generally, countries, including Russia and France, were very cooperative and gave investigators access to correspondence and files in their foreign ministries. Only in a few cases was "soft pressure" necessary. Whereas it was Paul Volckers's job to calm down the excited Australian government (the Australian Wheat Board was found to have paid over $230 million of illegal surcharges to Saddam Hussein's government),[25] my role was to suggest to financial centers to rapidly cooperate and to prevent public exposure.

Switzerland intervened after the first interviews on Swiss territory, as the government maintained this amounted to an official inquiry on Swiss territory on behalf of a foreign entity (criminalized by Article 271 Criminal Code). However, Federal Councilor Deiss (minister of foreign affairs)

25. Meyer and Califano 2006, 117 et seq., 120 et seq.

rapidly agreed to grant a general authorization to the IIC, as long as the IIC allowed domestic officials to participate in those hearings.

One of the major challenges was to obtain the documents in Iraq. The relevant ministries (especially the minister of Oil) were seriously damaged by bombing; furthermore they were outside the so-called "green zone" in the dangerous parts of Bagdad. Our staff, led by Mary Schreiber of Deloitte, had to use military protection to collect the so-called "side letters" (written promises of companies to make illegal payments to the regime of Saddam Hussein in order to obtain contracts).

Findings

The overall finding was that the Programme was influenced by politics from the outset, that the oversight structures in the UN were insufficient, that some individuals enriched themselves, and that the private sector was more than happy to make illegal payments in order to obtain contracts (be it in the acquisition of oil or in the sale of humanitarian goods).[26]

Clearly, it went beyond the means of an international organization to feed an entire country for several years and to prevent graft against a government intent on generating additional funds in order to buy arms. Under these circumstances it was certainly a fundamental mistake to allow the administration of Iraq to continue to choose its contracting partners.

The Iraqi officials managed to bribe key UN officials, including a Security Council chairman. They made buyers of oil and contracting partners in humanitarian goods contribute illegal "surcharges" (typically 10 percent of the contract value).

It must be added, though, that also key Security Council Member Countries participated in bid rigging when it came to support their national inspection companies or banks in the initial contest to obtain jobs. Other countries struck hopeful bidders off the list for political reasons.

Overall, it turned out that political motivation frequently trumped sound governance.

The IIC presented its findings in several reports.[27] Orally it presented them to the Secretary-General, to the Security Council, and to the General Assembly of the UN as well as to the media. However, the UN has so far been reluctant to act upon the major Recommendations made in its direction in the Final Report. The diplomats listened politely and then went back to "business as usual." It is uncertain if the lessons have been learned: an

26. Meyer and Califano 2006, 106 et seq.

27. Volcker, Goldstone, and Pieth 2005d, 2005e, 2005f, 2005a.

analysis of the aid operations after the tsunami in South Eastern Asia or the earthquake in Haiti would tell.

Since the publication of the report by the IIC in 2005 some domestic law enforcement agencies have picked up cases and have reached convictions, especially in the United States and in Switzerland. More recently, the French judiciary has, however, freed all the companies of the accusation of corruption;[28] the trials on embargo violation have been neglected due to the short statute of limitation.

7. THE CONTRIBUTION OF THE IFIS

Over the last years, the international debate on aid effectiveness has picked up momentum. Faced with substantial losses through mismanagement and theft, the World Bank in particular has intensified its work on *"Governance and Anti-Corruption."* A new generation of *"GAC policies"* has been developed.[29] At the same time the sanctions systems of the IFIs have been further upgraded, especially through an agreement to accord each other's sanctions against companies and managers mutual recognition through a system of cross-debarment.[30] The IFIs have all given themselves investigative institutions and typically two-tier sanctions boards. In cases of fraud (especially misrepresentation of past experience in infrastructure projects), corruption, coercive, collusive, or obstructive practices,[31] the sanction boards dispose of several sanctions (reprimand, conditional non-debarment, debarment, debarment with conditional release, restitution, or remedy[32]). Whereas the sanctions boards express the sanctions at the end of an extensive process, ensuring a fair hearing,[33] the institutions are

28. Le Monde, June 18, 2015; The FCPA Blog, June 19, 2015: "French Court clears Renault Trucks and others in oil for food case."

29. Kunicová 2013, 44 et seq.

30. Agreement for Mutual Enforcement of Debarment Decisions, 9 April 2010 (African Development Bank, AfDB; Asian Development Bank, ADB; European Bank of Reconstruction and Development, EBRD; Inter-American Development Bank, IADB; World Bank, WB), cf. below 214.

31. See World Bank Sanctions Procedures 2012, Appendix 1; cf. below 214.

32. See World Bank Sanctions Procedures 2012, Article IX, Section 9.01. and World Bank Sanctioning Guidelines 2011; cf. below 214.

33. World Bank Sanctions Procedures 2012, Article VI, Section 6.01. et seq.; cf. below 214.

also able to close cases by means of settlement. These tools are used increasingly and are typically leading to financial sanctions.[34]

Supporting INT: the Independent Advisory Board of the World Bank

The former World Bank president Paul Wolfowitz had an open ear for the neoconservative approach to foreign aid: it was basically considered a waste of money, and the conservative press in the United States, especially the *Wall Street Journal*, demanded sanctions for badly governed states (the code word was "conditionality"). It was part of his policy to toughen up the integrity department of the Bank, when he nominated Suzanne Folsom to head INT. Suzanne Folsom had some experience as a prosecutor in the Southern District of New York, but she was essentially the wife of a firm supporter and fundraiser of George W. Bush. During her term of office, INT took on some large systemic investigations, such as the "India Detailed Implementation Review,"[35] an attempt to give a full picture of waste and graft in India's health service. The report was—in marked deviation from established practice and rules—leaked to the media before it had been shown to the country and to the operational bank staff. This led to an immediate breakdown of relations between India and the World Bank. It also had serious consequences within the Bank: distrust between Bank staff and INT culminated to an extent that relations are still not totally mended ten years after. Rumors said that Ms. Folsom needed to be guarded within the Bank.

At any rate Suzanne Folsom left the Bank with Paul Wolfowitz (in order to take a position as the legal counsel of the company formerly called Blackwater, now Academi). The successor to Paul Wolfowitz, Bob Zoellick, asked Paul Volcker to give an opinion on how to reorganize INT. Volcker came up with a comprehensive report, amongst other recommendations asking for an independent supervisory (or advisory) committee (the IAB) to be created to oversee INT's work, but also to protect INT from the operational part of the Bank. At the same time INT was elevated to a vice-presidency.[36] A new head for INT was elected in the person of Leonard McCarthy, the former head of the South African "Scorpions," a police unit created to combat organized crime.

34. World Bank Sanctions Procedures 2012, Article XI, Section 11.01. et seq.; cf. below 215.

35. World Bank 2007.

36. World Bank Panel Review 2007, 3 et seq.

The IAB—made up of Peter Costello, a former governor of the World Bank and longtime treasurer of Australia; Chester Crocker, a former US assistant secretary of state for Africa; Simeon Marcello, a former ombudsman of the Philippines; and myself—was to report to the president of the Bank and the Audit Board. It spent an intensive six years interviewing Bank staff, visiting locations where Bank loans and grants had been misappropriated or wasted, or where they had been the object of corruption. It also commented on the sanctions reform of the Bank and the overall performance of INT. Its annual reports are public.[37] Unluckily, the new World Bank president has not renewed this essential outside sounding board after the end of our tenure.

Overall, the major challenges are not resolved: aid effectiveness remains an uncertainty. Bilateral and multilateral donors maintain that they have a major contribution to make to alleviate poverty and yet the concepts to prevent corruption are not fully satisfactory. As the example of the "Padma Multipurpose Bridge" in Bangladesh has shown,[38] it is rare that the MDBs muster the courage to step in and foreclose a loan. And interestingly, even the poorest of countries can now find alternative funding sources—sometimes, however, at the price of even greater political dependency (as the example of the new Development Bank sponsored by China demonstrates).

37. Cf. http://www.transparency.org/whatwedo/publications/doc/ar/.

38. See above 146 et seq.

PART FOUR

Criminal Law and other Forms of Regulation

This Part highlights responses available to discourage or punish perpetrators who engage in corruption. Starting with a discussion of the up- and downsides of criminal law responses, this Part also looks at administrative and preventive measures.

17

Strengths and Limitations of Criminal Law

MARK PIETH ■

1. IS CRIMINAL LAW REALLY THAT ESSENTIAL TO COMBATING BRIBERY?

The immediate reaction to news about a corruption scandal is the call for the prosecutor. Some authors criticize that criminal law misses the systemic nature of corruption; others prefer prevention to prosecution. Nevertheless, there can be no question that prosecution of bribery is necessary. Various experiences with self-governed bodies have demonstrated that without the legal risk of prosecution self-regulation rarely works: the inquiry into the Oil-for-Food Programme of the UN in Iraq has shown that the UN lacked the necessary oversight.[1] Likewise—even in a far more dramatic way—recent revelations about sports governing bodies, in particular the mismanagement of the International Federation of Association Football (FIFA), have shown how problematic institutions are that believe themselves above the law.[2] Probably the Vatican would be another illustration of such a body undeterred by legal constraints. On the other hand, the recent increase of the prosecution of managers and corporations in the private sector has demonstrated effectiveness of criminal law in turn motivating sound preventive concepts (compliance programs).

Criminal law, however, is a corner stone of sovereignty of traditional nation-states. To harmonize criminal law internationally is therefore a formidable

1. See above 186 et seq.

2. See above 167 et seq.

Confronting Corruption. Fritz Heimann and Mark Pieth.

task. In an ideal world one might wish to create a supranational Court to deal with large-scale corruption. This suggestion will be discussed below (211 et seq.). Currently, harmonization uses more modest means: international organizations act as facilitators helping states agree on a common standard. As pointed out (18, 59), the OECD's motive for criminalization is to create a level playing field among international commercial competitors. The UN, in turn, attempts a broader harmonization, allowing more general international cooperation among states. Both international instruments, however, rely on national implementation and application. In order to enforce the common standards various monitoring mechanisms have emerged. "Peer review" ensures that countries apply the rules they have signed up to. As these mechanisms rely on merely politically binding "recommendations," the harmonization process is rather slow.[3]

Harmonizing criminal law faces a number of challenges, be it in the translation of the standards into national law (so-called substantive law) as well as its application (criminal procedure).

Criminal law in general deals with public and private (commercial) corruption. Although both forms of corruption are expressions of abuse of power, the rationales of the offenses diverge: the law on public corruption defends unbiased decision-making by officials and—in a wider sense—the trust in public institutions (ultimately democracy and the rule of law). Commercial corruption is much closer to other attacks on private property; in a wider sense it is a kind of fraud or breach of trust, depending on whether one sees it from the vantage point of the briber or the bribee.

International instruments, if they address commercial corruption, are typically discretionary, whereas public corruption is at the core of mandatory international law against corruption.

2. WHO IS A "FOREIGN PUBLIC OFFICIAL"?

Both according to the UN and the OECD Conventions, bribery of a foreign public official is a criminal offense. However, the concepts diverge. Whereas the UN simply refers to the definition of the state in question, the OECD insists on a so-called "autonomous definition."[4] All this seems like legalese. However, the difference is fundamental. So, for instance, according to the OECD, state-owned

3. Cf. above UN 115, OECD 84.

4. Zerbes 2014, 74 et seq.

companies and their representatives (so-called "instrumentalities") are considered "functional" officials.[5] Although this is accepted in principle, there have been some serious struggles over possible exceptions.

The OECD, following the Foreign Corrupt Practices Act, contains a seemingly marginal exception for "parastatals" that are not in any way privileged over private companies. The typical example is the French car manufacturer who had collaborated with the Nazis during World War II and was as a consequence nationalized after the war. It has remained a purely fiscal public asset. But it does not enjoy any preferential treatment, for instance in providing police cars, and it does not receive subsidiaries.[6]

Enel Power

Nevertheless, the German Supreme Court, when discussing Siemens bribing representatives of the Italian power companies Enel Power and Enel Produzione, claimed that the companies were only 70 percent state-owned and were in competition with private power providers. In stark contrast to an Italian decision[7] they were not considered state-owned companies for the purposes of German anticorruption laws.[8] The German Court ruling, however, missed out on the fact that Enel Power and Enel Produzione were subject to public procurement rules. The decision was therefore to be considered highly unsatisfactory.[9]

O'Shea

In *United States v. John Joseph O'Shea*, the US District Court for the Southern District of Texas used Para. 15 of the OECD Commentaries 1997[10] to develop a carveout for the general manager of ABB: he authorized payments

5. Zerbes 2014, 80 et seq.

6. Para. 15 of the OECD Commentaries 1997 reads: "An official of a public enterprise shall be deemed to perform a public function unless the enterprise operates on a normal commercial basis in the relevant market *i.e.*, on a bases which is substantially equivalent to that of a private enterprise, without preferential subsidiaries or other privileges."

7. OECD WGB 2011, Italy Phase 3, 9 (para. 14).

8. Federal Court of Justice of Germany, Decision No. 2 StR 587/07, 29 August 2008.

9. Zerbes 2014, 83 et seq.

10. See above footnote 7.

to officials of the Mexican *Comisión Federal de Electricidad* (CFE) in return for profitable deals. The CFE is owned by the Mexican state, it acts under the control of the respective ministry, and its director is appointed by the Mexican president. By constitution and by law it enjoys the exclusive competence "to generate, conduct, transform, distribute, provide electric power with the purpose of providing a public service".[11] Nevertheless, the Court did not recognize the public function of its employees. Again, it is the view of experts that the exception has been overstretched.[12]

3. WHAT ABOUT THE PERPETUAL "FACILITATION PAYMENTS"?

Anybody doing business in developing countries is familiar with those small payments they are asked to make for virtually any administrative step. The individual payment may be a nuisance but accumulated, the payments become a real problem: imagine that you have to pay a so-called "finders-fee" for every container arriving at a port, usually immediately "lost" upon arrival in the pile of other containers. If you—as a logistics company—pay $50 once, one might be tempted to adopt a rather fatalistic view. If you pay a 1,000 times $50 to the same few people in one year, it is a real issue, and both from the perspective of the victim country and your home country it will be considered as a bribe or bribes of $50,000!

Although facilitation payments are generally recognized as a serious issue for local and foreign business alike, they are far more of a problem for the local population. Taken together, all these small payments needed to get through everyday life in a country drowning in systemic bribery amounts to a hefty and inefficient tax on the average household budget. Mexican sources have priced accumulated facilitation payments paid by an average family at 20 percent of the family income.

Now, legally there is no question that paying and taking of facilitation payments are offenses in the country where they are made. But so far, the host countries of exporters have been rather reticent to get involved. The US Foreign Corrupt Practices Act even contains an exception for "routine government

11. Mexican Electric Power Public Utility Service Law, Article 1.

12. Zerbes 2014, 84 on *United States v. John Joseph O'Shea*, no. 4:09-cr-629 (S.D. Tex. 2009), indictment of November 16, 2009.

action."[13] In real life, however, companies making recurring payments risk law enforcement summing up these repetitive small payments to the same officials. Other countries, such as the United Kingdom,[14] have taken the step to criminalize facilitation payments outright even if not every case will actually be prosecuted. A guideline gives the details on prosecution policy.[15]

Nongovernmental organizations (NGOs), such as Transparency International[16] as well as the OECD,[17] have been pushing industry to phase out facilitation payments. The United Nations Convention against Corruption (UNCAC) leaves no doubt that they are considered illegal bribes. The private sector has reacted rather insecurely: companies feel under pressure. Some, especially those domiciled in the United States, have adopted a zero tolerance approach to corruption. Typically, companies in the logistics industry adopt the attitude that facilitation payments are not made as they are forbidden by company policy. The risk of a simple zero tolerance approach is that third parties are hired to do the "dirty work." Therefore, some of their foreign competitors have adopted a markedly different stance: accepting that such payments cannot be rooted out immediately, they want at least to be informed about the scale. Obviously, this is a delicate approach in the face of law enforcement threats; however, it allows organizations to set targets toward phasing out such payments in specific countries (such as lowering them at the rate of 30 percent next year with the help of publishing one's policy).

A more creative approach has been developed by the logistics industry in the context of a recent *"collective action."* With the Basel Institute on Governance, the World Customs Organization, and the World Economic Forum (Partnering Against Corruption Initiative (PACI)) as facilitators, the companies suggested to the government of Vietnam to act as a pilot. The companies would supply Vietnam with an electronic customs clearance system allowing it to speed up and simplify procedures drastically and at the same time to reduce the risk of solicitation for bribes.[18] Like many such initiatives, this approach is time-consuming and still under development.

13. FCPA 1988; Urofsky and Moon 2014, 703.

14. UK Bribery Act 2010, cf. Raphael 2010, 71 et seq.

15. UK Joint Prosecution Guidance 2011.

16. TI Business Principles 2009, Section 5.5.

17. OECD Rec. 2009, Section VI.

18. Pieth 2012, 17.

4. INDIVIDUALS VERSUS CORPORATE LIABILITY

An intense discussion evolved both in the United States and in Europe on whether it would be preferable to punish corporations or individuals. In the United States—in the wake of astronomical monetary sanctions—there is a current move back to include sanctioning of managers. In some prominent cases, top managers have recently been sent to prison (such as Albert Jackson Stanley, former chief executive officer (CEO) of Kellogg, Brown and Root's, for thirty months[19]).

In a recent move the US Department of Justice (DOJ) has stepped up prosecution of managers on top of holding corporations responsible: the so-called "Yates Memo"[20] forces corporations to hand over responsible individuals if they want to benefit from the sentencing rebate for cooperative companies!

In Europe and also in Latin America the discussion has taken a different turn, in particular because corporate liability is a recent addition to criminal law. The goal of international treaties is to assure that all countries in the world are able to (be it criminally or quasi-criminally[21]) sanction corporations for corruption.

The main issue outside the United States concerning corporate liability is to ensure that not merely the willful wrongdoing by most senior staff triggers liability. The United Kingdom and other common law nations had to be motivated to broaden what they called an "identification model" applicable only to the senior management (the "brain" of the company as opposed to the "limbs") engaged with responsibility. Whereas according to the US approach, the company is responsible for bribery by any employee or agent (in legalese: "respondeat superior" or "vicarious liability"). The worldwide compromise struck in the OECD asks all industrialized nations to ensure that as a minimum, the lack of adequate supervision or deficient compliance programs trigger corporate responsibility when employees or agents resort to bribery. The focus is on systematic failure, on the lack of leadership.

RE: ARTICLE 2 OF THE OECD ANTI-BRIBERY CONVENTION: RESPONSIBILITY OF LEGAL PERSONS[22]

1) Member countries' systems for the liability of legal persons for the bribery of foreign public officials in international business

19. According to DOJ, February 23, 2012.

20. DOJ, September 9, 2015.

21. Both the UNCAC 2003 and the OECD Convention 1997 allow countries the choice between criminal and quasi-criminal approaches.

22. OECD Rec. 2009, Annex I B; cf. also UK Bribery Act 2010, Section 7.

transactions should not restrict the liability to cases where the natural person or persons who perpetrated the offence are prosecuted or convicted.

2) Member countries' systems for the liability of legal persons for the bribery of foreign public officials in international business transactions should take one of the following approaches:
   a) The level of authority of the person whose conduct triggers the liability of the legal person is flexible and reflects the wide variety of decision-making systems in legal persons; or
   b) The approach is functionally equivalent to the foregoing even though it is only triggered by acts of persons with the highest level managerial authority, because the following cases are covered:
      - A person with the highest level managerial authority offers, promises or gives a bribe to a foreign public official;
      - A person with the highest level managerial authority directs or authorizes a lower level person to offer, promise or give a bribe to a foreign public official; and
      - A person with the highest level managerial authority fails to prevent a lower level person from bribing a foreign public official, including through a failure to supervise him or her or through a failure to implement adequate internal controls, ethics and compliance programs or measures.

5. WATCH YOUR AGENTS!

If we are looking at statistics on corporate corruption around 70 percent of large-scale foreign bribery cases have involved intermediaries, agents, third parties—you name them.[23] Now, industry claims that there are many legitimate uses of agents, and in some cases even national law supposedly requires the use of a "sponsor" (typically a member of the local royal family).[24] Why are agents such a risk factor? There are two main reasons: on the one hand, the company may simply be tempted to farm out its dirty business and deliberately engage an agent for such purposes. Into this box fall also those cases where companies simply hope that the agent will "sort out the problems."

23. OECD Foreign Bribery Report 2014, 8, 29 (chart 16).

24. Davies 2008, 53 et seq.

When Fraport teamed up with a local company to build an airport terminal in Manila (Philippines), it needed to secure its loans. The creditors, however, asked for over seventy conditions in an already difficult project to be met before agreeing to the payments. Amongst these conditions were several discretionary decisions by government agencies and ministers. In order to secure these signatures in a matter of days and weeks, Fraport and its local partner used a retired pharmaceutical salesman with no experience in the infrastructure industry, but with personal acquaintances in high places. Based on a success fee he earned millions in a matter of days for securing signatures for discretionary decisions. These and many more red flags should have pointed toward the risks of bribery, if the employers were not altogether factoring bribery into their calculation.[25]

According to a second eventuality, the principal does not want to bribe, maybe he even asks the agent to sign a no-bribery pledge and reserves specific audit rights on the agent's company. Nevertheless, the agent resorts to bribery without the principal knowledge.

This was the claim of Glencore when its agents, dealing with the regime of Saddam Hussein in the Oil-for-Food Programme, provided 10 percent of specific oil contracts as "surcharges" to Iraq (especially via physical payment to the Geneva embassy of Iraq). Glencore had made its intermediaries sign a no-bribery covenant.[26]

Rightly law enforcement practice and official guidance[27] require corporations to apply due diligence in the selection, instruction, and supervision of their third parties. Deficiencies may trigger corporate liability.[28]

25. Fraport AG Frankfurt Airport Services Worldwide v. Republic of the Philippines (ICSID Case No. ARB/11/12); Betz 2017, 119 et seq.

26. Volcker, Goldstone, and Pieth 2005c, 143 f.

27. OECD Rec. 2009, Annex II, para. 6; Pieth 2011.

28. Pieth and Ivory 2011.

For purposes of preventing abuse, but also as indicators of bribery through third parties, a series of so called "red flags" has been developed. Most lists cover similar items. One comprehensive list is reproduced here:

- the company acting as agent neither has its seat in the country in which it provides its service, nor does it carry out any other business in this country;
- the agent company demands payment of its commission before it has concluded the contract in question;
- the accounts or bills for services rendered fail to specify in any detail either the content of the negotiations done or when they were carried out; instead they refer only in a general way to "services" and "expenses";
- the key factor is whether the commission fee demanded is a reasonable one, i.e. one which is proportionate to the job in question; the expenses claim should also be related to actual expenses incurred: an exorbitant commission or expenses claim will be a clear indicator of corrupt practices;
- the agent company demands payment via a third party or in a different country than the one in which it is situated;
- the agent company offers its services without being approached by the principal and does so shortly before conclusion of a contract or after unsuccessful negotiations by the principal;
- the agent company emphasizes that it alone can secure the conclusion of the contract, because only it knows the right people;
- the company structure and financial organization of the agent company is lacking in transparency; it appears to have hardly any staff;
- the agents are not bound to any particular codes of conduct;
- the competence of the agents working in the field is suspect;
- there are personal connections between the agents and the decision makers of the foreign state.[29]

6. THE PROOF IS IN THE PUDDING

As a consequence of the many anticorruption treaties, laws have been changed all over the world. However, they are applied very unevenly. In many cases anticorruption policies are subjected to political agendas: domestically, anticorruption

29. Zerbes 2014, 155.

agencies are used to restrain political opponents. Internationally, states are sometimes reluctant to bring cases against prominent companies. In particular concerning the defense industries, governments may find themselves in a conflict between fostering exports and applying the law.

Clean Nordics?

The Swedish company Saab found itself at a competitive disadvantage with its fighter plane "Gripen," as all competitors had large economic and political powers backing their products. It therefore went for fringe markets such as South Africa, Czech Republic, and Romania. Rapidly suspicion arose that Saab, like many of its competitors, was bribing politicians and officials in these countries to sell their products. We do not know if they are guilty. What we do know, however, is that the responsible senior Swedish prosecutor closed the cases and retired. At a press conference covered by Swedish state-owned television he gave a remarkable statement:

> "They have emphasized, that these inquiries are of course damaging to Swedish business," says van der Kwast.
> Q: "But who is it who says that?"
> "I don't want to go into that. I don't want to say more than that. But from my position, from the policeman's position, it is understood as a sort of indirect hint to take it carefully."
> Q: "Has it affected your decision to drop the inquiry?"
> "Not for a second."[30]

This example, like many others, demonstrates that even countries with a good reputation on corruption are reluctant to take key corporations to court when fundamental interests are at stake. A similar example involving the United Kingdom has already been discussed above;[31] another such example is the unconvincing way Finnish courts dealt with the defense corporation Patria.[32] The Austrian lack of enthusiasm when dealing with Steyr Daimler Puch has already been mentioned.[33]

30. SVT, Sverige Television AB, Uppdrag Granskning (Assignment: Investigate), Manuscript, The Final Battle (of the Grippenaffair), 10 June 2009.

31. See above 88, 97.

32. Yle Uutiset, June 30, 2015: "Appeals court rejects Patria's Slovenia bribery charges."

33. See above 34 et seq.

7. ARE PROSECUTORS AND COURTS OUT OF THEIR DEPTHS?

It is not unusual in international corruption investigations that one country comes to the conclusion that a bribe has been paid and the courts of another country come up with conflicting decisions. In several cases, however, courts of the victim country have—frequently battling considerable political pressure—come up with decisions against prominent political figures. A case in kind is the sanctioning of the vice minister of Interior of Thailand to an eleven-year prison sentence for receiving bribes from Steyr Daimler Puch.[34] Another such case is the conviction of the former prime minister of Slovenia in the Patria case.[35] In the Steyr Daimler Puch case the Vienna prosecutor did not even bother to look into the case;[36] in the Patria case Finland's first instance court due to lack of evidence liberated the company from suspicion of bribery. Do Finland and Austria follow a higher standard of proof? Do they apply a greater respect of the rule of law? It is more likely that the lack of aggressiveness by law enforcement in many industrialized states has political reasons. They are unwilling because a proactive approach is likely to harm their careers.

Prosecutors as well as defendants may be tempted to end long-drawn-out legal battles by settling early in the investigative phase. US prosecutors have an additional advantage. As cooperation is considered a key mitigating factor in sentencing of corporations,[37] companies most always resort to internal investigation[38] and frequently agree to hand over the work product to the prosecution in view of a favorable outcome of settlement negotiations. If at all possible, both US and German judges resort to Non-Prosecution Agreements (NPAs) or Deferred Prosecution Agreements (DPAs[39]) (in German, *Einstellung unter Auflage*)[40], thereby preventing additional administrative consequences (such as debarment). Only in more blatant cases would a guilty plea be necessary.

34. Bangkok Post, September 12, 2013: "Amlo mulls seizing Pracha assets."

35. However, after a successful appeal Prime Minister Jansa was released after spending only six months in prison. A retrial didn't take place because the charges had expired; cf. Reuters, September 7, 2015: "Slovenian bribery trial against ex-PM Jansa expires."

36. Stellungnahme Zentrale Staatsanwaltschaft zur Verfolgung von Wirtschaftsstrafsachen und Korruption, Aktenzeichen 7 St 141/10t.

37. Nanda 2011, 71 et seq.

38. Zerbes 2013, 551 et seq.; Duggin 2003, 859 et seq.

39. Nanda 2011, 80 et seq.

40. § 153a StPO Germany.

Typically, in the United States, the sanction could be additionally mitigated if the defendant agrees to a compliance monitor or advisor.

Even though already the Council of Europe Recommendation in 1988[41] had suggested the use of compliance monitors, the European countries have been resisting the use of this form of "probation officer" for companies.

Increasingly, further jurisdictions are testing plea agreements and the like (Italy has long been experimenting with its *"patteggiamento"*;[42] the United Kingdom has moved toward plea agreements;[43] France is gradually tiptoeing toward *"le plaider-coupable"*;[44] Switzerland has integrated in its new criminal procedure a form of abbreviated procedure for such settled outcomes[45]). Big differences prevail, however. In particular the question of the publication of the facts remains largely unresolved.

If the general public has to put up with secret negotiations, it needs at least to be fully informed about the outcome. Transparency and judicial review are the bottom line if one is to accept that a large part of big cases are "solved" by settlements. This is the minimum left of the legacy of the era of enlightenment in criminal procedure.

The Compliance Monitor

What do you do as a compliance monitor?

As a compliance monitor, one is in a delicate position. On the one hand, one is remunerated by the company. On the other hand, one is working independently from the company; in fact, the monitor has very far-reaching powers, as an averse report can seriously imperil the situation of the corporation.

The monitor is there to supervise the creation of a credible compliance program and a compliance structure. Beyond a paper exercise one needs to establish whether the system is implemented throughout the company, including the sub-entities such as foreign subsidiaries and joint ventures.

41. CoE 1988: Recommendation No. R (88) 18 Concerning Liability of Enterprises having Legal Personality for Offenses Committed in the Exercise of their Activities, adopted by the Committee of Ministers on 20 October 1988.

42. OECD WGB 2004, Italy Phase 2 report, 48, 50, 53; Davigo and Mannozzi 2007, 117 et seq.

43. OECD WGB 2005, 43; cf. also speech delivered by Alun Milford to the Annual Employed Bar Conference, 26 March 2014 on "Corporate criminal liability and Deferred Prosecution Agreements."

44. Even if Garapon and Servan-Schreiber 2013 have written a flamboyant critique.

45. Pieth 2016b, 255 et seq., 269 et seq.

The assessment would be done both by anonymous electronic surveys amongst employees and targeted interviews with specific employees in delicate positions as well as random checks. So, for example, in a construction company active in difficult markets, so-called site managers would be asked about their dilemmas and about the support they are receiving from the subsidiary as well as the parent company.

Additionally, the monitor would at regular intervals discuss company policy with the senior management. In particular one needs to insist on pre-acquisition due diligence when companies are on an expansion course. However, the monitor should abstain from being drawn into operational decisions himself ("should we sell our company in Nigeria?").

Yearly or half-yearly the monitor would report both to the company and to the agency with whom the monitorship has been agreed (e.g., a multilateral development bank, a procurement agency, the US DOJ or the US Securities and Exchange Commission).[46]

8. DO WE NEED A SUPRANATIONAL CRIMINAL COURT FOR LARGE-SCALE CORRUPTION?

It has become fashionable to suggest creating a Supranational Court for so-called "grand corruption." The Austrian Minister of Interior, Mr. Platter, has suggested what observers at the European Forum Alpbach 2007 considered a visionary idea: a "World Penal Code" or a "supranational court system" dealing with transnational corruption cases.[47] Apart from the difficulty in distinguishing petty and grand corruption, the idea is very much a brain child of populist politicians. It sounds great, even if it is unlikely to be implemented: one is reminded of the International Criminal Court in The Hague (the ICC) called to deal with genocide and other most serious forms of collective criminality.[48] It will be noted that the largest powers of the world still abstain from participating in the ICC.[49] Furthermore, the ICC has proven far less than effective even in

46. Personal experience in several cases involving companies of the financial, logistics, and infrastructure sectors.

47. European Forum Alpbach, Political Dialogues, EPAC 2007.

48. Rome Statute of the International Criminal Court (Rome, 17 July 1998, UN Doc. A/CONF.183/9), Article 5 et seq.

49. E.g. the United States, Russia, and China!

the most problematic areas of the world. The indicted head of state of Northern Sudan, Al-Bashir, is still able to move freely at least in fellow African states.[50] The ICC lacks a police force and subpoena powers.

It is of course possible that the political dividing lines run differently on the issue of corruption, for example, that the United States could be tempted to support the idea.[51] It is, however, a fact that the United States is already—if unilaterally—acting as a kind of supranational prosecutor on transnational bribery. But maybe this would actually make things more difficult: a supranational court acting in the interest of industrialized states would certainly deepen the North-South divide.

The most fundamental argument against the idea of a supranational anticorruption court is, however, that it misses the major problem: corruption is at its worst systemic, made up of thousands of small, medium-sized, and big criminal activities, and that it permeates entire societies. It cannot be the job of a judge abroad to tidy up an entire society with an endemic corruption problem. Take for instance India: of course, India has a widespread corruption problem, but it would be ludicrous to imagine that somebody from outside could solve the issue, India has to deal with its domestic problem itself. Obviously, host states of corporations bribing Indian officials have to take their share of the responsibility. However, there is—as far as we see—no way around the tedious task of forcing nation-states to stick to their international commitments, to implement the international rules, and to apply them. If necessary, international bodies have to enforce the harmonized rules by publicly exposing deficiencies. In doing so, they will be helped by the civil society, NGOs and the media. This will take time, but it is inevitable. One might further consider toughening up the sanctions available to peers—for example, trade sanctions or monetary sanctions against a noncompliant Member State of Treaty.

50. Decision of the African Union No. 547 (Assembly/AU/Dec.547[XXIV]), Section 17 (b).

51. Wolf 2014.

18

Beyond Criminal Law

Administrative Sanctions and Preventive Measures

MARK PIETH ■

1. REGULATORY SANCTIONS

Whereas criminal law is thought to exert an indirect preventive effect through deterrence, states and multilateral development banks (MDBs) have developed a set of regulatory sanctions more directly aimed at the prevention of abuses by companies and individuals, and protecting the interests of their respective institutions. Domestic procurement rules as well as the regulations developed by MDBs (and signed by clients and bidders) foresee cancellation of loans in the face of concrete misbehavior. Domestic agencies would also be able to stay subsidies or export insurance. Furthermore, domestic agencies and MDBs have introduced detailed sanctions procedures allowing debarment of corporations and individuals from future participation in procurement or from eligibility for export insurance. Whereas US agencies each have their individual procedures (such as the US Army or the US Air Force, with their own sanctions officers[1]), in the European Union (EU) there is a unified approach.[2]

1. E.g. the administrative agreement between the US Army and the German construction company Bilfinger.

2. EU Directive 2014/24/EU of the European Parliament and of the Council (OJ L 94/65, February 26, 2014).

Confronting Corruption. Fritz Heimann and Mark Pieth.

2. DEBARMENT BY MDBS

The debarment procedures established by MDBs may be regarded as a worldwide example of such administrative sanctioning: the front runner is the World Bank. Its sanctions procedures of April 15, 2012 define "sanctionable behavior" and "sanctions" as well as detailed rules on procedure and evidence.[3] The procedure navigates between a purely administrative approach and a more judicial process. Currently, it finds itself somewhere between the extremes. The procedure guarantees a fair hearing to parties. Based on an investigation by the in-house investigation unit called INT, the Sanctions Officer (in the World Bank system called evaluation and suspension officer) assesses whether the evidence is sufficient to warrant a sanctions procedure before the Sanctions Board. The Sanctions Board hears the case de novo; typically, it holds a hearing with the parties present; however, witnesses are heard only exceptionally, and there is no actual cross-examination of witnesses, even if the parties may pose questions through the Chairman of the Board. Already during the process, INT and the Sanctions Officer are able to order a temporary debarment for a limited stretch of time.

The regional international financial institutions (IFIs) have followed suit, even if they do not necessarily apply identical rules. Major differences are that whereas the World Bank has a predominantly external Sanctions Board deciding on cases prepared by an internal staff, some of the regional MDBs have moved even further toward external judges (in the African Development Bank (AfDB) both "tiers" are predominantly staffed externally[4]). Other sanctions boards are, however, still entirely run by bank staff (Asian Development Bank (ADB); European Bank for Reconstruction and Development (EBRD)). Most regional MDBs are less inclined than the World Bank to give parties a right to an oral hearing (the Inter-American Development Bank (IDB) and the AfDB put holding a hearing in the discretion of the Sanctions Board[5]).

Even though there are differences in the makeup of these sanctions systems, MDBs have concluded an agreement, foreseeing "cross debarment" once a corporation or an individual has been sanctioned by one of the MDBs.[6] In exceptional situations, an MDB has the possibility to opt out of the cross-debarment

3. World Bank Sanctions Procedures 2012; see also World Bank Sanctioning Guidelines 2011.

4. In the AfDB, the 1st tier (Sanctions Commissioner) consists of an external judge; the 2nd tier (Sanctions Advisory Board) consists of two external and one internal judge.

5. Sanctions Procedures of the African Development Bank Group 2013, Section 8.8; Sanctions Procedures of the Inter-American Development Bank 2015, Section 11.3.

6. Agreement for Mutual Enforcement of Debarment Decisions, 9 April 2010 (AfDB, EBRD, IADB, WB).

system for "legal or other institutional considerations." The debate is ongoing whether this constitutes a necessary escape valve or a giant loophole.[7]

3. AUTOMATIC DEBARMENT?

The EU has—maybe inadvertently—created a major problem for the entire world of settlements (criminal and administrative). Above a certain threshold it foresees within its area of competence automatic debarment for corruption and similar sanctionable behavior.[8]

What seems tough, develops into a serious impediment: if one wants to evade a totally disproportionate sanction, both domestic and international investigative bodies have had to cut corners (call straightforward corruption by a different name, such as "inadequate bookkeeping"[9]) in order to prevent the automatic debarment on all fronts from kicking in as a consequence of a settlement.

It is generally understood that a subtler approach will allow a tougher sanctioning practice.[10]

4. IS DEBARMENT ALWAYS THE BEST SOLUTION?

It is no coincidence that MDBs have in their sanctions manuals developed differentiating sanction scales, allowing admonishment of the respondent in light cases, and ability to decide on (partly) conditional debarment, possibly combined with additional measures such as a compliance monitorship or to allow revisiting a decision at a later stage in order to grant "probation." This approach has been copied in many variations into domestic laws. It is essential, though, to publish the sanctions and to keep registers. Increasingly, in the course of settlements monetary sanctions are imposed. They may be meant as direct compensation, as a form of confiscation of illegal profits or as a "fine." Some MDBs have found it difficult, however, to handle the funds. When the World Bank imposed a $100 million fine on Siemens to avert lengthy debarment of the parent company, it decided to leave it to a company-based foundation (the "Siemens Integrity Initiative") to decide on the distribution of the funds, keeping merely a veto right

7. Zimmermann and Fariello 2012, 198 et seq.

8. EU Directive 2014/24/EU of the European Parliament and of the Council (OJ L 94/65, February 26, 2014).

9. Cf. *United States v. BAE Systems PLC*, No. 1:10-cr-35 (JDB) (D.D.C. 2010).

10. Clark and Suprenant 2009.

for itself. This solution has been regarded as second-best by the Independent Advisory Committee advising the World Bank president. It suggested the creation of a separate fund within the Bank and a high-level committee to advise on its uses.[11] Such a solution has now been chosen by the AfDB.[12]

5. DEALING WITH CORRUPTION IN ARBITRATION PROCEDURES

Many of the biggest (infrastructure) contracts are subject to arbitration clauses. The parties prefer to solve their disputes outside a possibly cumbersome procedure before a public court. They want to have influence on the procedures, and the substantive law applicable to their case, and they want to have a say in the selection of judges. This is particularly essential because corruption is still widespread especially in the judiciary across the world.

On the other hand, arbitration tribunals lack the robust tools of the national judiciary (they have no police or prosecution agency or subpoena powers). They can, however, order parties to produce evidence, and draw adverse inferences if the party fails to deliver.[13]

Generally, there are two types of arbitration procedures: the public law investment arbitration (especially through the World Bank's International Centre for Settlement of Investment Disputes (ICSID) System) and the so-called commercial arbitration (be it through the mediation of the International Chamber of Commerce (ICC) or ad hoc tribunals).

In the past, arbitration tribunals have been reluctant to accept the "corruption-defense," in particular because it is often used by parties previously involved in illicit behavior. Nevertheless, there has been a sequence of "causes célèbres" where a party has been sent home because it did not come with "clean hands".[14] So far, there is no clear position of the standard of proof

11. See above 194 et seq.

12. See African Development Fund (https://www.afdb.org/en/about-us/corporate-information/african-development-fund-adf/) (last visited March 17, 2017).

13. Betz 2017, 266 et seq.

14. Cf. the Final Award in *Hesham Talaat M. Al-Warraq v. The Republic of Indonesia* of 15 December 2014 (at para. 646) and several ICSID and ICC cases where the clean hands doctrine was not named explicitly, but where the same result was achieved: *World Duty Free v. Kenya* (ICSID Case No. ARB/00/7); *Inceysa* v. *El Salvador* (ICSID Case No. ARB/03/26); *Metal-Tech v. Uzbekistan* (ICSID Case No. ARB/10/3); *Fraport v. Philippines I and II* (ICSID Cases No. ARB/03/25 and ARB/11/12); ICC Cases No. 1110 (the *Lagergren* case, named after the Sole Arbitrator), 8891.

required. Some tribunals demand the higher (close to) criminal standard of "clear and convincing" evidence; others are satisfied with "more likely than not" (also called preponderance of probability).[15] Considering that some of the most substantial international contracts are outside national jurisdiction, it would be preferable if such a fundamental question was clarified.

6. PREVENTION

It is a truism that preventing is better than healing. And the United Nations Convention against Corruption (UNCAC) recognizes the key role of preventing corruption by addressing it already in its second chapter, before touching on criminalization.[16] Prevention is fundamental; it has, however, on a worldwide base not yet received the attention it deserves.

In the preventive area, a variety of approaches is promoted. In particular authors from the global South demand better ethical education. This is a preoccupation especially in Africa. The general tendency in the North is rather to accept that we live in an imperfect world with citizens of all sorts. Here one would rather emphasize reducing opportunities and incentives than moralization.[17] Preventive approaches again come in different forms. Some are very hands on, practical. Such "administrative best practices"[18] may include the regular declaration of income and assets by officials and officeholders (including judges) as well as corresponding lifestyle checks on senior officials. Typically, best practices extend to regulating procurement. They would include the four-eye-principle and transparency in offering and publication of procurement decisions.[19] On a more generic level preventive approaches would attempt to strengthen key institutions such as the judiciary, the police, or the audit functions.[20] Overall, these suggestions aim at fostering transparency of procedures and accountability of decision-makers as well as impartiality.

15. Betz 2017, 276.

16. UNCAC 2003, Chapter II, Preventive Measures, Article 5 et seq.

17. Klitgaard 2014, 33.

18. Johnston 2014, 220 et seq., 237; cf. also UNCAC 2003, Chapter II, Preventive Measures, Article 5 et seq.

19. For the efforts on e-procurement in Latin-America, see Government at a Glance: Latin America and the Caribbean 2014, published by the OECD, 10, 106 et seq.; Compendium of Innovative E-Government Practices, Volume II, published by the United Nations (UN Doc. ST/ESA/PAD/SER.E/96), 310, 313, 321.

20. Cf. International Bar Association (IBA) Judicial Integrity Initiative, a new project aimed at combating judicial corruption, 19 February 2015.

Philippines

In the Philippines public officials and judges are obliged to regularly declare their income and their assets. The office of the ombudsman is in charge of so-called "life-style checks." In particular, the declared funds will be compared with the obvious cost of living (housing, cars, entertainment of friends, etc.). As an additional component of this system legislation contains an offense of "illicit enrichment," translating Article 20 of UNCAC into national law.

All these recipes addressing concrete risks of wrongdoing are essential; however, they do not replace a more holistic approach to reform, addressing the systemic nature of corruption. A credible reform program would need to be tailor-made for the specific society in question. Thereby a series of models may be used. There is a huge difference between challenging bribery in a society just emerging from an autocratic regime (be it a longtime dictatorship, the rule of clans or elites) or even a civil war[21] on the one hand, and an established democracy and state of law struggling with occasional power abuses on the other.[22] Such concepts will be further explored below in Chapter 23.

21. Johnston 2014, 57 et seq., 119 et seq.

22. Johnston 2014, 186 et seq.

PART FIVE

Private Sector Responses

It is often said that overcoming corruption is only possible if all stakeholders are actively engaged in the action. Thus, going beyond the measures available to states, this Part talks about remedies for the private sector. Again, featuring a variety of personal anecdotes by the authors, compliance as well as collective action are reviewed.

19

Private Sector Response to Corruption

FRITZ HEIMANN ■

1. MAJOR TRENDS

During the past quarter century corruption has become a key issue for the private sector. The level of government and public attention focused on corruption has risen sharply. Until the 1990s there was only episodic interest in spectacular scandals. Now articles about corruption appear in almost every issue of the *Economist*, the *Financial Times*, the *New York Times,* and the *Wall Street Journal.* There have been sharp increases in government enforcement, particularly by the United States, Germany, Switzerland, and the United Kingdom. Foreign bribery, which had been largely off the screen, has moved to the center of attention.

The rapid evolution of a global economy has been a transformative factor. For many leading companies, foreign business now represents more than half of their volume. The nature of foreign business has changed from export sales of domestically-manufactured products to manufacturing and sales, as well as research and development (R&D) and joint ventures on a worldwide basis.

The United States passed the Foreign Corrupt Practices Act (FCPA) in 1977. It was the first law that criminalized foreign bribery. The OECD Convention, which internationalized the FCPA, became effective in 1999. It prohibits foreign bribery of public officials by over forty countries. The UN Convention against Corruption (UNCAC), became effective in 2005, and has been ratified by more than 180 states. UNCAC deals with domestic as well as foreign bribery,

Confronting Corruption. Fritz Heimann and Mark Pieth.

bribery of public officials as well as bribery in the private sector.[1] Enforcement has greatly expanded in the past decade. The United States has adopted very flexible jurisdictional standards, making possible prosecution of foreign companies based on minimal American contacts, such as sales of their securities in the United States.

Four international organizations, Transparency International (TI), the International Chamber of Commerce (ICC), the World Economic Forum (WEF), and the UN Global Compact (UNGC), have actively developed and promoted corporate compliance rules.

Corporate responses have also evolved. Anticorruption compliance programs have been used by US companies for more than three decades. Widespread use of compliance programs in other countries was triggered by the prosecution of Siemens in 2008.

2. EVOLUTION OF COMPLIANCE

Corporate efforts typically began with a policy declaration disavowing bribery, with little follow-up effort. They were often regarded as "cover your rear end" exercises, enabling top management to characterize bribe payments as violation of company policy by "bad apples."

With bribery continuing and enforcement becoming stronger, companies began to adopt internal compliance programs. These became steadily more rigorous. Sound compliance programs call for active top management involvement, transparent communications up and down the line, regular reviews, administration by a compliance function independent of marketing and sales staffs, and most importantly strict disciplinary action, including firing when infractions are discovered. The scope of corporate compliance programs has been extended to cover not only the parent company, but also foreign subsidiaries, subcontractors, and the supply chain.

The need for rigorous compliance was driven home by the ever-increasing level of corporate fines. Fines collected by US prosecutors reached hundreds of million dollars. By way of example, Och-Ziff Capital Management, a US-based hedge fund, was ordered to pay a fine of $213 million to the US DOJ as part of a deferred prosecution agreement.[2] The OECD Report on Enforcement

1. The OECD Convention is discussed in detail in Chapter 7 and UNCAC in Chapter 8.

2. In addition, the hedge fund admitted to its role in paying more than $100 million in bribes to officials in the Democratic Republic of Congo, Libya, and others to secure natural resources deals; DOJ Justice News, September 29, 2016: "Och-Ziff Capital Management Admits to Role in Africa Bribery Conspiracies and Agrees to Pay $213 Million Criminal Fine."

published in December 2015 covers 530 cases brought by seventeen OECD members. Sanctions included large fines and prison terms.[3] Corruption has also been punished by blacklisting, and exclusion from bidding by procurement agencies and by the World Bank and other development agencies.

For large multinational enterprises (MNEs), the Siemens case was the turning point. In addition to fines in excess of $1 billion, the CEO and other top Siemens officers were fired. Many small and medium sized enterprises (SMEs) are still in a state of denial, believing that their conduct is below the radar screen of prosecutors. Some SMEs contend that it would be impossible to adopt compliance programs like those of MNEs. This ignores that compliance in SMEs is easier to achieve because the number of employees is smaller and communication channels are simpler. In typical family-owned *"Mittelstand"* companies, a management policy against bribery should be much easier to implement than in large, decentralized MNEs.

My experience at General Electric in the 1980s and 1990s made clear that compliance was hard to achieve. I accompanied a senior marketing officer on a trip to Geneva to explain a detailed compliance policy to European employees and sales representatives. At dinner that evening the top sales representative for the Middle East complimented us on the detailed nature of the new policy. He commented that the new policy would provide excellent protection against liability for the board of directors, but he assumed that marketing practices in the Middle East would not dispense with bribe payments. We tried to disabuse him of this misconception. On our return, we informed Jack Welch that the message of change would not be believed if it did not come directly from the CEO—a responsibility that was accepted.

In practice, it took a traumatic scandal involving sales of GE jet engines to the Israeli Air Force. In this transaction, the head of middle eastern sales for the jet engine division made payments to the head of procurement of the Israeli air force. Subsequently, Welch fired eighteen senior employees including several officers. They had had no direct involvement with bribe payments, but should have uncovered what was going on if they had been more diligent. That drove the message home without room for any further misunderstanding. Among those fired was GE's comptroller and the head of the corporate audit staff. What particularly rankled Welch was that the bribery was uncovered by the Mossad, Israel's intelligence service, but not by GE's highly regarded audit staff!

---

3. OECD WGB, November 2016: "2015 Data on Enforcement of the Anti-Bribery Convention."

a. Role of NGOs

The development of corporate anti-bribery policies has been influenced by a number of NGOs.

The International Chamber of Commerce (ICC) established a high-level committee against extortion and bribery in 1975, following worldwide publicity over bribe payments to Prime Minister Tanaka of Japan, the Italian defense minister Mario Tanassi, and Crown Prince Bernhard of the Netherlands. The ICC committee was chaired by Lord Shawcross, a former UK attorney general and Nuremberg prosecutor.

The discovery of bribes paid by Lockheed, Gulf, and others was an incidental result of the Watergate investigation of fundraising for President Nixon's 1972 campaign. A congressional committee and the SEC found that corporate contributions to the campaign had come from foreign bank accounts, which were used primarily to make bribe payments. This led to the enactment of the US Foreign Corrupt Practices Act in 1977.

The Shawcross committee published "Rules of Conduct to Combat Extortion and Bribery" in 1977. The timing of the Shawcross report was not opportune. Interest in curbing foreign bribery had subsided and did not revive until after the end of the Cold War, and the eruption of a new round of bribery scandals in Italy, France, and Germany in the early 1990s.

The ICC re-established its Committee on Extortion and Bribery in 1993, under the chairmanship of François Vincke, then general counsel of Petrofina, the Belgian oil company; I was vice chair. New ICC Rules of Conduct were published in 1994, an updated version of the Shawcross rules. The ICC committee has remained active ever since.

The ICC Rules of Conduct cover bribery as well as extortion in both the public sector and within the private sector. They became the model for the TI Business Principles and the World Economic Forum's PACI Principles (Partnership Against Corruption). ICC, TI, and WEF actively promoted adoption of their rules and principles by their member companies. ICC also published "Fighting Corruption: International Corporate Integrity Handbook".[4]

The development of three different sets of rules reflected the desire of each organization to have a document bearing its own logo. This produced useful competition that strengthened the individual rules and resulted over time in substantial similarity of content. A remaining area of difference is the treatment of facilitation payments, which are barred by TI, whereas ICC and WEF leave some room for management discretion.

4. Heimann and Vincke 2008.

TI has also successfully promoted the adoption of project-specific "Integrity Pacts," under which organizations running the projects and all prospective participants agree that no bribes will be paid. Hundreds of integrity pacts have been established all over the world. In Mexico alone integrity pacts have been implemented in contracts worth more than $30 billion.[5]

b. UN Global Compact

The UN Global Compact was first announced by UN Secretary General Kofi Annan in 1999 as a broad-based effort to improve labor and environmental standards. Member companies were asked to submit annual reports on nine principles. In 2004 Peter Eigen persuaded Kofi Annan to add corruption as the Global Compact's 10th Principle. In recent years corruption has become the principal focus of Global Compact activities with involvement by many thousand companies. The Global Compact operates out of the UN Secretary General's office in New York and was run by Georg Kell for fifteen years.

c. Industry Sector Initiatives: Wolfsberg

Anticorruption programs for specific industries have advantages over generic policies, such as the ICC Rules and the TI Business Principles, because they can focus on special industry issues. TI's first experience involved the private banking industry. It began with a dinner hosted by Shaukat Aziz, then the vice chair in charge of Citibank's private banking activities, to which he invited Peter Eigen, Frank Vogl, and me. Aziz complained that when Citibank explained the "Know Your Customer" (KYC) rules of the Federal Reserve System to a prospective client, the common response was that other banks did not insist on obtaining such information. This posed a dilemma: Citibank risked losing the client if they insisted, but would violate government rules if they did not. Aziz asked TI for help.

I called Mark Pieth who had close relations with the major Swiss banks. With Mark's assistance, a meeting was arranged in Zurich with a dozen leading Swiss, German, British, French, and US banks. Aziz laid out the problem. TI offered to work with the banks, including steps to avoid antitrust issues. The response from the European banks was reluctant and inconclusive. They did agree to meet again. A second meeting was hosted by Union Bank of Switzerland (UBS).

5. Cf. https://www.transparency.org/whatwedo/tools/integrity_pacts/4/.

As an opening step, we proposed that the banks make available copies of their KYC policies to TI and that Mark Pieth would prepare a comparative review. It took six months before they did so. After we completed the review and made recommendations, several further meetings took place before all the participating banks agreed to apply KYC rules to screen prospective customers. That success led to a decision to work on other common problems, beginning with correspondent banking (rules for extending trading privileges to foreign banks). UBS made available its conference center at Wolfsberg for these meetings, and Wolfsberg became the name for the banking group. Hans Peter Bauer of UBS became the chairman. (Shaukat Aziz had left Citibank to become finance minister of Pakistan.)

An eye-opener for the TI participants, and an explanation why progress was initially so slow, was that the compliance officers of the banks had never met each other before. Getting them together was a key step. It created a communication channel among individuals with a continuing interest in preventing corruption. Thereafter, the compliance officers were able to check with each other when they received allegations of questionable banking practices and seek to overcome them by joint action.

Developing a constituency of persons with a common interest is a crucial step for many industries seeking to make progress in curbing corruption.

d. Other Industry Sector Initiatives

Productive initiatives are underway in several industries that have long been bedeviled by endemic corruption. These include:

Extractive Industries Transparency Initiative (EITI)

This brings together governments and companies in oil, coal, and related industries. Corruption in these industries has long been characterized as "the oil curse." Because rights to explore and extract oil are commonly negotiated directly by heads of governments with heads of large companies, "grand corruption" is particularly common.

The EITI Standard requires countries and companies to publicly disclose information on the key steps in the governance of oil, gas, and mining revenues.[6] EITI has been in operation for more than a decade and has its headquarters in Oslo, long headed by Clare Short, the former UK minister for International development. Thus far, fifty-one countries have implemented the EITI standard and $1.9 trillion revenues have been disclosed in EITI Reports.[7]

6. EITI Factsheet (https://eiti.org/document/factsheet) (last visited March 13, 2017).

7. EITI Factsheet (https://eiti.org/document/factsheet) (last visited March 13, 2017).

Construction Sector Transparency (CoST)

Infrastructure construction projects are another common field for grand corruption. CoST[8] is a multinational effort to make the sector more transparent and accountable by reducing mismanagement, waste, and corruption. It works with governments, industry, and local communities in fifteen participating countries across four continents.

In each country, CoST brings together members of government, the private sector, and civil society to improve the quality of public services, inter alia, by reviewing and evaluating data on infrastructure investment disclosed by the governments.[9] CoST is headed by Christiaan Portman of TI, formerly vice president of the World Bank for Middle East and North Africa, and its headquarters are in London.

Aerospace and Defense (IFBEC)

Because of the magnitude of aerospace and defense projects and the close relationships between top government officials and senior officers of contractors, grand corruption is common.

IFBEC aims to promote and foster the development of industry-wide ethical standards for companies that are active in the aerospace and defense business sector. IFBEC is managed by a Steering Committee composed of various defense, security, and aerospace companies. The main goal is to exchange best practices and facilitate a robust dialogue regarding issues such as anticorruption and compliance as well as due diligence.[10]

3. COMMON PROBLEM AREAS

a. Gifts, Entertainment, and Travel Expenses

The danger that gifts, entertainment, and travel expenses for government officials are used as disguised bribes has been widely recognized. In the United States the adoption of restrictions has ended such practices as defense contractors paying for country club memberships for Pentagon officials. The rules are so strict that contractors no longer give pocket calendars to officials. In China President Xi Jinping has launched a sharp crackdown on gifts

8. Cf. above 147 et seq.

9. CoST Factsheet (http://www.constructiontransparency.org/the-initiative?forumboardid=1&forumtopicid=1) (last visited March 13, 2017).

10. IFBEC Charter (http://ifbec.info/about/) (last visited February 10, 2017).

and entertainment of top officials and their relatives. According to newspaper reports this has resulted in the closing of many top Beijing restaurants. Although there has been a worldwide trend to curb gifts, entertainment, and travel expenses, there continue to be major cultural differences in what is deemed appropriate.

Distinguishing between proper and excessive gifts and entertainment expenses remains a matter of judgment. A practical guide is the "newspaper test": how will the practice look if it is publicly reported. Using the newspaper test has become even more relevant in a digital age when improper practices are unlikely to remain secret. The test should be applied by a supervising level of management.

Gifts above nominal value should be prohibited. Entertainment and travel expenses should be limited based on strict business purposes. Visits to factories and laboratories are appropriate; visits to race tracks and nightclubs are not. Costs of accompanying family members should not be reimbursed.

b. Lobbyists and Sales Representatives

Lobbyists, sales representatives, and other intermediaries have been widely used as conduits for bribe payments. Inflating amounts paid to intermediaries is a ready way to create funds for bribery. There are, of course, proper ways to use intermediaries. The following criteria should be applied: Does the work involve activities that a company cannot readily perform with its own employees? Does the intermediary have sound qualifications for the work and a good reputation in the community? Is the compensation justified based on the time spent? Will it be paid by check, not in cash?

Because of the sensitivity of using lobbyists and sales representatives, due diligence should be used in selecting and supervising intermediaries, and high-level management approval should be obtained.

c. Political Contributions

This represents a troublesome and volatile field. In the United States, recent Supreme Court decisions striking down long-established restrictions on political contributions as violations of free speech have reversed a century of political regulations. These cases were decided by 5-4 votes and have aroused widespread public controversy.

It is difficult to differentiate between reasonable levels of political contributions, buying influence, and disguised forms of bribery. However, from the perspective of anticorruption policy, the Supreme Court decisions have undesirable consequences.

Even without volatility in legal rules, companies face difficult choices. Failing to make contributions to the party in power can result in political retribution. Contributing to the party in power can have adverse effects when the opposition wins. There are additional issues: Should companies make contributions to candidates in primaries, to ballot initiatives, etc.? For multinational companies, the issues are multiplied by decisions about what to do in other countries where the company does business in addition to the home country.

Decisions about political contributions should be subject to legal review and to top management and board approval.

d. Avoiding Extortion

Resisting demands for bribes is a difficult problem because such demands are often accompanied by threats, explicit or implicit, not to deal with a bidder who refuses to pay. ICC and TI conducted a study, named RESIST, which recommended that companies should appeal to management above the level of the employees who solicited the bribes. However, many companies indicated that they are reluctant to do so because of concerns that they would lose the order, or even be removed from the bidders list. Such concerns are realistic because higher levels often share in the proceeds of extortion.

OECD has proposed that governments establish high-level reporting channels, separate from the procurement agencies, which could intercede in response to claims of extortion. That proposal was developed by Nicola Bonucci, Mark Pieth, and me. It called for speedy, informal intervention by high-level officials that would result in the withdrawal of the extortion demand. The objective should be timely preventive action, allowing the procurement process to be completed and avoiding prolonged legal procedures. Some governments have expressed interest. Others have expressed concern about high-level intervention in procurement procedures.

e. Private-to-Private Bribery

Compliance programs should apply to bribery within the private sector, as well as to bribery of public officials. This is important because private sector bribery is a serious problem, particularly in procurement transactions. From the corporate compliance perspective, it is desirable to get employees to follow a consistent no-bribery policy. Major projects often involve both private and public participants. It is difficult in practice and wrong in principal to tolerate private sector bribery.

f. Facilitation Payments

When the FCPA and the OECD Convention were adopted, facilitation payments—small payments to low level officials—were not prohibited. In the intervening decades, corporate and public attitudes have changed and the facilitation payment exception now has little support. It remains part of the FCPA, but many OECD countries did not provide an exception for facilitation payments when they implemented the Convention. The UN Convention does not have such an exception.

The original justification for the facilitation payments exception was that such payments were relatively innocuous, and were considered necessary to do business in many developing countries. It is now widely recognized that payments to lower-level officials are rarely isolated transactions, but are often part of organized schemes where much of the money moves upstream to higher officials and ministers. Most MNEs believe that it is preferable to apply a consistent no-bribery policy than it would be to define and administer an exception for facilitation payments.

The difficulty of limiting facilitation payments to small payments to low-level officials was dramatically illustrated in the Oil-for-Food investigation, which found that the Australian Wheat Board had paid $300 million to the president of Iran, claiming that it was a facilitation payment!

g. Foreign Subsidiaries and Joint Ventures

The scope of corporate compliance programs has expanded beyond the parent company to cover foreign subsidiaries controlled by the parent as well as joint ventures. The UK Bribery Act makes clear that company management has a due-diligence obligation to ensure that joint ventures, agents, and other intermediaries comply with the company's no-bribery policy.

4. PSYCHOLOGY OF CORRUPT CONDUCT

My experience over many years at General Electric (GE) indicates that patterns of behavior resembling a bell curve apply to corrupt behavior by employees in companies and government agencies. There appear to be three types of employees.

a. Type A

A small percentage of employees have strong, unbending personal ethical standards and would not pay or accept bribes, irrespective of the behavior of their fellow employees.

b. Type B

A large majority of employees have flexible ethical standards that will be influenced by the culture of their organization. They are not rule breakers, but they will distinguish between rules that are enforced and those that are not enforced. If other employees are paying or accepting bribes they will not want to be deprived of advantages that other employees enjoy, for example, accepting gifts from suppliers or winning orders by paying bribes.

c. Type C

Another small percentage of employees are amoral. They feel that they are not bound by rules applicable to others, that they are smart enough to "beat the system."

The important point is that a large majority of employees are Type B, whereas only small percentages are Types A and C. The key objective of anticorruption policies should be to create an organizational culture where Type B employees observe high standards. Type A employees can serve as examples; they do not need to be influenced. Type C employees cannot be influenced. They need to be identified and discharged.

Dr. Paul Wolpe, director of the Emory Center for Ethics, agrees with the foregoing analysis. He indicates that it is supported by a substantial academic literature dealing with the psychology of ethics.[11]

5. FACTORS NEEDED TO INFLUENCE CORPORATE CULTURE

The proclivity to pay or accept bribes by the Type B employees, who make up the vast majority of company employees, is influenced by their perception of the prevailing corporate culture.

11. Trevino/Youngblood 1990; Bandura 2006.

a. Tone at the Top Is Important

What leaders practice is much more important than what they preach. Statements opposing bribery will be regarded with cynicism by many employees: What did you expect them to say?

b. Transparent Rules

Companies should adopt a transparent ethical system with published rules covering practical applications. There should be regular training programs and procedures for getting answers to tough questions. Regular monitoring should be conducted by the corporate compliance staff. Disciplinary action for violations is crucial and should be publicized throughout the organization.

c. Leadership Selection

Leaders for ethically sensitive functions should ideally be Type A individuals. When Type B individuals are selected, adequate supervision must be provided. Appointing Type C individuals presents unacceptable risks, particularly at the top level, where incumbents may come to believe that they are not bound by the rules. Selecting leaders for government jobs involves considerations generally similar to those for corporate positions.

In the political arena, these problems are aggravated. Type A political leaders are extremely rare because the political process requires compromises such as living with flawed campaign finance systems, or need for winning support from flawed allies. Maintaining effective controls over Type B individuals is more difficult than in the corporate sector. The problems presented by Type C politicians are most serious, as indicated by the tendency of powerful leaders to believe that rules don't apply to them.[12]

12. The life of Samuel Pepys, as described in Noonan 1984, illustrates the influence of leadership on organizational culture. During Cromwell's Commonwealth, high moral standards prevailed. After the Restoration of King Charles II practically everybody, including Pepys, took bribes and mistresses.

6. MOVING ANTICORRUPTION TO THE NEXT LEVEL

Combating corruption is like mountain climbing: making progress becomes more difficult the further you go. Publishing statements of ethical principles is popular and raises no objections. Formulating detailed compliance programs may arouse opposition from those whose activities would be constrained. Moving from words to deeds by enforcing compliance programs is much more difficult. It requires allocation of money and experienced staff and will arouse active opposition from those who benefit from continuing corrupt practices. To overcome such opposition requires strong commitment from top management.

Building a corruption-free corporate culture will be very difficult. It will require strong and persistent action over a period of years, including disciplining senior violators—going after tigers not just sparrows, in Xi Jinping words.

Two additional steps will accelerate progress in corporate compliance.

First, government prosecutors should give credit to companies that conduct rigorous compliance and that self-report violations. That should be made clear in sentencing guidelines and in the disposition of cases, as was done in the Morgan Stanley case.

Second, corporations should recognize that external verification of compliance can have important benefits. It will help rebuild public confidence in corporate self-regulation, following the disclosure of ineffective self-regulation by many banks revealed in the investigations following the 2007–2008 financial crisis. External verification can also provide top management with confirmation of the adequacy of their compliance programs.[13]

13. Cf. TI USA (2014), "Verification of Anti-Corruption Compliance Programs."

20

Collective Action

MARK PIETH

1. WHY COLLECTIVE ACTION?

Traditional anticorruption compliance has its limits. Most companies have given themselves comprehensive compliance programs as described above and they are—in everyday life—struggling to implement and apply them. Nevertheless, one should not delude oneself: corruption is—in particular in difficult areas of the world—a persistent problem. And, with law enforcement intensifying both in the host countries of corporations and some of the more prominent exporting nations (such as China), the question becomes more and more relevant whether the classic approach to compliance is really sufficient.

Critical experts consider it by and large "inward looking" and "reactive" as opposed to "dynamic":[1] they claim that the focus is exclusively on "the sphere of control that the company can influence directly." Therefore, compliance programs are continuously adapted, however, predominantly when something goes wrong or when the legal or regulatory framework changes.[2]

What is largely missing in the current world of compliance is a more proactive approach: "An alternative would be for the business to drive integrity and take the initiative to leverage anti-corruption compliance into a competitive advantage."[3] According to this position "[c]ollective action provides a means to address the wider context of corruption risks by bringing together competitors as well as other market participants and stakeholders to seek common ground

1. Aiolfi 2014, 129 et seq.

2. Aiolfi 2014, 129 et seq.

3. Aiolfi 2014, 129.

Confronting Corruption. Fritz Heimann and Mark Pieth.

to reduce corruption."[4] Collective action has the additional advantage of enabling an entire business sector to manage expectations: in its talks with regulators and the wider public it can indicate what it considers reasonable.

On a more concrete level there are simple advantages that should not be underestimated: participating in the same group makes it easier for compliance and legal staff to talk with each other about common challenges. Obviously, the operational staff needs to be kept out of this discourse in order to dispel any antitrust doubts.

2. FROM AN ACADEMIC THINK PIECE TO A PRACTICAL SOLUTION

Collective action is a very broad umbrella-term for industry standards, multi-stakeholder initiatives, public-private partnerships, and the like.[5] The World Bank Institute in its "Fighting Corruption through Collective Action, A Guide for Business"[6] defines "collective action" as:

> *A collaborative and sustained process of cooperation amongst stakeholders. It increases the impact and credibility of individual action, brings vulnerable individual players into an alliance of like-minded organizations and levels the playing field between competitors. Collective Action can complement or temporarily substitute for and strengthen weak local laws and anti-corruption practices.*

Collective action is not a new term. However, it was traditionally used to illustrate aspects of the so-called "prisoner's dilemma."[7] Kingston applied it to corruption: "The citizens or firms dealing with a corrupt government official would all benefit from an agreement not to pay bribes but each has an incentive to pay bribes to try to get preferential treatment."[8] With the continuous upgrading of legal and reputational risks connected to bribery, the academic illustration of "game theory" has shifted to very concrete policies for companies, stakeholders, and governments.

4. Aiolfi 2014, 125.

5. Klitgaard 2012, 41 et seq.; Pieth 2007, 81 et seq.

6. World Bank Institute 2008, slide 4.

7. Hardin 2013; Reuben 2003, 26 et seq.; Sandler 2010, 40 et seq.

8. Kingston 2004.

Already in 1999 Transparency International (TI) came up with the concept of "Islands of Integrity" or the "Integrity Pact" in public procurement,[9] a concept used in many contexts since. Roughly at the same time, TI and the Basel Institute on Governance (BIG), together with the twelve biggest private banks of the world, initiated an industry group focused on preventing money laundering, the "Wolfsberg Group."[10] It has since produced a multitude of standards and has managed to establish itself as a strong self-regulatory body in the financial sector and as an interlocutor with regulators. It focuses on money laundering, prevention of financing of terrorism, corruption, and embargo-busting.[11]

Shortly afterward the Extractive Industries Transparency Initiative (EITI) was founded, a public-private partnership sponsored by several developed states involving resource-rich countries in the global South and the extractive industries.[12]

Several other industry-focused initiatives were founded, in particular in defense[13] and in heavy industries.[14] However, initial attempts failed. Only over time have new attempts been more successful (in defense: the International Forum on Business Ethical Conduct for the Aerospace and Defense Industry, IFBEC; in power: the new Power Systems Initiative). The reasons for the original failure have a lot to do with companies (such as British Aerospace (BAE) or Siemens) getting caught up in scandals and the mutual trust amongst members of the initiative braking down.[15]

After a "generic intermezzo" seeing new general codes and standards emerging—especially the amended International Chamber of Commerce (ICC) Rules of Conduct[16] and the TI Business Principles,[17] roughly concurrent with international[18] and national guidance on compliance[19]—collective action is now again very much *en vogue:* the B20[20] Task Force on Transparency

9. Aiolfi 2014, 130; de Swardt and Wiehen 2012, 83 et seq.; Wiehen 1999, 304.

10. Pieth 2012, 9 et seq.; Pieth/Aiolfi 2003, 243 et seq.

11. Wolfsberg Principles 2012; Wolfsberg Guidance 2011; Wolfsberg Statement 2002.

12. See above 140 et seq., 226 et seq.

13. A European version of the US Defense Industry Initiative, see above 155.

14. Power Systems Initiative, initiated in 1999 and abandoned in December 2002.

15. Aiolfi 2014, 133; Pieth 2012, 11.

16. ICC Rules 2011 (first published in 1977).

17. TI Business Principles 2013 (first published in 2003).

18. OECD Rec. 2009.

19. UK Ministry of Justice Guidance 2011; FCPA Resource Guide 2012.

20. The Business 20 (B20) has been created to mirror the work of the Group of Twenty (G20).

and Anti-Corruption has decided to create a Collective Action-Hub and has charged the BIG in connection with the UN Global Compact to set up such a center.

3. WHAT IS COLLECTIVE ACTION?

This short historical overview indicates that collective action is a very flexible concept and allows for innovative strategies of all kind. Some initiatives have started off within an industry sector developing common standards; others were directed at certification.[21] A different type of collective action involves other stakeholders and government from the outset. This is where the "Integrity Pacts" fit in. Some collective actions have evolved top-down (driven by the head offices); others are more bottom-up, such as the Integrity Pact by companies in the energy transmission sector in Argentina.[22] Another public-private partnership, currently finding a lot of traction especially in Latin America and Eastern Europe, is the so-called High Level Reporting Mechanism (HLRM):

High Level Reporting Mechanisms (HLRMs)

"The idea of "HLRMs" was born originally of discussions between general counsels of the largest heavy industries (power systems) groups, which were mediated by the Basel Institute on Governance. Frequently, even large companies find themselves confronted with outright extortion and, in some of the most difficult markets, are uneasy with escalating the matter individually. Hence, participants suggested the creation of ombudsman offices close to heads of government or heads of state. The organization of the structure would obviously be a matter for each country. The central idea, though, is not primarily of a law enforcement agency. Rather, from a company perspective, a complaint to the ombudsman would be a last-ditch effort at corruption prevention.

With the help of TI-USA, the idea was picked up and developed beyond one sector. The OECD agreed to act as a platform to promote the concept. The G20 countries and their B20 business representatives expressed their interest in this initiative at the summits of Cannes and Los Cabos in 2011 and 2012 (respectively). Colombia is the current pilot country, and has

21. For specifics verify TI-US 2014; see also above Chapter 19.

22. Zindera and Forstnig-Errath, 185 et seq.; cf. also Aiolfi 2014, 131 et seq.

developed a concept in which complaints of solicitation trigger increased due diligence in specific procurement procedures."[23]

4. IS COLLECTIVE ACTION REALLY NECESSARY?

Many companies may still wonder why they should get involved in collective action. It is a practical experience facilitators have made over and over again: some protagonists may be willing to lead the way, whilst other major competitors are reluctant to join. Do they have something to hide? Rather, they will believe internal compliance is sufficient.

To go back to the beginning of this chapter: Why is this reactive style insufficient in the long run? Because it will not be able to reduce major risks. To give another example:

Six international oil companies got together and discussed the challenges they faced in Nigeria. One of the key problems pinpointed is that the royalties paid to Nigeria rarely trickle down to the communities most affected by the extraction process (e.g., the fishermen in the Niger Delta[24]). Understandably they are unhappy about operational spills stemming from extraction and illegal oil theft in the region.[25] The companies, on the other hand, have been struggling to secure their operations, and have seen themselves forced to use armed guards of questionable reliability. Overall, the challenges of distributing the funds, securing exploitation, and protecting the environment are far too big for any individual company to handle. Additionally, even individual "oil majors" would be out of their depth working on these issues solely with the government. This is a case for a round table with government officials and representatives of all relevant oil majors active in the country, together with a facilitator.

NIGERIA

To illustrate how tedious such a collective action process can be at times: in fact, the oil majors active in Nigeria got together in London, generally represented by their general counsels upon our invitation. They rapidly identified

23. Pieth 2012, 17 et seq.; cf. also Basel Institute on Governance, Impact Story: The High Level Reporting Mechanism (HLRM), 2014; Heimann 2012, 209 et seq.

24. Cf. Global Witness 2013: "Nigeria's Missing Billions."

25. BBC, January 7, 2015: "Shell agrees $84m deal over Niger Delta Oil Spill."

their major problem. Furthermore, a first step toward a cure was determined: one needed to find ways to allow some of the oil revenue to "trickle down" to the affected community. As a first step a letter to the minister of finance was going to be written. However, when we asked whether we could use the names of the oil majors participating in the initiative, they all pulled back, and we for the time being decided not to continue. Maybe a new effort will be more successful.

PART SIX

Moving Forward

Completing the book, this Part reasons what twenty-five years of intense anticorruption work have achieved as well as the shortfalls of the last two decades. Considering the heavy toll corruption takes on democratic institutions and initiatives, this Part then changes perspective and provides an outlook toward what needs to be done in the next decade. It identifies globalization and the digital revolution as the main drivers of the anticorruption movement in the years to come. This Part ends with distinct anticorruption strategies for countries on different ranks on the development scale.

21

What Have We Achieved?

MARK PIETH ■

1. ACHIEVEMENTS AND CHALLENGES

It is time to go back to the question of where we stand after twenty-five years of intense work on fighting corruption. Some will—rightly—point out that corruption remains a major problem encountered worldwide. Particularly in some areas of the world corruption is so endemic that it still holds entire societies hostage.[1] This cannot be denied. So, what then has been achieved?

2. ACCOMPLISHMENTS

First, we should not underrate that the issue has been pushed up on the political agenda. An indicator is that allegations of corruption make a "good media story": the process of scandalization is a reflection of the fact that we care about the topic. Also, governments are elected on an anticorruption ticket; others are deposed for corruption.

As a consequence of all the conventions enacted—predominantly to criminalize corruption—laws have been enacted in most nation-states. Even if enforcement remains uneven, including in industrialized states, the risks of being caught and subjected to trials have grown substantially. In particular in the private sector the need for compliance programs has become obvious. Around the compliance topic an entire industry has grown, offering manifold

1. Cf. above 33 et seq., 181 et seq.

Confronting Corruption. Fritz Heimann and Mark Pieth.

career opportunities. Again, this can be regarded as an indirect expression of how seriously the topic is now being taken.

The risks are, however, not limited to industrialized states. Increasingly, exporters or investors are facing enforcement action in emerging markets. An example concerning the pharmaceutical industry in China has been given above.[2] Another is the case of Rheinmetall Air Defence AG in India:

Rheinmetall Air Defence AG in India

In 2011 the defense company Rheinmetall Air Defence AG (RAD) intended to export antiaircraft guns to India. Subsequently, Indian authorities alleged that representatives of RAD had bribed the director general of the defense procurement body. On top of it, allegations were voiced that the company intended to bribe members of the debarment authority to escape sanctions. As a consequence of these alleged maneuvers, the company ended up with a ten-year debarment from the Indian market.[3]

Beyond criminalization and enforcement especially the United Nations Convention against Corruption (UNCAC) contains a—largely still dormant—preventive agenda. Its implementation will take time, as it implies in-depth change down to the local level (e.g., in public financial management and auditing as well as in public procurement).

There is more, though: we have all observed the spectacular "Arab Spring." In rapid sequence, popular uprisings toppled autocratic leaders (in Egypt, Yemen, Libya, and Tunisia). In other countries the movements were stopped (as in Bahrain) or the revolutions led to civil war (in Syria and now also in Yemen). What is new is that urban youth went beyond the traditional "bread riots" (as in Egypt).[4] They fought for a democratic order. It would be unreasonable to call the "Arab Spring" a success story (except maybe in Tunisia). Traditionally, new autocratic fractions struggle to seize power.[5] Opposition is torn between laical and Islamic fractions.[6] In Libya, the Gadhafi regime has made way for a myriad

2. Cf. above 164 et seq.

3. Spiegel Online, August 30, 2013: "Indische Polizei ermittelt gegen Rheinmetall"; Reuters, June 9, 2012: "India Police charge Rheinmetall official with bribery."

4. Hottinger 2013, 7.

5. Hottinger 2013, 3 et seq.

6. Hottinger 2013, 9.

of armed militias, now forming three feuding governments. And yet, the rising is an expression of a new awakening from century-old lethargy.

Not only in the Arab region but especially in India popular movements are forming and expressing their weariness with the corruption confronting the population constantly in everyday life. They will no longer tolerate leaders abusing power for personal benefit. The worldwide nongovernmental organizations (NGOs) who have been in the driving seat of the anticorruption movement over the last twenty years, focusing predominantly on governments and the private sector, are challenged to close ranks with these more vocal, more advocacy oriented, locally driven movements.[7]

Both the popular risings in the Arab region and the mobilization in India benefit from the digital revolution: "New Media," widely accessible especially by young people who are not ready to see corruption reproducing itself generation after generation, are a tool of choice. They may well develop into a game changer on anticorruption (for further detail see below Chapter 22).

3. CHALLENGES

There is definitely change. But it should not distract from the challenges.

It has become fashionable to talk about corruption. Every year there is at least one major conference uniting governments, NGOs, and increasingly also the private sector. The official anticorruption groups have multiplied (including now the OECD Working Group on Bribery, the Anti-Corruption Working Groups of the G20 and of the B20,[8] the work on corruption of the Global Compact etc.). The risk is that these gatherings offer anyone, including politicians with a dubious background, a platform to raise their own profile.[9] What is dearly needed is to follow the words by action.

At the risk of demanding "more of the same," the next steps on the anticorruption agenda need to bring the existing tools to life. This applies first and foremost to the criminalization conventions. It is still uncertain whether local law enforcement and the judiciary even in industrialized states are willing and able to run cases, in particular against foreign bribery. The international organizations acting as repositories of these instruments have introduced monitoring mechanisms, but their touch is still too soft, too diplomatic. Even the OECD, harboring the probably toughest evaluation mechanism, is not really ready to

7. Cf. above 27 et seq.

8. The Business 20 (B20) has been created to mirror the work of the Group of Twenty (G20).

9. Cf. Moene and Søreide 2015.

threaten meaningful sanctions against noncompliant countries. This applies in a far more general way to the regional instruments and to UNCAC.[10]

Now, if we take a step back from this more technical perspective, there are more fundamental reasons it is so difficult to reduce corruption decisively: the early years of the twenty-first century stand for peace in large parts of the world, but also for intense regional conflict. Conflict frequently goes hand in hand with deep poverty (cf. the situations in Syria or in South Sudan and East Congo). Again, typical for these troubled areas are human rights violations.[11] Corruption is part of the problem, and it deepens these difficulties. Corruption is a worldwide challenge, and it is felt more in many parts of the developing world. But it has its most problematic effects in failing or failed states, frequently torn by conflict, embroiled in civil wars.

Therefore, wider-reaching strategies addressing corruption in the future need to differentiate according to the situation of the respective country or area (for further detail see below Chapter 23).

10. Cf. above OECD, 85 and UN, 103 et seq., 107.

11. For a human rights case against corruption cf. International Council on Human Rights Policy, Integrating Human Rights in the Anti-Corruption Agenda: Challenges, Possibilities and Opportunities, 2010; cf. also UN Human Rights Council Resolution 23/9, 20 June 2013 (UN Doc. A/HRC/RES/23/9); Pearson 2001, 30 et seq.; Peters 2015.

22

Globalization and Digital Revolution

FRITZ HEIMANN AND STEFAN MBIYAVANGA ■

The period from the end of World War II until 1990 was characterized by the bipolar world of the Cold War. Economic life was conducted primarily at the level of nation-states operating within the ambit of the alliance system of the Cold War. The end of the Cold War stimulated the evolution of *globalization*, as well as a technology push which is rightfully referred to as the "*digital revolution*".[1] These two developments have been among the most influential of the past quarter century. They will continue to be the two inexorable macro forces redefining the arena within which corruption is conducted and will shape the focus of future anticorruption strategies.

1. GLOBALIZATION

The industrialized sectors of the economy are now dominated by dozens of multinational companies (MNEs). These have evolved from domestic manufacturers exporting a fraction of their output to global companies engaging in development, manufacturing, and marketing of products and services in numerous countries around the world. In 2001 General Electric (GE) had roughly 70 percent of its operations inside the United States. By 2012 60 percent of its operations were outside the United States.[2] For MNEs with headquarters

1. Pieth 2016a, 10.

2. The Financial Times, April 25, 2012: "GE chief upbeat on US manufacturing."

in countries with smaller domestic markets, the percentages of employees and sales outside the home countries are even larger. For instance, in 2016 the Swiss pharma company Novartis generated 98 percent of its sales outside of Switzerland.[3]

In developing countries, the export of commodities into the world economy has become the most rapidly growing element of their national economies. Arrangements under which foreign companies and governments play an active role in exploration, extraction, and local manufacturing in developing countries have become common. One example thereof is the concession granted to the Anglo-Australian company Rio Tinto for developing the Guinean Simandou iron ore mine worth an estimated $140 billion.[4]

a. Globalization of Corruption

Before 1990, foreign bribery could essentially be conducted unimpeded by legal constraints. Foreign bribery was not a crime, except in the United States, and bribe payments abroad could be treated as tax-deductible business expenses.

Only after the growth of global trade led to changes in law enforcement did the practice of global corruption begin to change. Thereafter, a cat-and-mouse process began. Corruption became steadily more complicated. Instead of handing over briefcases stuffed with cash, bribe payments were conducted through intermediaries, and sophisticated money-laundering techniques were utilized.

b. Impact of Globalization on Law Enforcement

Law enforcement has had to make major changes to deal with globalization. Before 1990 enforcement focused almost exclusively on activities conducted within national borders. Since then new international treaties have been enacted, including the OECD Anti-Bribery Convention and the UN Convention against Corruption. International organizations have been established to promote the enforcement of these treaties, including the OECD Working Group on Bribery, the UN Office of Drugs and Crime (UNODC), and G20. Transparency International (TI), the International Chamber of Commerce (ICC), and other nongovernmental organizations (NGOs) are also actively involved.

3. Novartis, 2016: "Novartis in Switzerland", 10.

4. Cf. The Guardian, July 30, 2013: "The Tycoon, the dictator's wife and the $2.5bn Guinea mining deal."

These changes have created a superstructure to assist national enforcement systems. The treaties are not self-enforcing. Under the Treaty of Rome there is a court dealing with human rights violations. The court is based in The Hague. It has been proposed that the human rights court should accept corruption cases. However, the court has not worked very efficiently because governmental approval is needed to obtain jurisdiction.[5] National enforcement remains very uneven, depending on the level of commitment of individual governments. Enforcement actions can only be brought in national courts; there is no international court in which global corruption cases can be brought.

Dealing with global corruption through national legal systems is difficult. Mutual legal assistance is complicated and time-consuming.

2. DIGITAL REVOLUTION

Advancements in "information and communication technology" (ICT) led to the launch of the Internet in the early 1990s, which has grown rapidly ever since. It makes instantaneous global communications possible and has encapsulated virtually every aspect of life. In 2011, US secretary of state Hillary Clinton proclaimed that "the internet has become the public space of the 21st century—the world's town square, classroom, marketplace, coffee house and nightclub." [6]

However, as technology is neutral by nature it empowers individuals for both good and ill. Accordingly, it does not come as a great surprise that "cybercrime" is almost as old as "cyberspace" itself.[7] Hacking and the infiltration of company servers to compromise customer data have tarnished the Internet's reputation ever since its inception.[8] With the increased availability and reach of the Internet, the opportunities for abuse and criminal infringement also grew, which is evidenced by an ever-increasing "cyber security" industry. In the twenty-first century, trade in illegal firearms, drugs, and child pornography, largely facilitated by the anonymous network structures making up the so called "Dark Net," have made the headlines.[9]

5. The idea of a supranational court for corruption is further discussed in Chapter 17, page 211 et seq.

6. Huffington Post, February 15, 2017: "Secretary Clinton doubles down on Internet freedom at the State Department."

7. Pieth 2016a, 130.

8. Pieth 2016a, 130; Foreign Affairs, November 16, 2015: "How to disappear completely."

9. NZZ, July 25, 2015, "Ein Schatten, der uns befreien kann"; The Guardian, October 5, 2014, "Dark net markets: The eBay of drug dealing."

In the fight against corruption, however, the digital revolution has arguably tipped the balance in favor of the anticorruption movement. In the following, a few areas in which technology has affected anticorruption efforts will be outlined.

a. Cyber Forensics

The digital revolution has transformed the terrain on which the fight against corruption is conducted by giving investigators unprecedented access to huge amounts of data. The so-called "data revolution" has changed the risk profile for corruption, expanded the extent of public interest and involvement, and enlarged the scope for anticorruption measures. The mechanism of transforming large amounts of data into more accessible information is made possible through *data mining and cleaning*. Data mining refers to the process by which large data sets are analyzed to discover suspicious patterns.[10] It involves methods of artificial intelligence, machine learning, and statistics. By way of example, in online shopping data mining makes it possible to profile customer preferences and predict purchasing patterns. In the anticorruption context, however, it can be used for auditing purposes in public procurement, by searching data sets on government bidding processes for abnormal patterns or "red flags," that is, indicators of corruption risks, such as exceptionally short bidding periods or bids repeatedly won by the same company.[11]

The Forensic Impact

The impact of the Internet on foreign bribery cases was first made clear to me at an International Bar Association meeting in 2013. A panel of prosecutors from Switzerland, Italy, and the United States discussed their success in winning foreign bribery cases because the Internet makes incriminating documents much easier to find.

Bribe payers and bribe recipients have traditionally operated in strict secrecy. That was easier to do in the time of carbon-paper copies. In the Internet age emails are widely produced, copied, and distributed. As a result, the trail left by emails is much larger than the old-fashioned paper trail and is practically impossible to eradicate. Because it has become much harder to

10. Knierim, Rübenstahl and Tsambikakis 2013, 193.

11. World Economic Forum, April 18, 2016: "4 technologies helping us to fight corruption."

maintain secrets, the ability to uncover and prosecute corruption has correspondingly increased.

One of the biggest obstacles in bringing foreign bribery cases is the difficulty of securing evidence from other countries. Procedures for "mutual legal assistance" have been complex and very time-consuming. Such problems can be overcome as prosecutors from different countries learn to work together using information technology. OECD is sponsoring regular meetings among prosecutors. It would be helpful to include prosecutors from non-OECD countries where there is endemic corruption, such as Nigeria.

The perseverance and ingenuity of practitioners of corruption should never be underestimated. The use of tools made available by the digital revolution to rapidly launder bribe payments through multiple transactions, including banks in jurisdictions that continue to maintain bank secrecy, has become standard procedure. Money launderers also make extensive use of encryption. The cat-and-mouse game between practitioners of corruption and corruption fighters will of course continue, but a review of the current state of play provides a sound basis for optimism.

b. Digital Initiatives

When citizens file complaints with local officials, there is always a certain risk that the file is not adequately processed. A growing field of online reporting platforms addresses this problem by providing citizens with an outlet to report corrupt acts online, usually operating on a national basis. These *upward initiatives* can be established by NGOs or by government agencies. If civil society and citizens are enabled to gather data and to monitor government activities, the likelihood that abuses and corrupt behavior are reported increases substantially.[12] Where reports are made publicly available, media attention may also create political traction for change.[13]

12. U4 Expert Answer, March 28, 2013: "Technological innovations to identify and reduce corruption," 3.

13. U4 Issue, June 2014: "Mixed incentives: Adopting ICT innovations for transparency, accountability, and anti-corruption," 9.

IPAIDABRIBE.COM

Perhaps the most renowned corruption reporting website is the Janaagraha Centre for Citizenship's ipaidabribe.com. Through this website, citizens can report on the nature, number, location, and other values of actual corrupt acts that they experienced. The initiative started in India, but has been duplicated in Greece, Kenya, Zimbabwe, and other countries.

The data collected through the initiative was used to push for the establishment of online application procedures to receive driver's licenses from a local motor vehicle department.[14]

The World Bank (WB) has caught on to the trend and launched its own "Integrity" mobile phone app. The app enables users to submit confidential reports detailing concerns of fraud or corruption. Users can directly send information relevant to projects funded by the WB, for example recordings of a bribe or photos of half-erect schools. Furthermore, the app provides access to the WB list of debarred firms and individuals.[15] "Infomex" established by the Mexican government provides a similar capability by enabling users to obtain information to appeal agency decisions to an oversight board.

Furthermore, so-called *downward initiatives* seek to give the citizenry greater access to government-held data and information.[16] Through web-based portals, government agencies routinely publish sets of information on issues such as government spending and departmental budget allocations.[17] National transparency portals have been used across Latin America since the early 2000s and have become well established since then.[18] However, in many contexts direct

14. For further information about IPaidABribe: (http://ipaidabribe.com/about-us#gsc.tab=0) (last visited February 10, 2017).

15. World Bank Blog, November 19, 2012: "Leveraging New Tools to Report Fraud and Corruption: The World Bank Launches Its Integrity App" (http://blogs.worldbank.org/publicsphere/leveraging-new-tools-report-fraud-and-corruption-world-bank-launches-its-integrity-app (last visited February 13, 2017).

16. U4 Issue, June 2014: "Mixed incentives: Adopting ICT innovations for transparency, accountability, and anti-corruption," 23.

17. U4 Issue, June 2014: "Mixed incentives: Adopting ICT innovations for transparency, accountability, and anti-corruption," 6.

18. eGovernment for Development, eTransparency Case Study No. 15, 2003: "Portales de Transparencia" (http://www.egov4dev.org/transparency/case/laportals.shtml) (last visited March 10, 2017); see for example the Transparency Portal of Peru, "Portal de Transparencia Estàndar" (http://sgp.pcm.gob.pe/portal-de-transparencia-estandar/) (March 10, 2017).

action from local citizens and civil society based on the information they contain remains unsatisfactory.[19] Criticism has already been raised at open data portals that purport an appearance of government transparency yet either leave out any politically sensitive content or remain, in practice, inaccessible to the broad majority of the citizenry.[20]

c. The Political Impact

Instant mass communications over the Internet have expanded the political dimension of the fight against corruption. Masses of people can now become involved. This was vividly demonstrated by the Arab Spring, which caused the downfall of deeply entrenched dictators such as Mubarrak in Egypt, Qaddafi in Libya, and Ben Ali in Tunisia. They had been in power for decades and ruled with impunity. The public protests against corruption leading up to the overthrows erupted in response to calls for action over Twitter and Facebook.[21] Tens of thousands of protesters assembled in Tahrir Square in Cairo and its counterparts in Tunisia and Libya and stayed out until the dictators resigned or fled. The wave of elation produced by the Arab Spring was intense but short-lived. It was followed by disappointment, as corruption persisted and follow-up governments turned their backs on sustainable democratic reforms.

However, the Arab Spring made clear that widespread popular opposition to corruption can overthrow powerful governments. Corrupt governments now recognize that there are limits to corruption beyond which they become vulnerable. How much corruption they can get away with will vary from place to place depending on political conditions, including the strength of the government and the power of the opposition. The digital revolution will curtail the areas where corruption is tolerated. The rate of progress in curbing corruption is unclear, but change is moving in the right direction.

d. Awareness Raising

There is now much greater publicity surrounding corruption and the efforts to fight it. This may have resulted in a misleading public perception that

19. U4 Issue, June 2014: "Mixed incentives: Adopting ICT innovations for transparency, accountability, and anti-corruption," 8.

20. U4 Issue, June 2014: "Mixed incentives: Adopting ICT innovations for transparency, accountability, and anti-corruption," 2.

21. New York Times, February 17, 2012: "How an Egyptian revolution began on Facebook."

corruption has been on the rise in recent years. However, the increased focus on corruption has been the result of an awareness-raising strategy conducted by Transparency International, Public Witness, and other organizations, an effort largely facilitated by social media. Because bribery had always been conducted in secrecy, its extent had been hidden from public view. Awareness raising was a critical precursor to securing political support for reforms. The contention that increased awareness of corruption indicates that there is more corruption is a topsy-turvy view of developments.

23

Different Strategies for Different Countries

FRITZ HEIMANN ■

Public awareness of the damage done by corruption is now widespread. This is an important achievement of Transparency International (TI) and other reformers. However, there is still substantial public skepticism regarding the ability of reformers to reduce corruption. This was made clear to me some years ago when a colleague at General Electric commenting on my work for TI observed that: "You are doing the Lord's work." After some reflection I realized that this was not really a compliment. What he meant was that working against corruption was of no earthly use.

Building confidence in the effectiveness of reforms must be a key objective. To that end, tangible successes in reducing corruption must be achieved and widely publicized. Before starting new programs, realistic assessments of the chances of success should be made, recognizing that combating corruption is difficult and that risks must be taken. The level of care should be commensurate with the degree of risk.

Avoiding failures is important. For example, US government anticorruption programs in Afghanistan, while Hamid Karzai was president, and in Iraq while Nuri al-Maliki was prime minister, were not just unproductive, but had negative effects, reinforcing arguments that fighting corruption is futile and a waste of money.

The chances that reform programs can succeed will differ substantially, depending on the political system of the country. Four different political

Confronting Corruption. Fritz Heimann and Mark Pieth.

systems should be distinguished. In descending order of the potential for curbing corruption, they are:

- First, countries with strong democratic institutions.
- Second, countries with weaker democratic institutions.
- Third, countries with autocratic government.
- Fourth, failed states.

Because the funds available to combat corruption are limited, this classification should guide the selection of programs and the allocation of funds. It should be considered by nongovernmental organization (NGOs), by national governments, and by international organizations.

1. COUNTRIES WITH STRONG DEMOCRATIC INSTITUTIONS

Countries with strong democratic institutions typically have checks and balances in place that serve to curb corruption. The most important checks and balances are access to information, independent and effective judicial systems, freedom of the press, and active civil societies. These create transparency and accountability as a result of which abuses can be identified and addressed.

Examples include the Scandinavian countries, Great Britain, Switzerland, Canada, the United States, New Zealand, Australia, Chile, and Uruguay.

The key priority in countries with strong democratic institutions will be to maintain and strengthen the effectiveness of checks and balances. The incentives for corruption never disappear. Politicians seek money to get re-elected and companies seek political influence. The corrupt are resourceful, developing new techniques to circumvent controls. In response to reforms, corruption is likely to move further below the surface and take more sophisticated forms.

Continuing vigilance in maintaining anticorruption programs is also needed because of changing economic and political conditions. During periods of recession there will be increased pressure to win a smaller number of orders, making resort to bribes more likely. At the same time a recession will result in reduced government spending including cuts in anticorruption programs.

The need to confront new political challenges is illustrated by recent legal changes in the United States. Restrictions on contributions to political campaigns that had been in effect for much of the twentieth century have been eviscerated by two recent Supreme Court decisions, *Citizens United* and *McCutcheon*. To overcome this damaging setback will require a long and difficult political battle.

Even in countries with good controls at the national level, corruption is often widespread at the state and municipal levels. In Connecticut, a state with a strong legal system, a governor who had previously been imprisoned for accepting bribes has been sent to jail for a second time. Experience in the United States (and Canada) indicates that different, locally-based organizations are needed to cope with corruption at the state and municipal levels.

Dealing with corruption in countries with strong democratic institutions should be considered the primary responsibility of domestic organizations. Surveillance of these countries under OECD and United Nations Convention against Corruption (UNCAC) monitoring programs should continue. However, the limited resources of international anticorruption organizations should be devoted primarily to other countries.

The countries with strong democratic institutions are the best places to demonstrate tangible successes. They generally have good record-keeping practices and strong access to information laws. Greater efforts are needed to collect success stories that can then be broadly publicized.

2. COUNTRIES WITH WEAKER DEMOCRATIC INSTITUTIONS

In countries with weaker democratic institutions, transparency and accountability are insufficient to bring abuses to the surface until they reach a high level. Consequently, dealing with the abuses will be harder. However, popular support for reforms is aroused by prominent scandals. Examples include: Greece, Italy, Spain, Portugal, Colombia, Mexico, Brazil, India, Indonesia, Nigeria, Turkey, and South Africa.

In these countries, the focus should be on improving transparency and accountability by strengthening access to information laws, independence of the judiciary and the media, and civil society organizations.

Strengthening the capability of these countries to confront corruption should be a top priority for the anticorruption movement and particularly for Transparency International and the World Bank. The benefits obtainable are likely to be much greater than working in the other three categories. Countries with weaker democratic institutions are in greater need of external assistance than countries with strong democratic institutions. The chances of success will be much greater than in countries with autocratic governments or in failed states.

It is now widely recognized that anticorruption programs require an underlying institutional framework. In countries with weaker democratic institutions improving the existing framework should be manageable and external assistance will generally be welcome. In countries with autocratic governments outside assistance is generally unwelcome and governments will oppose reforms to strengthen transparency and accountability. In failed states, there will be no institutional framework to build on.

There are a range of available techniques for providing support.

- Transparency International has experience providing assistance to national chapters in countries with weaker institutions using its international secretariat, as well as national chapters in countries with strong institutions.
- In the private sector, major multinational enterprises (MNEs) have successfully promoted transparency and accountability utilizing their networks of subsidiaries and suppliers.
- Assistance can also come from the World Bank, the European Development Bank, and other regional development banks, as well as from bilateral agencies in Canada, Scandinavia, Great Britain, and the United States.

There are encouraging examples of progress in curbing corruption by strengthening democratic institutions. Examples include Colombia, Indonesia, Rwanda, and Georgia. Progress should also be possible in countries with governments strongly committed to reform including India, Italy, and Mexico.

In Brazil major improvements have been made at the national government level, but without adequate attention to state-owned enterprises. The massive Petrobras scandal illustrates this problem. Brazil also has serious problems at the subnational level, including the large cities where many services are delivered and infrastructure work takes place.

3. COUNTRIES WITH AUTOCRATIC GOVERNMENTS

In considering anticorruption strategy for autocratic countries, the major difference, compared with democratic governments, lies in the control that autocratic governments can be expected to exercise over anticorruption programs within their countries. In recent years several major autocratic governments have prohibited foreign NGOs from working in their countries and have barred domestic NGOs from obtaining external support.

Levels of corruption in autocratic countries differ greatly. Two of the least corrupt countries in the world are Hong Kong and Singapore, both autocracies. Corruption is deeply entrenched in many autocratic countries, with the leader and his entourage actively involved as organizers and as beneficiaries. Other autocratic governments are conducting strong anticorruption programs.

Examples of autocratic countries include China, Russia, Belarus, Saudi Arabia, Iran, Algeria, Qatar, Kuwait, the Emirates, Egypt, Zimbabwe, and Kazakhstan, as well as Hong Kong and Singapore.

As a broad generalization, it is easier for the anticorruption movement to work in democratic countries where their help is more often welcome and their activities will not be rigidly controlled. However, there are areas of work in autocratic countries that could be beneficial to the country and to the anticorruption movement.

Areas of mutual benefit include work on implementation of international conventions particularly UNCAC and OECD, as well as G20. The monitoring mechanisms of UNCAC and OECD can provide leverage for reforms. NGOs and companies active in the anticorruption movement could also assist companies based in autocratic countries to function in the global economy. Autocratic governments may be interested in getting help to curb corruption in activities such as collection of taxes and customs and public procurement.

Corrupt governments often issue public statements opposing corruption. This may reflect the desire to demonstrate adherence to international standards or may respond to domestic concerns. Such public positions may provide some leverage for reforms. However, international comments on such statements should be careful to avoid giving unwarranted credibility to what may only be window dressing.

Providing support for NGOs opposed to corruption would be desirable, but would probably be opposed by a number of autocratic governments.

If we go beyond generalizations about relations with autocratic governments, it is pertinent to look at the prospects for work in China and Russia, and to consider the implications of the Arab Spring on relations with countries in the Middle East and North Africa.

a. Working with China

In view of China's enormous influence on the global economy, working with China is critically important for the international anticorruption movement. Whether China curbs foreign bribery by Chinese firms will largely determine whether the OECD's prohibition of foreign bribery will become the global norm.

Although there are strong incentives for working with China, serious obstacles must be addressed. The Chinese government is determined to stand on its own feet. It is suspicious of Western influences and distrusts foreign NGOs. However, there are also important benefits for China. The experience of TI shows that the obstacles can be overcome and productive relationships can be established. Prolonged efforts were required to understand Chinese concerns and to develop mutually beneficial programs.

First Trip to China

TI's invitation to come to China was arranged by Professor Thomas Lee of MIT who had a unique background. He was born in China, educated in electrical engineering in Shanghai, and went to work for GE's Chinese subsidiary. In 1947 GE sent him and his wife to Schenectady for a year's experience. The Communist revolution in 1948 resulted in the takeover of GE's subsidiary. Tom stayed in Schenectady, obtained a PhD at Rensselaer Polytechnic Institute (RPI), and became a world authority on electrical transmission systems.

Tom was not allowed to visit China for over three decades, until his mother died in 1984. On this visit he re-established relations with his engineering school classmates, including Deng Ziaoping, who had risen to top jobs in the Chinese government. Thereafter Tom went to Beijing regularly, becoming an advisor to Deng.

Tom and I had become friends when we worked together in GE's power business, where he was the top scientist and I was the top lawyer. We stayed in close touch after he went to MIT. I talked to him about TI, and he offered to set up a meeting in Beijing. The meeting took place in 2000 hosted by the Ministry of Supervision. Tom Lee participated. TI was represented by Peter Eigen, Tunku Abdul Aziz from Malaysia, and me.

In the initial discussions TI expressed its interest in establishing a national chapter in China. The Chinese government proposed that the Ministry of Supervision should serve as TI's Chinese chapter. We explained that TI and its national chapters were civil society organizations, that national chapters had to be able to operate independently of their governments, and that the Ministry of Supervision could not function in such a role.

Thanks to Tom Lee's relationships, the impasse at the first meeting was overcome and a long relationship-building process evolved. As a first step, a law professor at Tsinghua University was designated by the government as a liaison representative. He attended TI meetings in Berlin. After a time, additional Tsinghua professors became involved. This process was nurtured by Liao Ran, a Chinese-speaking member of the TI Secretariat in Berlin, who traveled regularly to China.

Huguette Labelle, TI's chair from 2005 to 2014, played an influential role in developing TI's national chapter in China. This was facilitated by relationships with Chinese officials she had built when she ran the Canadian International Development Agency (CIDA), including serving as vice chair of the China Council on Environment and Development.

There can be no question about the Chinese government's long-standing and deeply-held concerns about corruption in China. The government has openly attributed the success of the Communist Party in overthrowing the Chiang Kai-shek government in 1948 to popular opposition aroused by Chiang Kai-shek's endemic corruption. This is still stressed by Party leaders after more than six decades.

Popular concern about growing corruption is considered the most serious threat to the Party's continuing in power. This was made clear to the TI team when it visited China in 2000. Party concern about this threat has been expressed most recently by President Xi Jinping, who has made action against corruption a top priority.

The scope and determination of Xi Jinping's program has overcome initial suspicion that his primary interest was to build his power base by using bribery charges to dismiss officials remaining from the prior regime. He has stressed the need for action against corrupt "tigers as well as swallows" and criticized the amassing of great wealth by relatives of Party leaders.

China has enacted legislation prohibiting bribery by Chinese enterprises outside China. It is unclear how actively that prohibition is enforced. Chinese companies doing business in Africa and elsewhere are widely believed to engage in bribery of foreign officials. (The Chinese government has had observers at the OECD Working Group on Bribery for some time but has given no indication that it will sign the OECD Anti-Bribery Convention.)

Interaction between Enforcement by China and OECD

It has become apparent that there have been adverse effects as a result of inadequate enforcement by the Chinese government of the prohibition of foreign bribery by Chinese exporters. China rigorously enforces the prohibition of bribery within China. However, there is only limited, if any, enforcement of the prohibition against foreign bribery by Chinese exporters. The Chinese government has justified this by pointing to very uneven levels of enforcement of the OECD Anti-Bribery Convention by OECD members. TI reports have indicated that there is strong enforcement in four countries, moderate enforcement in nine countries, and little or no enforcement by over half of OECD countries.[1]

OECD governments have expressed concern about increasing levels of Chinese competition and indicated that this has influenced their interest in stronger enforcement.

Efforts by OECD to encourage China and OECD member governments to improve their enforcements efforts have been unavailing.

A fundamental question raised by Western experts is whether China's top-down approach against corruption by Party leaders can be sustained longer term. Although the Ministry of Supervision has broad power to combat corruption at other levels, action against Party leaders can only be taken by the Disciplinary Committee of the Central Committee of the Communist Party.

Those of us trained in the Western legal tradition consider public transparency and accountability and independent checks and balances crucial to success in the fight against corruption. The Chinese government emphasizes the primacy of the Communist Party and opposes public checks and balances such as an independent judiciary, access to information laws and whistle-blowers, and an active civil society role.

A centralized system run by the Disciplinary Committee of the Central Committee is clearly able to punish high officials. The open question is whether such a centralized system, without independent checks and balances, can effectively curb corruption in the long run, after Xi Jinping has retired.

Until recently there was widespread belief in the superiority of the Western approach to combating corruption. It now has become a two-sided debate. There is increasing recognition that in other fields, the centralized Chinese system can produce results more quickly than a decentralized Western system. This has been demonstrated by China's ability to develop high-speed trains and a nationwide electrical transmission system.

With respect to curbing corruption, it can be argued that tone at the top is crucial to success and that Xi Jinping has set the right tone. The open question is: Will the same tone will be maintained by his successors?

The debate between believers in a highly centralized approach, and believers in public checks and balances will not be resolved by discussion and debate. The views of both sides are shaped by their training and traditions. It will almost certainly take several decades of experience to determine which approach is

1. Transparency International, May 2015: "Exporting Corruption, Progress Report 2015: Assessing Enforcement of the OECD Convention on Combatting Foreign Bribery."

more effective. There may be no single answer. One approach may be better for China, another for countries following Western legal traditions.

Areas for cooperation with China include:

- Encouraging adoption of the OECD Convention;
- Working with Chinese companies on development of compliance programs;
- Working with Chinese government agencies on procurement reforms such as High Level Reporting Mechanism and Integrity Pacts.

b. Working with Russia

The potential benefits from working with Russia to curb corruption are not promising as long as the current policies of President Putin remain in effect. The Putin government has shown little interest in systemic, as distinct from sporadic, programs to combat corruption. Putin has allowed his inner circle to pursue the same corrupt arrangements previously practiced by oligarchs during the Yeltsin era. The partners in Russia's economic sphere are Belarus and Kazakhstan, both very corrupt and uninterested in reforming.

Russia joined the OECD Convention during the Medvedev presidency when it showed greater interest in international cooperation. It is uncertain how Russian OECD membership will play out: Will Russia adopt better compliance policies in response to OECD monitoring, or will Russia work to weaken OECD monitoring?

The Putin government has tolerated the existence of a TI national chapter in Russia. TI-Russia has had courageous leadership by Elena Panfilova, who is now TI's vice chair. But its scope of operation and its future are kept uncertain by government threats. Preserving TI-Russia and improving its scope is important.

c. The Arab Spring and Its Implications for the Middle East and North Africa

Autocracy and widespread corruption have long been prevalent in the Middle East and North Africa. The popular uprisings in 2011 in Tunisia, Libya, and Egypt, popularly called the Arab Spring, were totally unexpected. They demonstrated that widespread indignation over pervasive corruption could trigger popular uprising powerful enough to overthrow dictatorships that had been in power for decades.

The initial media reaction to the Arab Spring was rapturous. That changed to deep disappointment by the fall of 2011 over the failure to establish sound successor governments. The Arab Spring is now widely characterized as a dismal failure and a defeat for the cause of fighting corruption. That fails to recognize the deeper effects.

The Arab Spring was a profoundly important development. The recognition of the power of popular movements and the vulnerability of entrenched dictatorships has stimulated new and more radical thinking by opponents of corruption. Transparency International's "No Impunity" campaign is a direct result. At the same time, corrupt dictators now recognize that they are more vulnerable than they previously believed. For some, such as Russia's Putin, the response has been to become even more repressive. Others have concluded that addressing popular concerns is a preferable response.

The decision of Iran's Supreme Leader Ayatollah Khamenei not to limit candidates at the 2013 presidential election to hardliners, which led to the election of President Rouhani, was almost certainly influenced by the Arab Spring. Morocco has become somewhat more democratic. Algeria has refused to change its rigid system. Saudi Arabia has retained autocratic control while seeking to build popularity by massive distributions of money.

The aftermath in the three countries where the Arab Spring occurred varies greatly. Tunisia appears to be building democratic institutions. Libya remains in disarray with different tribal groups seeking to control different sections. In Egypt, by far the largest Arabic country, the overthrow of President Mubarak led to an election that was won by the Moslem Brotherhood. The new government became progressively less popular as it sought to introduce Islamic rules. It was overthrown by another popular revolt supported by the army. The successor government dominated by the army has restored a measure of stability by violently suppressing the Moslem Brotherhood. President Al Sisi has indicated a desire to move toward democratic governance, but he has released Mubarak from prison. The return to stability is popular, but the future remains uncertain, except for continuing army control.

The second lesson of the Arab Spring is the difficulty of making a transition to stable democratic rule after dictators have been overthrown. This should be no surprise to students of history. Following the French revolution of 1789 it took eight turbulent decades, including the bloody reign of terror, military control by Napoleon, re-establishment of Bourbon kings, and additional revolutions in 1830 and 1848. It was not until after defeat by Germany in 1870–1871 before stable democratic institutions finally began to function.

Following a revolution, the key question is: How sweeping are the effects on preexisting institutions? New political institutions need years to grow roots, and there is little that can be done from the outside to speed up the process. If preexisting institutions survive and have popular support, the transition can proceed more quickly. That appears to be the case in Tunisia. In Libya, Quadafi ran a purely personal dictatorship. He did not even bother to occupy any political position. There was nothing to build on after his downfall.

Developments in Egypt make clear that after prolonged turmoil stability becomes the dominant concern. That explains why the army was able to take over, notwithstanding widespread Egyptian interest in building democratic institutions. It will be interesting to see whether President Al Sisi's expressed interest in moving toward democracy is only window dressing, or whether he has learned a lesson from the downfall of Mubarak.

In sum, the Arab Spring has shown that corrupt autocracies are not permanent fixtures and are vulnerable to popular uprisings. This is a very positive development for the anticorruption movement. What comes after a revolution will vary greatly from case to case. To encourage a positive transition will require careful analysis of post-revolutionary conditions, realism, and patience.

4. FAILED STATES

Failed states are characterized by dysfunctional and often predatory governments. Causes of state failure include prolonged misgovernment, wars, natural disasters, lack of resources, famines, and epidemics. Corruption may be an aggravating factor, but is usually dwarfed by other causes.

Failed states can be divided into two categories: hopeless cases and those trying to recover from their afflictions. The first category consists of governments that have been captured by corrupt interests. They serve as bases for a wide range of illicit activities including narcotics production and distribution, prostitution, counterfeiting, money laundering, and smuggling. In all of these activities corruption plays a central role.

The second category consists of governments that are trying to overcome their afflictions. These governments have not been captured by corrupt interests and do not serve as bases for illicit activities.

Examples of failed states include: Haiti, Congo, Somalia, Libya, Moldova, Central African Republic, and North Korea, which fall into the first category, and Afghanistan and Iraq, which are in the second category.

Corruption is practically impossible to overcome where there has been state capture because the rulers thrive on the proceeds of corruption. Such rulers typically face no domestic checks and balances. Opposition groups are pushed underground, jailed, or exiled.

Governments of captured states may be interested in obtaining outside assistance, and to that end in improving their public image. They may invite representatives of NGOs and other international organizations and offer to undertake anticorruption activities. Such invitations should be assessed with skepticism. Working in such states is likely to be a waste of resources that are better applied elsewhere.

In recovering states, substantial outside help is crucial. The causes of their failure, such as wars and natural disasters, are of such magnitude that assistance must come primarily from governments and international aid agencies. Help from NGOs in dealing with corruption can be a useful addition to the recovery process.

Governments where state capture has occurred cannot be ignored, because of the damage done by illicit activities conducted from such states. Governments and international organizations should apply sanctions, for example exclusion from the global financial system, freezing funds, and prohibiting travel by government officials. Support should be given to exiled or underground opposition groups.

Because of the magnitude of the problems and the time required to deal with them, addressing corruption in failed states is not an appropriate field for NGOs, and should be left to governments and international organizations such as the World Bank and national governments.

5. LONG-TERM STRATEGY PERSPECTIVE

Realistic anticorruption strategy should be based on three premises:

- Corruption can never be completely eliminated. Among the reasons is that the line between legal and illegal activities is unclear (e.g., bribery versus political contributions), and the practitioners of corruption will exploit such lack of clarity.
  - Criminal prohibitions should be used where clear lines can be drawn.
  - Regulatory rules and public standards should be used to curtail corruption beyond the reach of criminal law.
- Curbing corruption will require continuing effort for the indefinite future because the economic, political, and technical conditions keep changing, and because the practitioners of corruption will be resilient.
- Reducing existing levels of corruption can produce great benefits. A good indicator is the difference between the quality of life in countries in the top quartile of the TI Index with those in the bottom quartile.

Maintaining public and government support for continuing anticorruption programs for the long term presents a major challenge. The key condition for success will be to demonstrate continuing progress. Transparency International and its allies must establish credible programs to collect and publicize relevant data. A useful step would be to expand the TI Index by correlating national rankings of corruption with the state of economic and political health. Where there is insufficient progress, advocacy programs must be launched to improve progress.

BIBLIOGRAPHY

Books and Articles

Aiolfi, G. (2014), "Mitigating the Risks of Corruption through Collective Action" in D. Brodowski et al., (eds.) *Regulating Criminal Corporate Liability*, Cham et al., 125 et seq.

Balmelli, M. (1996), *Die Bestechungstatbestände des Schweizerischen Strafgesetzbuches*, Diss. Basel

Bandura, A. (2006), "Toward a Psychology of Human Agency," *Stanford University, Perspectives on Psychological Science*, no. 1, 164 et seq.

Banning, L. (1980), *The Jeffersonian Persuasion*, New York

Ben Jelloun, T. (1994), *L'homme rompu*, Paris

Betz, K. (2017), *Proving Bribery, Fraud and Money Laundering in International Arbitration, On Applicable Criminal Law and Evidence*, Cambridge

Beveridge, A.J. (1919), The Life of John Marshall, vol. 3, Boston

Bircher, D. and S. Scherler (2001), *Missbräuche bei der Vergabe öffentlicher Bauaufträge. Analysen, Beispiele und Lösungsvorschläge*, Bern

Bonucci, N. (2014), "Article 12, Monitoring and Follow-Up" in Pieth, Low, and Bonucci 2014, 534 et seq.

Brun, J.-P. et al. (eds.) (2011), *Asset Recovery Handbook, A Guide for Practitioners*, StAR, Washington, 17 et seq.

Bueno de Mesquita, B. and A. Smith (2011), *The Dictator's Handbook: Why Bad Behavior Is Almost Always Good Politics*, New York

Carver, J. (2004) (Clifford Chance law firm, Britain), "The Hunt for Looted State Assets: The Case of Benazir Bhutto" in Transparency International (ed.), *Global Corruption Report 2004, Special Focus: Political Corruption*, London, 102 et seq.

Clark, P. B. and J. Suprenant (2009), "Siemens—Potential Interplay of FCPA Charges and Mandatory Debarment under the Public Procurement Directive of the European Union," *ABA White Collar Conference*

Cover, O. and S. Mustafa (2014), "Identifying Corruption Risks in the Defense and Security Sector: Empirical Evidence Using the Government Defense Anti-Corruption Index," 9 *The Economics of Peace and Security Journal*, 27 et seq.

Confronting Corruption. Fritz Heimann and Mark Pieth.

Dannacher, M. (2012), *Diktatorengelder in der Schweiz, Einziehung und Herausgabe von unrechtmässig erworbenen Vermögenswerten politisch exponierter Personen*, Basel

Datzova, B. (2003), *Health Care Reform and Inequality of Access to Health Care in Bulgaria,* September 2003

Davies, M. N. (2008), "The Role of Agents and Other Intermediaries" in Heimann and Vincke 2008, 53 et seq.

Davigo, P. and G. Mannozzi (2007), *La corruzione in Italia, Percezione sociale e controllo penale*, Bari

Davis, J. (2004), "Corruption in Public Service Delivery: Experience from South Asia's Water and Sanitation Sector," 32 *World Development Report*, No. 1, 53 et seq.

De Swardt, C. and M. Wiehen, "Islands of Integrity" in Pieth 2012, 83 et seq.

Duggin, S. H. (2003), "Internal Corporate Investigations: Legal Ethics, Professionalism and the Employee Interview," *Columbia Business Law Review*, no. 3, 859 et seq.

Falcone, G. and M. Padovani (1992), *Inside Mafia,* Munich

Fenner Zinkernagel, G., C. Monteith, and P. Gomes Pereira (eds.) (2013), *Emerging Trends in Asset Recovery,* Bern

Fox, T. (2013), *GSK in China: A Game Changer in Compliance,* (ebook)

Gabus, P. and A.-L. Bandle (2014), *L'art a-t-il un prix? The Art of Pricing the Priceless, L'évaluation des œuvres d'art, ses défis pratiques et juridiques—On the Valuation of Art, Its Challenges and Liabilities (français-anglais),* Zurich

Garapon, A. and P. Servan-Schreiber (2013), *Deals de Justice, Le Marché Américain de L'obéissance Mondialisée,* Paris

Goijman, M. (2006), "Volleygate—The Breathtaking Story of King Rubén and Queen Malú" in Weinreich 2006, 94 et seq.

Goldsmith, L. P. (2014), 'Foreword' in Pieth 2014b, 3 et seq.

Goldsmith, S. (2014) "Digital Transformation: Wiring the Responsive City," *Center for State and Local Leadership Civic Report,* No. 87, 1 et seq.

Hardin, R. (2013), "The Free Rider Problem" in E. N. Zalta (ed.), *The Stanford Encyclopedia of Philosophy* (Spring 2013 Edition), (available at http://plato.stanford.edu/archives/spr2013/entries/free-rider/ (last visited February 10, 2017)

Heimann, F. (2012), "High-Level Reporting: Overcoming Extortion" in Pieth 2012, 209 et seq.

Heimann, F. and F. Vincke (2008), *Fighting Corruption: International Corporate Integrity Handbook,* Paris

Heineman, B. W. and F. Heimann (2007), "Arrested Development: The Fight against International Corporate Bribery," *The National Interest*, November/December 2007, 80 et seq.

Hershman, M. (2014), "The Need for Reform" in Pieth 2014b, 17 et seq.

Hobbes, T. (1992), *Leviathan* (1651), Stuttgart

Hottinger, A. (2013), "Two Years Later: The Arab Revolutions in Transition" in Fenner et al. 2013, 3 et seq.

Jean-Pierre, T. (2003), *Taïwan Connection, Scandales et Meurtres au Cœur de la République,* Paris

Jennings, A. (2006), *Foul! The Secret World of FIFA: Bribes, Vote Rigging and Ticket Scandals,* London

Jennings, A. and C. Sambrook (2000), *The Olympic Swindle, When the World Wanted Its Games Back*, London

Johnston, M. (2014), *Corruption Contention and Reform, The Power of Deep Democratization*, Cambridge

Johnston, M. (2005), *Syndromes of Corruption, Wealth, Power, and Democracy*, Cambridge and New York

Kaufmann, D. and P. C. Vicente (2005), "Legal Corruption," 23 *Economics & Politics*, no. 2, 195 et seq.

Kistner, T. and J. Weinreich (2000), *Der olympische Sumpf, Die Machenschaften des IOC*, Munich

Klitgaard, R. (2014), *Addressing Corruption Together*, Stocktaking paper prepared for the Symposium on Anti-Corruption Development Assistance: Good Practices among Providers of Development Cooperation, OECD Development Cooperation Directorate, Paris, December 11–12, 2014

Klitgaard, R. (2012), "Public-Private Collaboration and Corruption" in Pieth 2012, 41 et seq.

Knierim, T., M. Rübenstahl, and M. Tsambikakis (2013), *Internal Investigations: Ermittlungen im Unternehmen*, Heidelberg et al.

Kunicová, J. (2013), "The Role of the World Bank in Promoting Good Governance and Anti-Corruption Reforms: A View from the Europe and Central Asia Region" in S. Rose-Ackerman and P.-D. Carrington (eds.), *Anti-corruption Policy: Can International Actors Play a Constructive Role?*, Durham, 41 et seq.

Langer, S. H. and J. Pelzman (2001), "An Analysis of the OECD Convention on Combating Bribery of Foreign Officials" in K. Fatemi (ed.), *International Public Policy and Regionalism at the Turn of the Century*, Amsterdam/New York, 60 et seq.

Low, L. A. (2014), "Preventing and Defending against Vicarious and Successor Liability under National and International Transnational Bribery Regimes" in Pieth, Low, and Bonucci 2014, 611 et seq.

Machiavelli, N. (1961), *Il Principe* (Florence 1513), Stuttgart

Marcelo, S. (2008), "The Long Road from Zurich to Manila: The Recovery of the Marcos Swiss Dollar Deposits" in Pieth 2008, 89 et seq.

Meyer, J. A. and M. G. Califano (2006), *Good Intentions Corrupted: The Oil-for-Food Scandal and the Threat to the U.N.*, New York

Mill, J. St. (2009), *On Liberty* (1859), Stuttgart

Moene, K. and T. Søreide (2015), *Good Governance Facades*, Working Paper WP 2015:2

Moody-Stuart, G. (1997), *Grand Corruption*, Oxford

Moyo, D. (2009), *Dead Aid: Why Aid Is Not Working and How There Is Another Way for Africa*, New York

Mungiu-Pippidi, A. (2014), *MS2 Quantitative Report on Causes of Performance and Stagnation in the Global Fight against Corruption*, March 28, 2014

Nanda, V. P. (2011), "Corporate Criminal Liability in the United States: Is a New Approach Warranted?" in Pieth and Ivory 2011, 63 et seq.

Neugebauer, G. (1978), *Grundzüge einer ökonomischen Theorie der Korruption*, Diss. Basel

Nicholls, C., Daniel, D., Bacarese, A. and J. Hatchard (2011), *Corruption and Misuse of Public Office*, 2nd ed., Oxford

Noonan, J. T. (1984), *Bribes: The Intellectual History of a Moral Idea*, Berkeley et al.

Obermayer, B. and F. Obermaier (2016), *The Panama Papers, Breaking the Story of How the Rich and Powerful Hide Their Money*, Cologne

OECD (ed.) (2000), *No Longer Business as Usual: Fighting Bribery and Corruption*, Paris

O'Shea, E. (2011), *The Bribery Act 2010, A Practical Guide*, Bristol

Pearson Z. (2001), "An international Human Rights Approach to Corruption" in P. Lamour and N. Wolanin (eds.), *Corruption and Anti-corruption*, Canberra, 30 et seq.

Peters, A. (2015), "Corruption and Human Rights" in Basel Institute on Governance (ed.), *Working Paper No. 20*, 1 et seq.

Pieth, M. (2016a), "*Wirtschaftsstrafrecht*," Basel

Pieth, M. (2016b), *Schweizerisches Strafprozessrecht*, 3rd ed., Basel

Pieth, M. (2014a), 'Introduction', 'Article 2, The Responsibility of Legal Persons', 'Article 7, Money Laundering' in Pieth, Low, and Bonucci 2014, 3 et seq., 212 et seq., 422 et seq.

Pieth, M. (ed.) (2014b), *Reforming FIFA*, Zurich/St. Gall

Pieth, M. (2014c), 'Do ut des' in S. Reindl-Krauskopf et al. (eds.), *Festschrift für Helmut Fuchs*, Vienna, 367 et seq.

Pieth, M. (2013a), 'Korruptionsstrafrecht' in J.-B. Ackermann and G. Heine (eds.), *Wirtschaftsstrafrecht der Schweiz*, Bern, 677 et seq.

Pieth, M. (2013b), "Kommentierung von Art. 305bis und Vor Art. 322ter" in M.-A. Niggli and H. Wiprächtiger (eds.), *Basler Kommentar Strafrecht II*, 3rd ed., Basel

Pieth, M. (ed.) (2012), *Collective Action: Innovative Strategies to Prevent Corruption*, Zurich/St. Gall

Pieth, M. (2011), *Harmonising Anti-corruption Compliance, The OECD Good Practice Guidance 2010*, Zurich/St. Gall

Pieth, M. (2008), "Recovering Stolen Assets—A New Issue?" in M. Pieth (ed.), *Recovering Stolen Assets*, Bern, 3 et seq.

Pieth, M. (2007), "Multi-Stakeholder Initiatives to Combat Money Laundering and Bribery" in C. Brütsch and D. Lehmkuhl (eds.), *Law and Legalization in Transnational Relations*, London/New York, 81 et seq.

Pieth, M. (2000), "From Ideal to Reality: Making the New Global Standard Stick" in OECD 2000, 51 et seq.

Pieth, M. (1999), "International Efforts to Combat Corruption," *International Trade Corruption Monitor (ITCM)*, A-1038

Pieth, M. and G. Aiolfi (eds.) (2004), *A Comparative Guide to Anti-money Laundering: A Critical Analysis of Systems in Singapore, Switzerland, the UK and the USA* (study by the Basel Institute on Governance, commissioned by the Stiftung Finanzplatz Schweiz), Cheltenham (UK)/Northampton (US), 462 et seq.

Pieth, M. and G. Aiolfi (2003), "The Private Sector Becomes Active: The Wolfsberg process" in A. Clark and P. Borrell (eds.), *A Practitioner's Guide to International Money Laundering, Law and Regulation*, Old Woking, 267 et seq.

Pieth, M. and P. Eigen (eds.) (1999), *Korruption im internationalen Geschäftsverkehr: B estandsaufnahme, Bekämpfung, Prävention*, Neuwied et al.

Pieth, M. and R. Ivory (2011), "Emergence and Convergence: Corporate Criminal Liability Principles in Overview" in M. Pieth and R. Ivory (eds.), *Corporate Criminal Liability: Emergence, Convergence, and Risk,* Dordrecht et al., 3 et seq.

Pieth, M., L. A. Low, and N. Bonucci (eds.) (2014), *The OECD Convention on Bribery, A Commentary,* 2nd ed., Cambridge

Pocock, J. G. A. (1975), *The Machiavellian Moment: Florentine Political Thought and the Atlantic Republican Tradition,* Princeton

Public Eye (formerly known as 'Berne Declaration') (ed.) (2012), *Commodities—Switzerland's Most Dangerous Business,* Zurich

Raphael, M. (2010), *Blackstone's Guide to the Bribery Act 2010,* Oxford/New York

Recanatini, F. (2013), "Tackling Corruption and Promoting Better Governance: The Road Ahead" in S. Rose-Ackerman and P.-D. Carrington (eds.), *Anti-corruption Policy: Can International Actors Play a Constructive Role?,* Durham, 55 et seq.

Reuben, E. (2003), *The Evolution of Theories of Collective Action,* Masters Thesis, Tinbergen Institute

Richter, H.-E. (1989), *Die hohe Kunst der Korruption: Erkenntnisse eines Politik-Beraters,* 3rd ed., Hamburg

Rose-Ackerman, S. and B. Billa (2008), "Treaties and National Security," 40 *New York University Journal of International Law and Politics,* 437 et seq.

Rose-Ackerman, S. and T. Søreide (2011), *International Handbook on the Economics of Corruption, Volume 2,* Cheltenham/Northampton

Roth, M. (2015), *Wir betreten den Kunstmarkt, Geldwäscherei/Zollfreilager—ein zu diskretes Geschäft?/Interessenkonflikte, Manipulationen und Preisabsprachen,* Zurich/St. Gall

Sandler, T. (2010), "Overcoming Global and Regional Collective Action Impediments," 1 *Global Policy,* 40 et seq.

Stålgren, P. (2006), "Corruption in the Water Sector: Causes, Consequences and Potential Reform," *Swedish Water House Policy Brief Nr. 4 SIWI*

Stiglitz, J. E. (2012), *The Price of Inequality: How Today's Divided Society Endangers Our Future,* New York

Stiglitz, J. E. and Pieth M. (2016), *Overcoming the Shadow Economy,* Berlin

Tarullo, D.-K. (2004), "The Limits of Institutional Design: Implementing the OECD Anti-Bribery Convention," 44 *Vanderbilt Journal of International Law,* 665 et seq.

Teachout, Z. (2014), *Corruption in America,* Cambridge Massachusetts and London

Trevino L. K. and Youngblood S. A. (1990), "Bad Apples in Bad Barrels: A Causal Analysis of Ethical Decision-Making Behavior" *Texas A&M University Journal of Applied Psychology,* no. 75, 378 et seq.

Urofsky, P. and H. W. Moon (2014), "A Resource Guide to the US Foreign Corrupt Practices Act: The US Government's Perspective on Enforcing the FCPA" in Pieth, Low, and Bonucci 2014, 684 et seq.

Vincke, F. and J. Kassum (eds.) (2013), *ICC Ethics and Compliance Training Handbook, Anti-corruption Guidance by Practitioners for Practitioners,* Paris

Vogl, F. (2012), *Waging War on Corruption: Inside the Movement Fighting the Abuse of Power,* Plymouth

Volcker, P. A., R. J. Goldstone, and M. Pieth (2005), Independent Inquiry Committee into the United Nations Oil-for-Food Programme:

Volcker, Goldstone, and Pieth (2005a), *The Management of the United Nations Oil-for-Food Programme*, Volume I—The Report of the Committee, 7 September

Volcker, Goldstone, and Pieth (2005b), *The Management of the United Nations Oil-for-Food Programme*, Volume II—Report of Investigation Programme Background, 7 September

Volcker, Goldstone, and Pieth (2005c), *Manipulation of the Oil-for-Food Programme by the Iraqi Regime*, Report on Programme Manipulation, 27 October

Volcker, Goldstone, and Pieth (2005d), *Interim Report*, 3 February

Volcker, Goldstone, and Pieth (2005e), *Second Interim Report*, 29 March

Volcker, Goldstone, and Pieth (2005f), *Third Interim Report*, 8 August

Warin, F. J., C. Falconer, and M. S. Diamant (2010), "Somebody's Watching Me: FCPA Monitorships and How They Can Work Better" 13 *University of Pennsylvania Journal of Business Law*, 321 et seq.

Weidenfeld, U. (ed.) (2011), Nützliche Aufwendungen? Der Fall Siemens und die Lehren für das Unternehmen, die Industrie und Gesellschaft, Munich et al.

Weinreich, J. (ed.) (2006), *Korruption im Sport: Mafiose Dribblings, Organisiertes Schweigen*, Leipzig

Weinstein, M. J., R.-J. Meyer, and J.-D. Clark (2012), *The Foreign Corrupt Practices Act: Compliance, Investigations and Enforcement*, New York

Wiehen, M. (1999), "Transparency International" in Pieth and Eigen 1999, 297 et seq.

Wolf, M. L. (2014), "The Case for an International Anti-corruption Court," *Governance Studies at Brookings*, July 2014

Wrong, M. (2009), *It's Our Turn to Eat: The Story of a Kenyan Whistle Blower*, Fourth Estate (London)

Zerbes, I. (2014), "Article 1, The Offence of Bribery of Foreign Public Officials" in Pieth, Low, and Bonucci 2014, 59 et seq.

Zerbes, I. (2013), "Unternehmensinterne Untersuchungen," 125 *Zeitschrift für die gesamte Strafrechtswissenschaft*, no. 3, 551 et seq.

Zimmermann, S. S. and F. A. Fariello Jr. (2012), "Coordinating the Fight against Fraud and Corruption, Agreement on Cross-Debarment among Multilateral Development Banks" in H. Cissé, D. D. Bradlow, and B. Kingsbury (eds.), *The World Bank Legal Review, Volume 3, International Financial Institutions and Global Legal Governance*, Washington, 189 et seq.

Zindera, S. and B. Forstnig-Errath (2012), "Siemens: Promoting Collective Action—from Theory to Practice" in Pieth 2012, 177 et seq.

Selected Documents

African Union 2003, Convention on Preventing and Combating Corruption, adopted by the 2nd Ordinary Session of the Assembly of the Union on 11 July 2003

Basel Art Trade Guidelines 2012, Basel Institute on Governance, edited by Christ, T. and C. von Selle, Intermediary Report of a Self-Regulation Initiative, Working Paper Series, No. 12

Centre for Media Studies 2012, India Corruption Study 2012: Expanding Slums . . . Growing Corruption, New Delhi
Centre for Media Studies 2011, India Corruption Study 2011: Is The Scenario Changing?, New Delhi
CoE 2014, Convention on the Manipulation of Sports Competitions, signed by 15 states at the 13th Council of Europe Conference of Ministers responsible for Sport in Magglingen/Macolin, Switzerland, 18 September 2014, CETS. No. 215 (not yet in force)
CoE 2005, Convention on Laundering, Search, Seizure and Confiscation of the Proceeds from Crime and the Financing of Terrorism, ETS No. 198, 16 May 2005
CoE 2004, Resolution I on the Principles of Good Governance in Sport, adopted in Budapest on 14/15 October 2004
CoE 2005, Recommendation Rec(2005)8 on the Principles of Good Governance in Sport, adopted by the Committee of Ministers on 20 April 2005
CoE 1999, Criminal Law Convention on Corruption, CETS No. 173, 27 January 1999
CoE 1990, Convention on Money Laundering, Search, Seizure and Confiscation of the Proceeds from Crime, ETS No. 141, 8 November 1990
CoE 1988, Recommendation No. R (88) 18 Concerning Liability of Enterprises having Legal Personality for Offenses Committed in the Exercise of their Activities, adopted by the Committee of Ministers on 20 October 1988
EBK-Report "Oil-for-Food" 2005, Eidgenössische Bankenkommission (EBK) (Swiss Banking Commission), Bericht über die Tätigkeiten der Banken mit Sitz in der Schweiz im Rahmen des Programms "Oil-for-Food" der Vereinten Nationen, 27 October 2005
EITI Rules 2011, Extractive Industries Transparency Initiative, EITI Rules, 2011 Edition, 4 April 2011
EITI Standard 2015, Extractive Industries Transparency Initiative, The EITI Standard, 1 January 2015
EU 1997, Convention drawn up on the basis of Article K.3 (2) (c) of the Treaty on European Union on the fight against corruption involving officials of the European Communities or officials of Member States of the European Union, OJ C 195, 25 June 1997, 2 et seq.
FATF 40/2012, International Standards on Combating Money Laundering and the Financing of Terrorism & Proliferation, The Financial Action Task Force Recommendations, adopted 15 February 2012
FATF 40/1990, The Forty Recommendations of the Financial Action Task Force on Money Laundering, 29 July 1990
FATF Best Practices 2013, Financial Action Task Force, Best Practices Paper: The Use of the FATF Recommendations to Combat Corruption, October 2013
FATF Guidance 2013, Politically Exposed Persons (Recommendations 12 and 22), Financial Action Task Force Guidance, June 2013
FATF NCCT Report 2000, Financial Action Task Force, Report on Non Co-operative Countries or Territories, 14 February 2000
FATF Reference Guide 2012, Corruption: A Reference Guide and Information Note on the use of the FATF Recommendations in the fight against Corruption, February 2012

FATF Report 2012, Specific Risk Factors in Laundering the Proceeds of Corruption: Assistance to Reporting Institutions, FATF Report, June 2012

FATF Report 2011, Laundering the Proceeds of Corruption, Financial Action Task Force Report, July 2011

FATF Report 1989, Report of the Financial Action Task Force Working Group on Statistics and Methods, December 1989

FCPA Resource Guide 2012, A Resource Guide to the US Foreign Corrupt Practices Act, By the Criminal Division of the US Department of Justice and the Enforcement Division of the US Securities and Exchange Commission, November 14, 2012

FCPA 1988, United States Foreign Corrupt Practices Act, Amendments of 1988, Pub. L. No. 100-418, S. 5003, 102 Stat. 1107, August 3, 1988

FCPA 1977, United States Foreign Corrupt Practices Act, Pub. L. No. 95-213, 91 Stat. 1494, December 19, 1977

Global Witness 2013, Nigeria's Missing Billions, Report from 13 June 2013

Global Witness 2004, Time for Transparency, coming clean on oil, mining and gas revenues, Report from March 2004

Global Witness 1999, A Crude Awakening, Report from 1 December 1999

ICC Rules 2011, International Chamber of Commerce Rules on Combating Corruption, 2011 edition, first published in 1977, 17 October 2011

ICC Whistleblowing Guidelines, International Chamber of Commerce, Commission on Anti-Corruption, Guidelines on Whistleblowing Prepared by the ICC Commission on Anti-Corruption, 12 June 2008

IFBEC Principles 2009, International Forum on Business Ethical Conduct for the Aerospace and Defense Industry (IFBEC), Global Principles of Business Ethics for the Aerospace and Defence Industry, 2 October 2009

IFPMA Code of Practice 2012, International Federation of Pharmaceutical Manufacturers and of Association, Code of Practice 2012, first published in 1981

Intergovernmental Expert Group 1991, Recommendations of the Intergovernmental Expert Group to Study the Economic and Social Consequences of Illicit Traffic in Drugs, UN Doc. E/CN.7/1991/25

IOC 2014, International Olympic Committee, Factsheet, IOC Financial Summary, 8 July 2014

OAS 1996, Organization of American States, Inter-American Convention against Corruption, 29 March 1996

OECD 1989, United States Proposal on the Issue of Illicit Payments, OECD Council, Note by the Secretary-General, 23 March 1989, incl. Annex, United States Proposal for an International Agreement on Illicit Payments, C(89)49, 14 March 1989

OECD Commentaries 1997, OECD Commentaries on the Convention on Combating Bribery of Foreign Public Officials in International Business Transactions, adopted by the Negotiating Conference on 21 November 1997

OECD Convention 1997, Convention on Combating Bribery of Foreign Public Officials in International Business Transactions, adopted by the Negotiating Conference on 21 November 1997, entered into force on 15 February 1999

OECD Foreign Bribery Report 2014, OECD Foreign Bribery Report: An Analysis of the Crime of Bribery of Foreign Public Officials, OECD publishing, 2 December 2014

OECD MAI 1998, The Multilateral Agreement on Investment, Draft consolidated text, 22 April 1998, also DAFFE/MAI(98)7/REV1

OECD Rec. 2009, Recommendation of the Council for Further Combating Bribery of Foreign Public Officials in International Business Transactions, 26 November 2009 (with amendments adopted by Council 18 February 2010 to reflect the inclusion of Annex II, Good Practice Guidance on Internal Controls, Ethics and Compliance)

OECD Rec. 1994, Recommendation of the Council of the OECD on Bribery in International Business Transactions, adopted by the Council on 27 May 1994

OECD Revised Rec. 1997, Revised Recommendation of the Council of the OECD on Combating Bribery in International Business Transactions, adopted by the Council on 23 May 1997, C/M(97)12/PROV

OECD Travaux Préparatoires 1999, Travaux Préparatoires of the OECD Convention on Combating Bribery of Foreign Officials, International Trade Corruption Monitor (ITCM), DAFFE/IME/BR(97)14, 1001 et seq.

OECD WGB 2013, OECD Working Group on Bribery, Annual Report 2013

OECD WGB 2012, OECD Working Group on Bribery, Phase 3 Report on Implementing the OECD Anti-Bribery Convention in France, October 2012

OECD WGB 2011, OECD Working Group on Bribery, Phase 3 Report on Implementing the OECD Anti-Bribery Convention in Italy, December 2011

OECD WGB 2009, OECD Working Group on Bribery, OECD Anti-Bribery Convention, Phase 3 Monitoring Information Resources, 17 December 2009, DAF/INV/BR(2008)25/FINAL

OECD WGB 2008, OECD Working Group on Bribery, Phase 2bis Report on Implementing the OECD Anti-Bribery Convention in the United Kingdom, adopted by the WGB on 16 October 2008

OECD WGB 2006, OECD Working Group on Bribery, Mid-Term Study of Phase 2 reports, 22 May 2006

OECD WGB 2005, OECD Working Group on Bribery, Phase 2 Report on Implementing the OECD Anti-Bribery Convention in the United Kingdom, adopted by the WGB on 17 March 2005

OECD WGB 2004, OECD Working Group on Bribery, Phase 2 Report on Implementing the OECD Anti-Bribery Convention in Italy, 29 November 2004

OECD WGB 1999, OECD Working Group on Bribery, Phase 1 Report on Implementing the OECD Anti-Bribery Convention in the United Kingdom, December 1999

OECD WGB Typologies 2009, OECD Working Group on Bribery, Typologies on the Role of Intermediaries in International Business Transactions, Final Report, 9 October 2009

PwC 2014, PricewaterhouseCoopers, Economic crime: A threat to business globally, Global Economic Crime Survey

Report of the US Department of the Treasury, US Customs Service to the Subgroup "Statistics and Methods" of the FATF, Typology of Money Laundering, October 6–8, 1989

TI Business Principles 2013, Transparency International, Business Principles for Countering Bribery, A Multi-stakeholder Initiative

TI Business Principles 2009, Transparency International, Business Principles for Countering Bribery, February 2009

TI CPI 2014, Transparency International, Corruption Perception Index 2014: Full Source Description

TI Progress Report 2015, Transparency International, Exporting Corruption, Progress Report 2015: Assessing Enforcement of the OECD Convention on Combating Foreign Bribery

TI Progress Report 2013, Transparency International, Exporting Corruption, Progress Report 2013: Assessing Enforcement of the OECD Convention on Combating Foreign Bribery

TI-UK 2015, Transparency International UK, Defence Companies Anti-Corruption Index 2015, published in April 2015

TI-UK 2013, Transparency International UK, Government Defence Anti-Corruption Index 2013, first published in January 2013

TI UK 2011, Transparency International UIK, Building Integrity and Countering Corruption Defense and Security, first published in February 2011

TI-UK 2010, Transparency International UK, Defence Offsets, Addressing the Risks of Corruption & Raising Transparency, first published in April 2010

TI-US 2014, Transparency International USA, Verification of Anti-corruption Compliance Programs

Trace 2010, Trace Anti-Bribery Compliance Solutions, Trace Due Diligence Guidebook: Doing Business with Intermediaries Internationally

UK Bribery Act 2010, United Kingdom Bribery Act 2010, 8 April 2010

UK Joint Prosecution Guidance 2011, United Kingdom Bribery Act 2010, Joint Prosecution Guidance of the Director of the Serious Fraud Office and the Director of Public Prosecutions, 30 March 2011

UK Ministry of Justice Guidance 2011, United Kingdom Bribery Act 2010, Guidance about procedures which relevant commercial organisations can put into place to prevent persons associated with them from bribing (section 9 of the Bribery Act 2010)

UN 2006, Assessment of Justice Sector Integrity and Capacity in Two Indonesian Provinces, Technical Assessment Report, Vienna/Jakarta, March 2006

UN 1989, International Action to Combat Drug Abuse and Illicit Trafficking, UN Doc. A/RES/44/142, 15 December 1989

UN 1988, United Nations Convention against Illicit Traffic in Narcotic Drugs and Psychotropic Substances, adopted on 20 December 1988

UNCAC 2003, United Nations Conventions against Corruption, UN Doc. A/RES/58/4, 31 October 2003

UNESCO 1999, UNESCO International Code of Ethics for Dealers in Cultural Property

UNESCO 1970, UNESCO Convention on the Means of Prohibiting and Preventing the Illicit Import, Export and Transfer of Ownership of Cultural Property

UNIDROIT 1995, The International Institute for the Unification of Private Law (UNIDROIT), Convention on Stolen or Illegally Exported Cultural Objects

US DII Principles 1997, United States Defense Industry Initiative on Business Ethics and Conduct, The DII Principles, February 1997 (updated 2010/2013)

US Department of Commerce 2008, Offsets in Defense Trade, Fourteenth Study, December 2009

Wolfsberg Guidance 2011, Wolfsberg Anti-Corruption Guidance, August 2011

Wolfsberg Guidelines 2000, Wolfsberg Global Anti-Money-Laundering Guidelines for Private Banking, first issued 30 October 2000, updated in 2002
Wolfsberg Principles 2012, Wolfsberg Anti-Money Laundering Principles for Private Banking
Wolfsberg Principles 2002, Wolfsberg Anti-Money Laundering Principles for Correspondent Banking, October 2002
Wolfsberg Statement 2006, Wolfsberg Guidance on a Risk-Based Approach for Managing Money Laundering Risks
Wolfsberg Statement 2002, Wolfsberg Statement on the Suppression of the Financing of Terrorism
World Bank 2013, Integrity Vice Presidency of the World Bank Group, Fiscal Year 2013 Annual Update
World Bank 2007, Department of Institutional Integrity, Detailed Implementation Review, India Health Sector, 2006–2007, volumes I/II, issued: 19 December 2007
World Bank 2005, Voice of the World's Poor: Selected Speeches and Writings of World Bank President James D. Wolfensohn, 1995–2005, Washington DC
World Bank External Panel 2013, External Panel of Experts of the World Bank, The Padma Multipurpose Bridge Project, Final Report, 20 February 2013
World Bank Institute 2008, Fighting Corruption through Collective Action, A Guide for Business
World Bank Panel Review 2007, Independent Panel Review of the World Bank Group Department of Institutional Integrity, Washington DC, 13 September 2007, 3 et seq.
World Bank Sanctioning Guidelines 2011, 1 January 2011
World Bank Sanctions Procedures 2012, adopted 15 April 2012
WJP Rule of Law Index 2014, World Justice Project Rule of Law Index
WTO Revised Agreement on Government Procurement, World Trade Organization, 30 March 2012

INDEX

The manufacturer's authorised representative in the EU for product safety is Oxford University Press España S.A. of El Parque Empresarial San Fernando de Henares, Avenida de Castilla, 2 - 28830 Madrid (www.oup.es/en or product.safety@oup.com). OUP España S.A. also acts as importer into Spain of products made by the manufacturer.
Printed and bound by CPI Group (UK) Ltd, Croydon, CR0 4YY
14/09/2026
02216304-0016